Prophecies, Visions, Occurrences, and Dreams

from Jehovah God, Jesus Christ, and the Holy Spirit given to Raymond Aguilera Book 4

Raymond Aguilera

EARTHQUAKE 68

Writers Club Press
San Jose New York Lincoln Shanghai

Prophecies, Visions, Occurrences, and Dreams
from Jehovah God, Jesus Christ, and the Holy Spirit
given to Raymond Aguilera Book 4

All Rights Reserved © 2000 by Raymond Aguilera

No part of this book may be reproduced or transmitted in any form or by any means, graphic, electronic, or mechanical, including photocopying, recording, taping, or by any information storage or retrieval system, without the permission in writing from the publisher.

Published by Writers Club Press
an imprint of iUniverse.com, Inc.

For information address:
iUniverse.com, Inc.
620 North 48th Street
Suite 201
Lincoln, NE 68504-3467
www.iuniverse.com

ISBN: 0-595-09323-X

Printed in the United States of America

P63 JAPAN IS ONE OF 10 HORNS
P120 LAST TRAIN LEAVES AT 7AM
166 4 INVASIONS = SATAN CONTROLS WORLD
182 DEVIL IN COSTA RICA
189 DEC 2 1990 BEGINNING OF END
224-6→ MT. SHASTA VOLCANO
265 WOLF & BEAR CLASH IN Nov.

Prophecy Book 4
(Prophecies 876 through 1175)

Preface Prophecy

Prophecy given to Raymond on 26 October 1994 at 11:33 AM. in English.

The Lord Jehovah gave me this prophecy to be placed here.

Jehovah God said, "The prophecy of Joel is being fulfilled today."

From King James Bible:

Joel 2:28 And it shall come to pass afterward, that I will pour out my spirit upon all flesh; and your sons and your daughters shall prophesy, your old men shall dream dreams, your young men shall see visions:

Joel 2:29 And also upon the servants and upon the handmaids in those days will I pour out my spirit.

Joel 2:30 And I will show wonders in the heavens and in the earth, blood, and fire, and pillars of smoke.

Joel 2:31 The sun shall be turned into darkness, and the moon into blood, before the great and the terrible day of the LORD come.

Joel 2:32 And it shall come to pass, that whosoever shall call on the name of the LORD shall be delivered: for in mount Zion and in Jerusalem shall be deliverance, as the LORD hath said, and in the remnant whom the LORD shall call.

Acts 2:16 But this is that which was spoken by the prophet Joel;

Acts 2:17 And it shall come to pass in the last days, saith God, I will pour out of my Spirit upon all flesh: and your sons and your daughters shall prophesy, and your young men shall see visions, and your old men shall dream dreams:

Acts 2:18 And on my servants and on my handmaidens I will pour out in those days of my Spirit; and they shall prophesy:

Acts 2:19 And I will show wonders in heaven above, and signs in the earth beneath; blood, and fire, and vapour of smoke:

Acts 2:20 The sun shall be turned into darkness, and the moon into blood, before that great and notable day of the Lord come:

Acts 2:21 And it shall come to pass, that whosoever shall call on the name of the Lord shall be saved.

Today's Calling
by Gerald O. Lukehart*

What if a man, a Catholic man, one not familiar with or desiring the Supernatural, begins to receive prophecies and warnings from God? These warnings include a major California earthquake, a nuclear explosion in Paris, and the world ending by a collision with a star.

This man has a calling to be a prophet, something he has never wanted to be. To this day this is something he never fully wanted. All he wanted was to be able to lead his own life, to follow his own path, never desiring to be called a fool, a heretic, a charlatan, or worse. This man has received over six hundred messages ranging from Abortion, to the New Age movement, to Pastors who mislead the flock. These messages reveal things to come, things that now are and things that should not be…From hope, to love, to doom, to a new beginning, herein lies a broad range of insight from a whole new perspective. From God's…

Really not a new perspective for these messages reach out from an earlier time, the time of Joel, Jeremiah and Daniel, giving us an insight to the inner workings of the Lord. With a warning and with a possibility of the end coming soon there is an urgency and a relevance to these messages that must get out to one and all.

We, Ray's extended spiritual family, want to share with you of the struggles to have faith ourselves and of the reality of what we have received from Ray and of the miracles that have followed.

We find the prophecies:
> To be simple and straight forward, written from a first hand perspective.
> To fly in the face of orthodox tradition.
> To be a thorn in the side to everyone who has already made up their mind and heart on how the end is to come and who God is...

This has the potential to be one of the most controversial books of the year. Since April of 1992 the prophecies and the spiritual warfare has increased around Mr. Aguilera. The Prophecies are spreading across the United States and around the world. People have sensed the presence of God, some cry, some shake, some pray, some find God...We hope you will too.

* Mr. Gerald O. Lukehart is a grassroots born again Charismatic Christian with a Southern Baptist family heritage.

Dedicated Man
*An explanation of the Ray Aguilera phenomenon, by Robert Thompson.**

To understand Ray Aguilera, two key words must be defined.

First, the definition of *Dedicate:* According to the American Heritage Dictionary,

1. To set apart for a special purpose.
2. To commit (oneself) fully; devote.
3. To inscribe (e.g. a book) to someone.

Secondly, the definition of *Phenomenon:* Again, according to the American Heritage Dictionary,

1. An occurrence or fact that can be perceived by the senses.
2. a. An unusual fact or occurrence.
   b. A person outstanding for an extreme quality or achievement.

During the first three years of Ray's "Journey" he encountered a multitude of obstacles, all of which he challenged and conquered, as his Christian walk strengthened with the knowledge that he was chosen for a very special purpose.

Without formal bible training or any past theological interests, other than a desire to be a good Christian, Ray has accepted the greatest responsibility of his life. Criticism from leaders within the church, disbelief from friends and acquaintances, and his own insecurities as a human being have not deterred Ray from completing his task. As if these reasons were not enough, to deter Ray from his work, there were also constant battles and tests visited upon him from the Spiritual world. For Ray's battles, on behalf of God, were with the devil, who never sleeps. (Eph. 6:12) Therefore Ray's vigilance over these matters required weekly, daily, and hourly attention.

Ray professes not to be a prophet, yet he receives prophecies. He understands not symbolism, yet he receives visions and symbols. He lacks biblical expertise, yet he is told to use the bible. He aspires not lofty rank within the church, yet he challenges those of authority and questionable repute. He detests radicalism and revolution, yet his work is radical and revolutionary in thought and design.

Ray's life appears complicated, troubled, and disturbed at times. Nevertheless, Ray has kept to his task and pursued goals given him by God: Write everything down; put it into a book form; and spread the word worldwide. Ray was told to do this and have unconditional faith in God's ability to open doors and provide contacts to insure the successful completion of this powerful project.

Ray is a dedicated man. He is set apart from others, by God, for a special purpose. He is devoted and fully committed to his task. And, he has sacrificed all to write a book, not about God, but from God.

This book is not about Ray's life, his beliefs, or even his experiences. This book is about change; this book is about perceptions; this book is about getting back to God. Ray feels there is a disturbance in the church. He hopes this book will bring about change that will be positive for all Christians and non-Christians alike. More importantly, Ray wants to see change in the church.

Ray faces an uphill battle. He feels threatened and intimidated by leaders in the church because of what has been written. But it is precisely what has been written, and disseminated, that will bring the needed change. Force, violence, and radical actions will not be the catalyst for change. The written word, just the word of God, will be enough to bring universal change in the body.

The greatest change in the church occurred in the 1500's by a theologian named Martin Luther. He challenged the dogmatic practices of the Catholic Church. He was a prolific writer and charismatic speaker. The German people of the 1520's would have violently revolted or turned to radical activities had Martin Luther suggested that course of action. However, Martin Luther wrote and published God's word. The word of God was spread by individuals that networked and challenged the authority of the existing church. Martin Luther knew also that Satan could attack individuals, but when the work of God is being done, by spreading words, it is very distressing to the devil.

Ray Aguilera is not a theologian. Nevertheless, he is spreading the word of God just as he has been instructed. He is experiencing divine intervention through visions and occurrences. He records and documents every event in his own words and style. Ray is not a writer so he puts everything down as if he were conversing with a friend. Ray's work is personal, not for commercial gain, and written for everyone, Christian and non-Christian alike.

Ray's mission in life is simple: Get the word of God to everyone. Through his dedication he is accomplishing this very goal. It is phenomenal that Ray's writings, although incomplete, are being read and distributed throughout the United States and abroad. Bits and pieces are scattered throughout the world. When this work is finished it will be available to everyone because it is the will of God that the word of God be read by all.

* Robert Thompson is a Teacher/Historian who stated that the Lord gave him several dreams and restless nights and placed a burden to write this preface and to use scripture.

Comments

Many people have related to me that the material in this Book gives them joy and peace in knowing that the Lord is coming. My suggestion would be to **pray** before you read any part of this Book for guidance and wisdom, for some people sense the **Presence of the Lord** in a supernatural way when they read certain Prophecies. If possible read the Holy Bible at the same time with an **open mind** on the **true reality** of how God deals with mankind.

    This Book certainly will not tickle your ears concerning the wrath of God, but it will show you **His love** for **mankind** and so states it many times. At the same time some people are afraid, due to the frankness of how the wrath of God is stated. The beginning Prophecies have many words that are repeated, I believe that the Lord was training me to receive His Word, and in some cases I believe He wanted people to hear it over and over. So I prayed about it, and was instructed to leave it as I received it. I would like to also add that I am a Catholic going to a Protestant church at the present time. God bless you all.

Raymond Aguilera

PS: The Lord instructed me to enclose this scripture here on 21 September 1994.

King James Bible:
John 11:25 Jesus said unto her, **I am** the **resurrection**, and the **life**: he that believeth in me, though he were dead, yet shall he live:
John 11:26 And whosoever liveth and believeth in me shall never die. **Believest thou this?**

Acknowledgments

My Personal thanks to all the men and women that have helped in putting this Book together with prayers, knowledge, wisdom, technical help, supplies, finances, and for the uplifting spiritual help I received in the spiritual warfare. I would like to add that as of September 1992 five months after I started typing the Prophecies, people have mailed them to missionaries around the world. The Prophecies have spread to approximately twenty countries and forty U.S. states by mail, fax, and from hand to hand within and outside the Body of Christ. May Jehovah, Jesus Christ, and the Holy Spirit our only God Bless you all.

Pastors:
    Catholic Church
    Covenant Church
    Four Square Church

Individuals from:
    The Baptist Church
    The Catholic Church
    The Covenant Church
    The Four Square Church
    The Full Gospel Business Men's Fellowship International
    The Mormon Church

The Presbyterian Church
The Vineyard Church
Non-Denominational Churches
And:
Non-Practicing Christians
Non-Christians

Table of contents

Preface Prophecy v
Today's Calling vii
Dedicated Man ix
Comments xiii
Acknowledgments xv
Part 1
    The Story of how Prophecies, Visions, Occurrences, and Dreams began with Raymond Aguilera 3
Part 2
    Prophecies, Visions, Occurrences, and Dreams. 61
        876. Vision and Prophecy given to Raymond Aguilera on 14 March 1996 at 3 AM. 63
        877. Vision given to Raymond Aguilera on 16 March 1996 at 9:00 PM. 63
        878. Vision given to Raymond Aguilera on 17 March 1996 at 8:00 PM. 64
        879. Vision: 64
        880. Vision: 64
        881. Prophecy given to Raymond Aguilera on 20 March 1996 at 1:15 AM in Spanish. 64
        882. Vision given to Raymond Aguilera on 21 March 1996 at 7 AM. 67
        883. Prophecy given to Raymond Aguilera on 25 March 1996 at 12:44 AM. in Spanish. 67

884. Vision given to Raymond Aguilera
on 25 March 1996 at 9 AM. 72
885. Vision given to Raymond Aguilera
on 27 March 1996 at 8:30 PM. 72
886. Vision given to Raymond Aguilera
on 2 April 1996 at 9:42 AM. 73
887. Prophecy given to Raymond Aguilera
on 2 April 1996 at in 9:58 AM. Spanish. 73
888. Vision given to Raymond Aguilera
on 2 April 1996 at 9:38 PM. 75
889. Prophecy given to Raymond Aguilera
on 2 April 1996 at 9:40 PM. in Spanish. 75
890. Vision given to Raymond Aguilera
on 3 April 1996 at 8:30 PM. 79
891. Occurrence and Prophecy given to Raymond Aguilera
on 3 April 1996 8:30 PM. in English. 79
892. Prophecy given to Raymond Aguilera
on 3 April 1996 at 11 PM. 80
893. Prophecy given to Raymond Aguilera
on 4 April 1996 at 1:30 AM in English. 80
894. Vision given to Raymond Aguilera
on 6 April 1996 at 1:00 PM. in English. 80
895. Vision given to Raymond Aguilera
on 10 April 1996 at 1:30 PM. 80
896. Vision given to Raymond Aguilera
on 10 April 1996 at 8:30 PM. 80
897. Vision given to Raymond Aguilera
on 16 April 1996 at 1:30 PM. 81
898. Occurrence and Visions given to Raymond Aguilera
on 16 April 1996 at 10:30 PM. 81
899. Prophecy given to Raymond Aguilera
on 24 April 1996 at 8:15 AM 85
900. Prophecy given to Raymond Aguilera
on 25 April 1996 at 3:55 PM. in Spanish. 89
901. Prophecy given to Raymond Aguilera
on 1 May 1996 at 1 AM. in Spanish. 92
902. Vision given to Raymond Aguilera
on 2 May 1996. 95

903. Prophecy given Raymond Aguilera
     on 5 May 1996 at 8:19 AM. in Spanish and English. 95
904. Vision given to Raymond Aguilera
     on 5 May 1996 at 10 AM. 97
905. Vision given to Raymond Aguilera
     on 6 May 1996 at 10 PM. 97
906. Prophecy given to Raymond Aguilera
     on 7 May 1996 at 7:26 AM in Spanish. 97
907. Vision and Prophecy given to Raymond Aguilera
     on 10 May 1996 at 10:00 AM. 100
908. Prophecy given to Raymond Aguilera
     on 16 May 1996 at 7:35 AM. 100
909. Occurrences and a Vision given to Raymond Aguilera
     on 17–21 May 1996. 101
910. Vision given to Raymond Aguilera
     on 21 May 1996 at 3:16 PM. 104
911. Prophecy given to Raymond Aguilera
     on 23 May 1996 at 11:30 AM. in English. 104
912. Vision given to Raymond Aguilera
     on 27 May 1996. 104
913. Vision given to Raymond Aguilera
     on 29 May 1996 at 8:30 PM. 105
914. Vision given to Raymond Aguilera
     on 6 June 1996 at 1:33 PM. 105
915. Vision given to Raymond Aguilera
     on 11 June 1996 at 10:30 AM. 106
916. Prophecy given to Raymond Aguilera
     on the 16 June 1996. 106
917. Vision given to Raymond Aguilera
     on 21 June 1996 at 8:30 PM. 107
918. Vision given to Raymond Aguilera
     on 23 June 1996 at 10:25 AM. 108
919. Prophecy given to Raymond Aguilera
     on 23 June 1996 at 10:56 AM. 108
920. Occurrence given to Raymond Aguilera
     on 25 June 1996. 112
921. Occurrence given to Raymond Aguilera
     on 27 June 1996 at 10:00 AM. 113

922. Vision given to Raymond Aguilera
on 28 June 1996. 115
923. Prophecy given to Raymond Aguilera
on 3 July 1996 at 1:30 AM. in Spanish. 115
924. Vision given to Raymond Aguilera
on 4 July 1996 at 4:00 PM. 117
925. Occurrence given to Raymond Aguilera
on 21 July 1996. 117
926. Occurrence given to Raymond Aguilera
on 10 July 1996 at 4:10 PM. 117
927. Occurrence, Vision, and Prophecy given to Raymond Aguilera
on 12 July 1996 at 6:15 PM. 119
928. Prophecy given to Raymond Aguilera
on 15 July 1996 at 10:30 AM. in English. 120
929. Vision and Prophecy given to Raymond Aguilera
on 17 July 1996 at 8:00 PM. 121
930. Vision given to Raymond Aguilera
on 21 July 1996 at 7:52 AM. 121
931. Prophecy given to Raymond Aguilera
on 21 July 1996 at 2:20 PM. 121
932. Occurrence given to Raymond Aguilera
on 22 July 1996 at 4:30 PM. 122
933. Prophecy given to Raymond Aguilera
on 23 July 1996 at 4:55 PM in English. 122
934. Prophecy given to Raymond Aguilera
on 23 July 1996 at 7:07 PM. in Spanish. 123
935. Occurrence given to Raymond Aguilera
on 31 July 1996 at 11:18 PM 127
936. Vision given Raymond Aguilera
12 August 1996 at 10 PM. 142
937. Prophecy given to Raymond Aguilera
on the 13 August 1996 at 12:42 PM. in Spanish. 142
938. Occurrence given to Raymond Aguilera
on 13 August 1996 at 7:54 AM. 146
939. Occurrence given to Raymond Aguilera
on 8 August 1996 at 9 AM. 150
940. Prophecy given to Raymond Aguilera
on 13 August 1996. 151

941. Vision given to Raymond Aguilera
on 14 August 1996 at 2:02 PM. 151
942. Prophecy given to Raymond Aguilera
18 August 1996 at 2:12 PM. in Spanish. 151
943. Prophecy given to Raymond Aguilera
on 19 August 1996 at 2:30 AM. in Spanish. 153
944. Prophecy given to Raymond Aguilera
on 19 August 1996 at 2:01 PM. in Spanish. 153
945. Prophecy given to Raymond Aguilera
on 21 August 1996 at 2:00 PM. 155
946. Prophecy given to Raymond Aguilera
on 21 August 1996 at 8:00 PM. 156
947. Prophecy and Vision given to Raymond Aguilera
on 28 August 1996 at 8:00 PM. 157
948. Vision given to Raymond Aguilera
on 30 August 1996 at 6:48 PM. 157
949. Vision given to Raymond Aguilera
on 30 August 1996 at 6:48 PM. 157
950. Vision given to Raymond Aguilera
on 30 August 1996 at 6:48 PM. 158
951. Vision given to Raymond Aguilera
on 30 August 1996 at 6:48 PM. 158
952. Vision given to Raymond Aguilera
on 30 August 1996 at 6:48 PM. 158
953. Vision given to Raymond Aguilera
on 30 August 1996 at 6:48 PM. 159
954. Prophecy given to Raymond Aguilera
on 30 August 1996 at 6:48 PM. 159
955. Vision given to Raymond Aguilera
on 30 August 1996 at 6:48 PM. 159
956. Vision given to Raymond Aguilera
on 31 August 1996 at 7:24 AM. 159
957. Vision given to Raymond Aguilera
on 31 August 1996 at 7:24 PM. 159
958. Prophecy given to Raymond Aguilera
on 1 September 1996 at 4:33 PM. in Spanish. 160
959. Vision given to Raymond Aguilera
on 3 September 1996 at 4:30 PM. 160

960. Prophecy given to Raymond Aguilera
on 3 September 1996 at 7:01 PM. in English. 161
961. Prophecy given to Raymond Aguilera
on 5 September 1996 at 6:19 PM. in Spanish. 161
962. Prophecy given to Raymond Aguilera
on 9 September 1996 at 8:12 PM. in Spanish. 162
963. Prophecy, Vision and Occurrence given to Raymond Aguilera
on 11 September 1996 at 10:30 AM 163
964. Occurrence given to Raymond Aguilera
on 13 September 1996 at 1:02 PM. 165
965. Vision given to Raymond Aguilera
on 18 September 1996 at 4:10 PM. 166
966. Visions given to Raymond Aguilera
on 25 September 1996 at 7:37 AM. 166
967. Vision given to Raymond Aguilera
on 19 September 1996 at 12:30 AM. 167
968. Occurrence given to Raymond Aguilera
on 25 September 1996 1:30 PM. 167
969. Vision given to Raymond Aguilera
on 25 September 1996 at 8 PM. 168
970. Occurrence given to Raymond Aguilera
on 26 September 1996 at 6 PM. 168
971. Occurrence given to Raymond Aguilera
on 30 September 96 at 11:30 PM. 170
972. Prophecy given to Raymond Aguilera
on 1 October 1996 at 8:40 AM in Spanish. 170
973. Prophecy given to Raymond Aguilera
4 October 1996 at 8:53 AM. 171
974. Prophecy given to Raymond Aguilera
on 7 October 1996 at 8:45 PM. 172
975. Vision given to Raymond Aguilera
on 9 October 1996 at 8:00 PM. 173
976. Prophecy given to Raymond Aguilera
on 10 October 1996 at 12 AM. 175
977. Vision given to Raymond Aguilera
on 10 October 1996 at 1:46 PM. 176
978. Prophecy and Vision given to Raymond Aguilera
on 17 October 1996 at 10 PM. 176

979. Vision given to Raymond Aguilera
on 17 October 1996 at 7:15 PM. 177
980. Occurrence given to Raymond Aguilera
on 21 October 1996 at 11:05 PM. 177
981. Occurrence given to Raymond Aguilera
on 22 October 1996 at 11:44 PM. 178
982. Prophecy given to Raymond Aguilera
23 October 1996 at 9 AM. 180
983. Prophecy given to Raymond Aguilera
on 24 October 1996 at 3:34 PM. in Spanish. 182
984. Occurrence and Prophecy given to Raymond Aguilera
on 29 October 1996 at 9:06 AM. in Spanish. 182
985. Vision given to Raymond Aguilera
on 29 October 1996. 183
986. Vision given to Raymond Aguilera
on 29 November 1996 at 1:30 AM. 184
987. Vision and Prophecy given to Raymond Aguilera
on 4 December 1996. 184
988. Vision given to Raymond Aguilera
on 1 December 1996 at 8:00 PM. 184
989. Vision given to Raymond Aguilera
on 2 December 1996 at 2:30 AM. 185
990. Vision given to Raymond Aguilera
on 5 December 1996 at 2:37 PM. 185
991. Vision given to Raymond Aguilera
on 7 December 1996 at 10:03 PM. 185
992. Vision given to Raymond Aguilera
on 7 December 1996 at 11:30 PM. 186
993. Vision given to Raymond Aguilera
on 8 December 1996 at 11:00 AM. 186
994. Prophecy given to Raymond Aguilera
on 9 December 1996 at 8:45 PM. 186
995. Vision given to Raymond Aguilera
on 12 December 1996 at 7:15 PM. 187
996. Vision given to Raymond Aguilera
on 16 December 1996 at 2 AM. 187
997. Occurrence, Vision, Prophecy given to Raymond Aguilera
on 18 December 1996 at 3:17 PM. in English. 188

998. Vision given to Raymond Aguilera
on 19 December 1996 at 11:10 PM. 190
999. Prophecy given to Raymond Aguilera
22 December 1996 at 5:28 PM. 190
1000. Prophecy given to Raymond Aguilera
on 23 December 1996 at 6:47 AM. in English. 191
1001. Occurrence given to Raymond Aguilera
on 7 January 1997 at 10:15 PM. 192
1002. Vision given to Raymond Aguilera
on 13 January 1997 at 2:02 AM. 195
1003. Vision given to Raymond Aguilera
on 19 January 1997 at 10:54 AM. 195
1004. Vision given to Raymond Aguilera
on 21 January 1997 at 2:30 AM. 195
1005. Vision given to Raymond Aguilera
on 25 January 1997 at 12:30 AM. 195
1006. Prophecy (story) given to Raymond Aguilera
on 31 January 1997. 195
1007. Vision given to Raymond Aguilera
on 3 February 1997 at 9 AM. 197
1008. Prophecy given to Raymond Aguilera
on 7 February 1997 at 11:55 AM. 197
1009. Occurrence given to Raymond Aguilera
on 12 February 1997 at 7:45 AM. 198
1010. Prophecy given to Raymond Aguilera
on 16 February 1997 at 9:30 AM. 201
1011. Vision given to Raymond Aguilera
on 16 February 1997 at 9:52 AM. 201
1012. Prophecy (Song) given to Raymond Aguilera
on 18 February 1997 201
1013. Prophecy given to Raymond Aguilera
on 18 February 1997 at 3 PM. 202
1014. Dream given to Raymond Aguilera
on 26 February 1997. 202
1015. Prophecy given to Raymond Aguilera
on 27 February 1997 at 7:00 AM. 203
1016. Vision given to Raymond Aguilera
on 28 February 1997 at 12:16 AM. 203

1017. Vision given to Raymond Aguilera
on 5 March 1997 at 5 AM. 203

1018. Vision given to Raymond Aguilera
on 5 March 1997 204

1019. Vision given to Raymond Aguilera
on 6 March 1997 at 3:49 AM. 204

1020. Vision given to Raymond Aguilera
on 10 March 1997 at 1:26 AM. 204

1021. Prophecy given to Raymond Aguilera
on 15 March 1997 at 8:02 AM. in Spanish. 204

1022. Vision given to Raymond Aguilera
on 15 March 1997 at 10:34 AM. 206

1023. Prophecy and Vision given to Raymond Aguilera
on 19 March 1997 at 8:06 AM. 206

1024. Prophecy given to Raymond Aguilera
on 21 March 1997 at 11:49 PM. 207

1025. Vision given to Raymond Aguilera
on 23 March 1997 at 12:15 AM. 207

1026. Prophecy given to Raymond Aguilera
on 26 March 1997 at 7:56 AM. in Spanish. 207

1027. Prophecy given to Raymond Aguilera
on 26 March 1996 at 8:13 AM. in English. 209

1028. Prophecy given to Raymond Aguilera
on 10 April 1997 at 12:27 AM. in Spanish. 209

1029. Occurrence given to Raymond Aguilera
on 14 April 1997 at 5:30 PM. 213

1030. Vision given to Raymond Aguilera
on 14 April 1997 at 9 PM. 214

1031. Vision given to Raymond Aguilera
on 18 April 1997 at 9:30 AM. 214

1032. Vision given to Raymond Aguilera
on 19 April 1997 at 9:30 PM. 214

1033. Vision given to Raymond Aguilera
on 24 April 1997 at 6:00 PM. 215

1034. Prophecy given to Raymond Aguilera
on 25 April 1997 at 11:30 PM. 215

1035. Vision given to Raymond Aguilera
on 25 April 1997 at 5:00 PM. 215

1036. Vision given to Raymond Aguilera
on 29 April 1997 at 6:00 AM. 216
1037. Prophecy given to Raymond Aguilera
on 29 April 1997 at 9:01 AM in English. 216
1038. Vision given to Raymond Aguilera
on 29 April 1997 at 9:00 PM. 218
1039. Prophecy given to Raymond Aguilera
on 6 May 1997 at 11:08 AM. in Spanish. 219
1040. Prophecy given to Raymond Aguilera
on 7 May 1997 at 1:10 AM. in Spanish. 220
1041. Vision given to Raymond Aguilera
on 7 May 1997 at 1:20 AM. 222
1042. Prophecy given to Raymond Aguilera
on 7 May 1997 at 8:13 AM. in Spanish. 222
1043. Vision given to Raymond Aguilera
on 7 May 1997 at 2:02 PM. 223
1044. Vision given to Raymond Aguilera
on 8 May 1997 at 1:35 AM. 223
1045. Vision given to Raymond Aguilera
on 9 May 1997 at 8:00 PM. 223
1046. Prophecy given to Raymond Aguilera
on 11 May 1997 at 8:00 AM. 224
1047. Vision given to Raymond Aguilera
on 11 May 1997. 224
1048. Prophecy given to Raymond Aguilera
on 12 May 1997 at 12:30 AM. in Spanish. 224
1049. Vision given to Raymond Aguilera
on 12 May 1997 at 3:45 PM. 225
1050. Occurrence given to Raymond Aguilera
on 16 May 1997. 226
1051. Prophecy given to Raymond Aguilera
on 28 May 1997 at 6:56 PM. in Spanish. 230
1052. Prophecy given to Raymond Aguilera
on 30 May 1997 at 8:23 PM. 231
1053. Prophecy given to Raymond Aguilera
on 30 May 1997 at 3:53 PM. 231
1054. Vision given to Raymond Aguilera
on 2 June 1997 at 2:37 PM. 231

1055. Prophecy given to Raymond Aguilera
on 2 June 1997 at 11:45 PM. in Spanish. 232
1056. Prophecy given to Raymond Aguilera
on 8 June 1997 at 3 AM. 232
1057. Prophecy given to Raymond Aguilera
on 10 June 1997 at 4:15 AM. 232
1058. Vision given to Raymond Aguilera
on 12 June 1997 at 2:16 PM. 232
1059. Prophecy given to Raymond Aguilera
on 13 June 1997. 233
1060. Prophecy given to Raymond Aguilera
on 14 June 1997 at 1:45 AM. in Spanish. 234
1061. Vision given to Raymond Aguilera
on 14 June 1997. 235
1062. Occurrence given to Raymond Aguilera
on 14 June 1997. 235
1063. Vision given to Raymond Aguilera
on 15 June 1997 at 11:30 PM. 236
1064. Vision given to Raymond Aguilera
on 16 June 1997 at 8:45 PM. 236
1065. Vision given to Raymond Aguilera
on 23 June 1997. 237
1066. Prophecy given to Raymond Aguilera
on 23 June 1997 at 6:56 AM. in English. 237
1067. Vision given to Raymond Aguilera
on 26 June 1997 at 5:52 PM. 238
1068. Prophecy given to Raymond Aguilera
on 29 June 1997 at 6:52 PM in Spanish. 239
1069. Prophecy given to Raymond Aguilera
on 29 June 1997 at 7:23 in English. 239
1070. Prophecy given to Raymond Aguilera
on 8 July 1997 at 8:15 AM. 240
1071. Prophecy given to Raymond Aguilera
on 13 July 1997 at 9:55 AM. in Spanish. 243
1072. Prophecy given to Raymond Aguilera
on 14 July 1997 at 9:30 AM. 244
1073. Prophecy given to Raymond Aguilera
on 17 July 1997 at 1:30 PM. in English. 246

1074. Prophecy given to Raymond Aguilera
on 22 July 1997 at 8:04 AM. in English. 246
1075. Prophecy given to Raymond Aguilera
on 22 July 1997 at 8:20 AM. 247
1076. Prophecy given to Raymond Aguilera
on 25 July 1997 at 4 AM. in Spanish. 247
1077. Prophecy given to Raymond Aguilera
on 25 July 1997 at 5:30 AM. in Spanish. 248
1078. Vision given to Raymond Aguilera
on 25 July 1997 at 6 AM. 248
1079. Vision given to Raymond Aguilera
on 25 July 1997 at 6 AM. 249
1080. Prophecy given to Raymond Aguilera
on 25 July 1997 at 6 AM. 249
1081. Prophecy given to Raymond Aguilera
on 25 July 1997 at 6 AM. 249
1082. Prophecy given to Raymond Aguilera
on 25 July 1997 at 6:30 AM. in English. 249
1083. Prophecy given to Raymond Aguilera
on 26 July 1997 at 1:45 AM. in English. 250
1084. Vision given to Raymond Aguilera
on 26 July 1997 at 3:30 AM. 250
1085. Occurrence given to Raymond Aguilera
on 26 July 1997 at 2:53 PM. 250
1086. Prophecy given to Raymond Aguilera
on 26 July 1997 at 8:17 PM. 253
1087. Occurrence given to Raymond Aguilera
on 27 July 1997 at 3:30 AM. 253
1088. Vision given to Raymond Aguilera
on 27 July 1997 at 3:45 AM. 256
1089. Vision: 256
1090. Vision: 257
1091. Vision: 257
1092. Vision: 257
1093. Vision: 257
1094. Vision: 257
1095. Vision: 257
1096. Vision: 258

1097. Vision given to Raymond Aguilera
on 28 July 1997 at 1:20 AM. 258
1098. Prophecy given to Raymond Aguilera
on 28 July 1997 at 1:20 AM. 258
1099. Vision given to Raymond Aguilera
on 28 July 1997 at 1:20 AM. 259
1100. Vision given to Raymond Aguilera
on 28 July 1997 at 1:20 AM. 259
1101. Vision given to Raymond Aguilera
on 28 July 1997 at 1:20 AM. 260
1102. Occurrence given to Raymond Aguilera
on 28 July 1997 at 4:15 AM. 260
1103. Prophecy given to Raymond Aguilera
on 28 July 1997 at 4:30 AM. 260
1104. Occurrence given to Raymond Aguilera
29 July 1997 at 10:36 PM. 261
1105. Vision given to Raymond Aguilera
on 30 July 1997 at 3:25AM. 261
1106. Vision given to Raymond Aguilera
on 30 July 1997 at 5:03 AM. 261
1107. Prophecy given to Raymond Aguilera
on 3 August 1997 at 5:20 PM. in English. 261
1108. Vision given to Raymond Aguilera
on 8 August 1997 at 8:42 AM. 263
1109. Vision given to Raymond Aguilera
on 29 August 1997 at 1:14 PM. 263
1110. Occurrence given to Raymond Aguilera
on 29 August 1997. 263
1111. Vision given to Raymond Aguilera
on 9 September 1997 at 1:10 PM. 263
1112. Occurrence given to Raymond Aguilera
on 9 September 1997 at 8:30 PM. 264
1113. Vision given to Raymond Aguilera
on 16 September 1997 at 9:10 AM. 264
1114. Vision given to Raymond Aguilera
on 27 September 1997 at 7:31 AM. 264
1115. Prophecy given to Raymond Aguilera
on 7 October 1997at 3:36 PM. 265
1116. 3:43 PM. 265

1117. Prophecy given to Raymond Aguilera
on 14 October 1997 at 7:12 PM. in Spanish. 265
1118. Occurrence given to Raymond Aguilera
on 20 October 1997 at 12:30 PM. 265
1119. Occurrence given to Raymond Aguilera
on 3 November 1997 at 9:00 AM. 266
1120. Prophecy given to Raymond Aguilera
on 3 November 1997 at 9:15 AM. 267
1121. Occurrence given to Raymond Aguilera
on 3 November 1997 at 9:15 AM. to 9:00 PM. 267
1122. Occurrence given to Raymond Aguilera
on 14 November 1997 at 8:30 PM. 268
1123. Prophecy given to Raymond Aguilera
on 14 November 1997 at 8:30 PM. 271
1124. Occurrence given to Raymond Aguilera
on 14 November 1997 at 11:00 PM. 271
1125. Vision given to Raymond Aguilera
on 21 November 1997 at 1:30 AM. 273
1126. Vision given to Raymond Aguilera
on 23 November 1997 at 10:45 AM. 275
1127. Vision given to Raymond Aguilera
on 28 November 1997 at 8:35 AM. 275
1128. Prophecy given to Raymond Aguilera
on 29 November 1997 at 11:15 PM. in Spanish. 276
1129. Prophecy given to Raymond Aguilera
on 1 December 1997 at 12:10 AM. in Spanish. 277
1130. Prophecy given to Raymond Aguilera
on 2 December 1997 at 5:45 PM. 278
1131. Prophecy given to Raymond Aguilera
on 3 December 1997 at 11:30 PM. 279
1132. Prophecy given to Raymond Aguilera
on 7 December 1997 at 8:30 AM. 279
1133. Vision given to Raymond Aguilera
on 7 December 1997 at 9 AM. 280
1134. Prophecy given to Raymond Aguilera
on 7 December 1997 at 12:15 PM. 280
1135. Prophecy given to Raymond Aguilera
on 17 December 1997 at 8:30 AM. 280

1136. Prophecy given to Raymond Aguilera
on 18 December 1997 at 1:30 PM. 280
1137. Prophecy given to Raymond Aguilera
on 21 December 97 at 11:15 PM. in Spanish. 282
1138. Prophecy given to Raymond Aguilera
on 22 December 1997 at 1:27 AM. 283
1139. Prophecy given to Raymond Aguilera
on 23 December 1997 at 7:14 AM. in Spanish. 283
1140. Vision and Prophecy given to Raymond Aguilera
on 28 December 1997 at 7:28 AM. 283
1141. Prophecy given to Raymond Aguilera
on 29 December 1997 at 6:45 PM 285
1142. Prophecy given to Raymond Aguilera
on 31 Dec 1997 at 9:15 AM. 285
1143. Vision given to Raymond Aguilera
on 11 January 1998 at 8:01 AM. 286
1144. Vision given to Raymond Aguilera
on 11 January 1998 at 8:13 AM. 286
1145. Prophecy given to Raymond Aguilera
on 13 January 1998 at 6:45 PM. 286
1146. Vision given to Raymond Aguilera
on 20 January 1998 at 11:20 PM. 287
1147. Prophecy given to Raymond Aguilera
on 2 February 1998 at 1:10 AM. in Spanish. 287
1148. Prophecy given to Raymond Aguilera
on 6 February 1998 at 9:30AM. in Spanish. 288
1149. Occurrence given to Raymond Aguilera
on 23 February 1998 at 2 PM. 288
1150. Prophecy given to Raymond Aguilera
on 24 February 1998 at 10:45 PM. in Spanish. 290
1151. Prophecy and Vision given to Raymond Aguilera
on 26 February 1998 at 11:45 PM. 292
1152. Prophecy and Vision given to Raymond Aguilera
on 27 Feb 1998 at 7 AM. 294
1153. Occurrence given to Raymond Aguilera
on 27 February 1998 at 5:10 PM. 295
1154. Prophecy and Vision given to Raymond Aguilera
on 2 March 1998 at 8:00 AM. 295

1155. Vision and Prophecy given to Raymond Aguilera
on 5 March 1998 at 8:20 AM. 296
1156. Prophecy given to Raymond Aguilera
on 7 March 1998 at 7:13 AM. 296
1157. Prophecy given to Raymond Aguilera
on 13 March 1998 at 8:32 AM. 297
1158. Prophecy and Vision given to Raymond Aguilera
on 17 March 1998 at 3:34 PM. 299
1159. Vision given to Raymond Aguilera
on 18 March 1998 at 4:00 PM. 300
1160. Occurrence given to Raymond Aguilera
on 19 March 1998 at 7:30 PM. 301
1161. Prophecy given to Raymond Aguilera
on 21 March 1998 at 8:00 AM. 302
1162. Vision given to Raymond Aguilera
on 22 March 1998 at 9:49 PM. 302
1163. Vision given to Raymond Aguilera
on 25 March 1998 at 12:56 AM. 303
1164. Vision given to Raymond Aguilera
on 3 April 1998 at 10:00AM. 304
1165. Vision given to Raymond Aguilera
on 6 April 1998 at 8:30 AM. 304
1166. Vision given to Raymond Aguilera
on 14 April 1998 at 9:45 PM. 305
1167. Vision given to Raymond Aguilera
on 30 April 1998 at 9:30 PM. 306
1168. Vision given to Raymond Aguilera
on 4 May 1998 at 5:20 PM. 306
1169. Vision given to Raymond
on 9 May 9:32 AM. 306
1170. Occurrence given to Raymond Aguilera
on 13 May 1998 at 8:17 AM. 306
1171. Prophecy given to Raymond Aguilera
on 28 May 98 at 8:00 PM. 308
1172. Vision given to Raymond Aguilera
on 1 June 1998 at 9:45 PM. 308
1173. Vision given to Raymond Aguilera
on 3 June 1998 at 12:15 AM. 308

1174. *Prophecy given to Raymond Aguilera*
   on 3 June 1998 at 9:15 PM. in English. 308
1175. *Prophecy given to Raymond Aguilera*
   on 5 June 1998 at 4:42 PM. in Spanish. 310
Daily Communion
Communion Bible Scripture 315
Daily Communion 319
About the Author 321

Part 1

The Story of how Prophecies, Visions, Occurrences, and Dreams began with Raymond Aguilera

Prophecies, Visions, Occurrences, and Dreams given to Raymond Aguilera.

(Written from my recorded journal tapes. **Almost totally written as recorded word for word.** Tape recorded two months after the first occurrence and visions, and not yet completed three years later. The names of some of the people have been changed.) Copyright 1990-1999 Raymond Aguilera

April 1990:

Well, I don't know where to begin my story, for it is so long. So, I'll start on the night before the first appearance of the Holy Spirit. It was a Wednesday night. I went to a church service and during that service, I approached a very close female friend and asked her to pray with me, for we were having problems. As I approached her, I remember her fear as she agreed to pray. We were both tense, because we were having problems relating to each other. I knew she cared for me, and she had become very special to me.

As we were praying, I sensed her fear. I could tell she wanted this prayer to be over and done with, but I pushed it. For she asked me if we had prayed for all of my needs and I quickly said "No." So we prayed some more and exchanged comments of the feeling we both had for each other. I was aware of her very personal problems of abuse, she had experienced in her past, which made it extremely hard for her to relate to anyone of the opposite sex.

She had mentioned to me, a number of times, that she cared, but was trying to deal with her problem. Well, with all of this tension, she lost control. She started to build this wall around herself, and it was extremely difficult for her to relate or even to talk. I felt her tension, and anxiety. I can still visualize her nervousness. She didn't want to sit next to me because it made her nervous, but she did anyway. This tension, fear, anxiety, and the anger was not directed toward me, but it was directed toward herself. I could see that she was having a battle within herself and it hurt me. I hurt down to the gut, but there wasn't anything I could do, and my presence was making it worse, and it hurt me inside for I didn't know what to do.

Here was a woman who I believe really cared for me and I couldn't reach her. By this time everyone had left the service and we were still there trying to communicate. I could tell that she wanted this meeting to be over, but she and I were suffering through it. When it was finished, she was a complete wreck. I mean her hands were soaking wet with perspiration and she was shaking. She just wanted to get this prayer over with, and she wanted me to go so she could leave, but then, she couldn't move, because of the distress. So, I got up and left, and she went down to talk to the pastor. I could see her nervousness by the way she handled herself. I went to talk to a church member, and then left for the parking lot.

As I was leaving I could see her walking out of the Church with two others. She was talking and trying to act normal, but I could tell she was still very nervous. I watched her as I drove slowly away. I hurt inside as I watched her standing there trembling. What was so unbelievable to me was we weren't fighting or arguing. We were simply talking about little things, nothing of any great significance. I drove home and I really felt bad. That meeting between us was so painful.

Well, the next morning I decided to dedicate my morning prayers to her. That's all I could do, for I couldn't reach her by talking. She said she couldn't hug or touch because of her past. She was just out of control and it wasn't like that before. Well, to proceed with my story. About a month before this prayer time with her I had been playing this game with the Bible. If I had a problem or question I would just open my Bible without looking and see if the Lord would give me the answer. If I remember correctly, I only used the New Testament. I had been fairly successful in the past in getting answers.

Generally, I opened the Bible and looked at the first chapter of the page that caught my eye. I ran my fingers through the edge of the pages of the Bible and opened it. They stopped at the Book of John, chapter eleven, concerning the death of Lazarus. I read the chapter from beginning to end. It was nine o'clock, Thursday morning, the day after my special friend and I prayed together.

I looked to see how the scriptures would fit and apply to her. I had given her scripture before on the phone or left them on her answering machine. At times she would tell me the scriptures applied. So maybe I had stumbled upon something here. As I was reading the chapter, I passed verse forty-four (where Christ was speaking) and proceeded on, but something told me I had read to far. I really didn't understand it, but I just sensed I had read to far. So I back tracked and stopped on verse forty-four. It was the last verse that Christ spoke about the rising of Lazarus.

From tape Journal as recorded:

My lips are dry and I have been sweating all night and it seems to be that way every night. I wake up in the morning in a cold sweat with my mouth dry. Sometimes I can't remember the words I am going to say because Satan attacks my mind, but I am going to proceed and go as far as I can, and say as much detail as I recall, and in the order I remember it. For I know that Satan attacks me when I repeat this story. I have relived these events many times, but he still attacks my mind. He makes my mind go totally blank of events just before I recall them.

I can't understand why this happens because I have relived this so many times, but my mind just goes blank and I know Satan is the cause. Sometimes he attacks me with anxiety, I shake and sweat with fear. I start thinking evil things, but I am going to try to tell you as much as I can and as thorough as I can. I have prayed for the Holy Spirit to help me in this process. Right now, while I am telling you this I feel...the presence of Satan. I feel nervous and I am shaking, but I am going to keep on describing these important events.

My mind just went blank—I can't remember where I left off...Lord Jesus in the name of Christ—help Me! Help me proceed. I told you, I was going to do it, so help me do it. Please help me with my memory. I can't remember where I left off. In the name of the Father, the Son, and the Holy Spirit, Lord Jesus protect me. In the name of Christ get out of here Satan. I mean it! In the name of the Father, and the Son, and the Holy Spirit—In the name of the Father, the Son, and Holy Spirit. Satan get out of here! Lord Jesus, Lord Jesus Help me right now! Please, I ask you.

Oh my God. I am so thirsty. I am...So thirsty. It must be three or four o'clock in the morning, Wednesday, the 28th of July 1990, I believe so, for the 26th of July was Monday. I don't know, for so many things have occurred and happened to me that I can't keep track of time following these occurrences. Time seems to have no meaning in both the spiritual and physical world to me lately.

My mind is still blank and my lips are dry. There are tears in my eyes. I see the sun coming up through my window and through the trees in my backyard. It's still dark outside, but I can see it coming up. I can't figure this out. I have always been able to repeat this story at the times when my mind goes blank, it would come back within a few seconds to a minute, but boy, this time...

Boy! Is my mouth dry, I seem to get to a point in my memory, then my mind goes totally blank with anything regarding this story—I mean blank, almost total amnesia. The evil one's presence is strong tonight. "In the name of Christ, Lord Jesus protect me! Put a Dome of protection around my bed like you did that morning." Great, I remember now. "Thank you Lord."

Back to the Story:

I read the Bible verses, then something struck me that this was important. I can't explain why or how. You could say a feeling, but I can't put a word to it. Sometimes it is hard to put words to what I see, maybe it's because my vocabulary isn't large enough, but what I experience sometimes is unexplainable in the flesh and extremely hard to describe, for they are so awesome. I wish I could relate how I see the Colors, the Power and Forces of both God and of Satan.

But when I read the Bible verses, in chapter eleven of the Book of John, I was compelled to call her. I knew she was at work, for it was nine o'clock Thursday morning when this occurrence happened. I felt like a fool, but I wanted to help her. But I had told her I was going to stay away because of the tension. This sensation was strong, like, "Ray, why don't you give her the information, give her a call, give her the chapter and verses? Maybe you'll do her some good…possibly." So I thought it out and said, "Okay," to myself. What could possibly go wrong by giving her the chapter and verses. I called her, even though this whole thing didn't make sense to me. Anyway, she was at work at nine in the morning so I called her at home.

Her recorder kicked on, and I said, "This is Ray, read chapter eleven and verse one through forty-four of the Book of John," and I hung up. Then I said to myself, "That was strange of me, let's see what I can get out of this." As I started to read it again, I felt this Presence, I don't know how I can explain it, but whatever this was, I had a strong sense to call her back. I don't know for sure what it was, but I sensed it was extremely important to make sure she got the right chapter and verses.

I cannot explain this feeling. It just came over me from nowhere. "No," I said to myself, "This is stupid. I just left a message a few minutes ago. She's really going to think I am nuts." But the feeling was so specific, and since I had already stuck my neck out that far. I said, "Why not," so I called her back and left this message on her answering machine, "I don't remember if I gave you the right chapter and verses, but be sure you read chapter eleven and verses one through forty-four in the Book of John, it's important." I don't know why I stressed that it was important, but I did stress it.

Since this whole thing was strange and not at all like me, I said to myself, "I better read this one more time." So, as I started to read the book of John, chapter eleven, verse one through forty-four, I must have read the first two or three verses, then, my God, I felt this sensation. I was laying in bed on my back and I felt this heat. This heat went through my heart, down through my legs, and out through both my arms. The warmth was incredible.

And I started to cry. I started to cry!! (I have to state here that parts of this section will sound different because, just my trying to tape record this event, I began to cry again uncontrollably.) I started to cry!!...I am crying...and I can't stop!...I can't stop crying to figure out what was going...I...I felt...I saw.

I saw this sphere, or a Dome of some sort that instantaneously came out of nowhere. I could see through it. This protective Dome went from the foot to the head of the bed as I was laying on my back. All I can say is that I could see through it. It covered the whole king-size bed. My body went into the fetal position and I started to perspire. Then I realized it was the Holy Spirit. The awesome Presence was just over powering. It felt so good, and so odd, all at the same time, and I felt so alive...I remember thinking, what's going on here? This was completely new...I have to stop here because I just can't talk right now for I am reliving it all over again...

Okay, I am back. During this whole thing all I could do was just cry, but during this crying I saw my female friend. I could see her, or I felt her, I guess you would say both, I don't exactly know how to explain it, but my soul went into her body or something like that. I guess, I really don't know. I experienced the sensations she was feeling, what her soul was feeling...(I lost control here during this section of the taping and started to cry.) Oh my God it's so awful...I felt the terror. I felt...the agony...the uncontrolled pain. I felt all the bad feelings that she felt...I just felt

The Story of how Prophecies, Visions, Occurrences, and Dreams began with... 9

them...I just felt them...My God...My God is this what she was feeling...Help her! Help her! My God.

Then I saw her trying to speak to me and something grabbed her by the throat. Then I saw some demon, or something. I don't know what it was, and it said, "I got her and I am not going to let her go. I don't care what you're going to do. I am not going to let her go!" And during this vision I was still crying, crying and crying to the Lord as I am seeing this happen before me in some other place, or world. The demon said, "I got her by the throat and I have her where I want her, and she's going to stay here. I don't care what you do, and I am going to keep her."

Then the next vision was of a merry-go-round, the kind you see in a school play yard. And this demon, whatever it was, was spinning my friend around and around on this merry-go-round, keeping her off balance. She couldn't get off the merry-go-round. I could see her trying, but this demon kept pushing it faster and faster as she moved to the edge to jump, so she couldn't jump, because of fear and the speed of the merry-go-round. I could see her move back to the center of the merry-go-round as the demon pushed the merry-go-round faster and faster. I felt so bad for her and so helpless. Then the image stopped.

I remember that the demon's face looked like Yoda of Star Wars. It's face had the same shaped head as Yoda with its pointed ears and small nose. Then I became aware of my surroundings, I became aware of myself crying like a baby, not alligator tears, I mean...I was crying from the depths of my heart, from my soul. I was crying like a three-year-old baby that had been swiped and left bleeding. My crying was totally out of control.

Then my crying changed to a feeling of fulfillment, and I sensed peace and felt cleansed. I knew it was the Holy Spirit, He had come to show me this event and release my pain. Things like this just don't happen to me, because I am the type of person that everything has to be like two plus two is four.

I remember when I would go to these Christian fellowship meetings. I would always be the one in the back of the room watching these people speaking in tongues and say to myself, "Look at these people make fools of themselves." Because most of them weren't even sincere, they just were making noises and wanted to be heard. My sister and I used to always talk about them. We were very judgmental, for they looked so phony, and I knew they were phony for there were certain individuals that always had something to say, or saw something that didn't make sense.

Even today I can still see, and say, some people just want to be heard, they want attention and want to look Christian. Basically, I sat in the back and watched and observed, and now here, something was happening to me. My two plus two wasn't four anymore. I have always been a Christian, at least most of my life. I believe in God, the Father, the Holy Spirit, and in the Son, Jesus Christ. Now that I think about it, I have had one or two unusual occurrences in the past, but not like this. My Christianity was out of control.

Sometimes I say to myself, "I was laying in bed seeing a Dome over my bed, experiencing the Presence of the Holy Spirit and feeling good inside, but the only way I could express it, was by crying my head off." "Yeah, Ray, you're normal." This experience was so awesome, words don't even come close to explaining it. Words are meaningless for what I am trying to say or explain. My earthly body, and my mind was thinking, "Ray, you're losing it, you're losing control." "Something is going on here, and it's not right. You're going out of your mind, a few minutes ago you were all right. Snap yourself to attention. Get control of yourself." But all I could do was cry.

I tried to control myself through parts of it, because it lasted, I'll guess, a half-hour to forty-five minutes. My body was sweating, in the fetal position. I felt the Power, the Glory of the Holy Spirit and it would not stop. So finally, I took a deep breath and shook myself together and said, "This has to end." So I got up and went to the rest room, I was a little dizzy. It was like I had been drinking or something. I soaked my face and climbed back into bed. I said to myself, "Ray, you're losing it, something else is going on here. It just..." but I knew in my heart that it was the Holy Spirit, and...(Boy, my mouth and lips are dry)

I said to myself, "Get yourself dressed and get something to eat." (For the past few months, I have been eating chef salads at Jack-in-the-Box, and I have been losing weight and I have been feeling good.) So I said, "Get your day going, you have to get yourself together." So I got dressed, hopped into my car, and drove down the driveway, a little shaken. I remember I turned left onto La Paloma, a steep downhill street, and as I reached approximately three-quarters down the bottom of the hill the Presence of the Holy Spirit **hit** me again.

Oh, my soul...you know, when you want to cry, and you get this lump in your throat, and you can't explain it. You get a wavering, shaking, and a feeling in your gut. You try to control it, but you can't. Then this lump disappears from your throat, and boy, then I started crying again. I started shaking my head and saying, "What's going on here, what's going on?" This is not normal. This is not me, I am losing it. I kept saying, "Ray get control, get control." "What's going on here?"

I am saying these things to myself, and maybe more, as I drove down to the bottom of the hill. I sat in my car thinking, "You need to talk to someone about this." "You're going to have to tell someone, I am out of control." I was going to the restaurant crying like a little child. So I wiped the tears from my eyes at the bottom of the street in front of the stop sign, saying to myself, "What am I going to do?" So I took a deep breath and tried to control myself.

As I drove into the Jack-in-the-Box parking lot, I saw the car of an old girl friend. I hadn't seen her in years, but I knew what kind of car she drove. I said, "This is funny, I had just said to myself that I needed someone to talk to." My friend is married and has several children. She was the person who got me back into the Catholic Church, twenty or so years ago.

I got out of my car and walked, as controlled as I could, into the restaurant, and saw her back, she was sitting by herself at a booth. There didn't seem to be anyone else there, so I went up to her and I asked, "Sherrill are you alone?"

She looked up at me and said, "Yes."

"Do you have a minute to talk?", I said.

"I only have a few minutes because I have to go to work," she said. Then she looked at me right in the face and said, "Ray, you look like you have seen a ghost."

"I think I have," I said. So, I went and ordered my food, and came back to the table and shared my experience with her.

I have known her for many years and had developed a good friendship for about three years, before she got married. We used to go to church together for a long time. We both knew each other well, and we knew where we both stood in our faith. I told her I have been out of control since this happened this morning, and I needed someone to talk to.

She said, "You know, every morning I eat at Carl's Jr. in Pinole, but for some reason I came here, I never have done this before."

I said, "Maybe it was because I needed to talk to someone," and we just stared at each other.

Then after talking for a while my self-control came back, and we proceeded to talk about old times and each others family. Then she left for work and I left for home. When I got home, my sister was there cleaning up my house because we were having a few friends over that night, and my son was helping her.

As I walked up the steps and into the kitchen I saw her cleaning the kitchen counter. The furniture was all over the place. I found a chair and I sat down.

I said, "Cristina, something happened to me this morning."

She looked right at me and said jokingly, "Have you been seeing spirits and visions?"

We always joked around about people with visions. I guess we were being unchristian, and we were always judgmental. We just didn't believe in that kind of stuff. I don't know, but when she said that, I felt like she had stuck a knife in my heart, and I started to cry. I had no control, I mean, I really started crying intensely. I could feel my soul crying in pain for what she had said and it hurt me. My son came out of the bedroom with a look that said, "What's wrong with Dad?"

I said to her, "I don't know what's going on. I just…you know."

Then she came over and put her arm around me, and we started to pray. It felt good to pray, but I was still out of control again. My son looked at me with those eyes that said, "Dad's flipping out." I guess this was about an hour and a half after my first real experience with the Holy Spirit. So that's where, and how…my first day and evening ended with the Presence of the Holy Spirit.

The Second visit of the Holy Spirit:

I'll tell you of some other occurrences but I don't know if the order is correct. So the sequence might not be correct but I will tell it as correctly as possible. They have been going on for over two months now.

A few days after the first occurrence, I called a friend of mine named Alice. Alice used to go to the Four Square Church I was attending, but she stopped going there because they didn't help her. She had a falling out with the Four Square Church. So she started going to a Mormon Church. This struck me funny, because before she started going to the Four Square church she was Catholic.

That gives a brief history of Alice, she was a very charismatic Christian. Well, I called Alice and I told her what had happened. I was telling her that I didn't understand all of this stuff, and that I didn't know why this happened and it was really confusing me.

Alice said, "The Holy Spirit appeared because you were praying for someone else and you weren't praying for yourself, and the Holy Spirit likes that." She said, "You should feel honored. I wish something like that would happen to me."

I said, "I didn't feel honored and special. I just felt like crying."

She said, "If it happens again, ask the Holy Spirit, Why? The Holy Spirit will tell you or you could pray for an answer."

So I said, "Okay."

So, that very evening, I don't remember if I had prayed for an answer or not; I just don't remember now, anyway, in my sleep…I just cannot explain the awesomeness of what happened: I was asleep when the Presence of the Holy Spirit came the second time. I felt His Presence, and it just filled my bedroom. It was indescribable, for He woke me up with this Powerful Force. He filled the whole room and in an instant my body went into the fetal position again, and started to shake. I knew it was the Holy Spirit because I sensed it and I started to cry. I mean, I cried again and loud, but this time the Holy Spirit's Presence was stronger than the first time. I mean **this was strong**. I had thought the first time was strong, but this time it was unbelievable.

The first time was sort of sensations with visions, but this time there was communication, not in the sense of spoken words, but mind to mind, or, Spirit to spirit. This was an **exchange of thoughts**. I wasn't saying words with my lips. It was sort of talking in pictures. The Holy Spirit didn't tell me, He showed me in my mind the reasons why He appeared to me. I just cried through most of the occurrence.

Try to understand this, I was crying, crying **LOUD**, but my mind was calm and communicating with the Holy Spirit and I was in control of my spirit, or whatever you want to call it. But my physical body, all it could do was cry, and I mean **CRY!** I don't mean alligator tears. My body started perspiring in the fetal position. I don't know if this fetal position was for protection, like in the womb, or for growing, but I knew the Holy Spirit was in my room and I remembered what Alice had said, "Ask why?"

During this crying experience I got enough nerve to ask, "Why me? What's going on?" I feel like I am losing my mind."

And the Holy Spirit said to me, "Ray, we are proud of you. You have been good, don't let your girl friend knock you off balance," and the Holy Spirit gave me reassurance.

I said, "Why? What's going on?"

And the Holy Spirit said, "I appeared because you have done three things."

I said, "Three things, what did I do?"

Maybe I was getting more confidence, because I felt safe and secure, like when I talk to a good friend. Or maybe because the Holy Spirit got my attention with His Glory, but I was still crying **LOUDLY**.

The Holy Spirit showed me pictures in my mind from October 1989, the weekend before the California earthquake. About twenty singles had gone to Yosemite on a Christian retreat. Most of us went on a hike up to this waterfall that was two to three miles up this sharp trail. On the way up the trail there was this young man about twenty-eight years old, He had a back pack with an eight or nine month old baby in it, and a cute little girl walking beside him, I guess she was three or four years old.

So our group walked around him because he was blocking the trail and walking slow and careful because of the sharp rocks all over the trail. The trail wasn't very defined, but there was a trail. Well, we all walked up the trail to the top to see the waterfall. We stayed at the top of the waterfall for about a half-hour then we proceeded back down this trail.

I was seeing this in my mind clearly, as if I was there. I was reliving it all over again. Well, about one quarter mile from the top of the hill this young man was sitting on this rock. This poor guy was sweating badly as if he had taken a shower with his clothes on. He even looked as if he was dizzy. His three-year-old child was looking over the side of the cliff and he still had his baby in his backpack. This guy was totally exhausted and there was no way in the world he could go any farther.

Then, when our Christian group walked around him and kept going, something made me stop and look back. I could see this guy was in trouble and I really didn't know what to do, as I looked at him. But I experienced this sharp pain inside of me, and I knew I couldn't leave him there.

I mustered the nerve and went up to him and said, "Can I help you?"

He looked up at me, his face was all sweaty. There were many people walking by him and I guess he felt his manliness threatened. He knew he was stuck on this hill with his two kids. He had reached that point in his mind where he realized he had done a stupid thing.

I could see him looking at me up and down, because I was a stranger. Then his pride showed and he said, "No, I am okay. I am just not going up to the waterfall, its just to hot and sticky."

I said, "Well if you're going back down let me give you a hand with the kids."

He looked up and down at me again and said, "No that's all right."

And I said, "It's no trouble."

He paused for a second and said, "Well, all right."

So he got up, and I tied my coat around my waist, because it was very hot that day and I didn't want to carry it, I reached out and took the little girl by the hand. He got up slowly and grabbed the other hand of his little girl, but He still had the other child in his backpack.

So we started down the trail. As we walked I told him I was here with a few Christian singles on a retreat. Then he started telling me about what he did for a living and we talked about religion and stuff like that. It was just small talk but it made the long walk back to the bottom easier. When we reached the bottom of the hill he introduced me to his wife and her family. It took us sometime to get down because we were walking at a snails pace.

But I relived the whole occurrence again. Then the Holy Spirit said, "That was the first thing you did." And I cried…and I cried…I couldn't believe what was going on here. So I just cried…

The next thing the Holy Spirit showed me was Mary. She is a woman that goes to my church. She's in a wheelchair. I don't know what's wrong with her, but she always has her arms crossed over her chest. I guess her muscles tighten up and so do her hands. She also has a difficult time speaking. She lives in a convalescent home and someone from the church picks her up for church every Sunday.

The Story of how Prophecies, Visions, Occurrences, and Dreams began with... 17

This particular Sunday, Roland, a friend of mine, took her to church. We had been talking outside the church, and if I remember correctly, I started to help him take her out of his car. On this particular Sunday there was a special musical concert by some Christian singing girls from the Los Angeles area, and Mary wanted to sit in the front row. Roland invited me to sit with them. (Boy, my mouth is dry) So we wheeled her down to the front row of the church but there was only one seat left for Roland. So the only other seat available was behind Mary, but to the left side of her.

The church service and the singing began. For some reason Mary caught my eye. I had never really watcher her before, and during the singing I could see her glow. I felt the Presence of God all over her. I can't explain this, but by watching her she touched me so. The Presence of God was all over her face and eyes, and she just radiated, sitting in that wheelchair. She seemed to be soaking up all the singing. For some reason I couldn't keep my eyes off of her as I watched her and listened to the songs myself. She was so in tune to the singing in this church service.

Now, these special groups of singers were all young girls, about forty of them. They ranged in age from thirteen to eighteen, all of them looked pretty in their red matching outfits. You could see that they all were in their prime and had all of their lives ahead of them. They all were lined up along the sides of the walls and across the front of the church. Well, Mary just sat there radiating. I tried to sense what she was feeling in that wheelchair.

Mary is about thirty years old. I understand she used to be a cheerleader or something like that in her youth before she was stricken with whatever she has. Here she was watching these young girls, thirteen to eighteen years of age, sitting in her body that can't even clap. Like I said, I just sat there watching her and not paying attention to anything else. My eyes were fixed on her. I felt the Presence of the Holy Spirit with her, but remember, this was before I had any real idea of the Holy Spirit's Power Presence.

After the service, I went over to her and I gave her a big hug and a kiss and I told her that I loved her. Everyone in this church hugs each other and most of the time they are phony hugs. So in Christ, I gave her a big, big loving hug, and I squeezed her tight. I can't explain why I did it. I just did it.

Then, after the church service, some single friends went to a wedding present opening party for some recently married friends. That afternoon, I spent a lot of time with Mary at this party. Just joking around with her, I'd tell her she was the wild one, because she was wearing this colorful handkerchief around her forehead. I remember, she turned, looked at me the best she could, and tried to speak to me. She said, "This is the best day I have had in a long, long time." It made me feel good inside and since that day she became special to me. Then my sister and I left the party. Then the image of Mary left, and the Holy Spirit said, "That was the second thing you did."

Then the third thing was shown to me. For some reason the third thing kind of perplexed me, for it was such a small thing, but the image began. It was a night at Gateway a Christian singles group. My Sister and I went together this one Monday night. She doesn't go much anymore, but this particular Monday night she went with me.

They were having a singer from the Los Angeles area. This singer, I guess, was working her way up north trying to sell her music tapes at mini-concerts in churches or wherever she could sing. She reminded me of Mama Cass of the Mama's and Papas singing group. She was big and heavy and she didn't look very good and she didn't sing very well either. I guess the other people didn't think she was very good also. I remember telling my sister, "She isn't very good," but she did sing three or four songs.

When she was finished singing they had an intermission break before the main meeting. The speaker of the meeting said the singer was selling her tapes in the back of the room if anyone wanted to buy one. Then the intermission took place, I looked around and no one moved. They all remained seated and then they slowly worked there way to the water, coffee, cookies, and other stuff that was offered, but no one went up to buy any music tapes.

I had twenty dollars in my pocket for gas and that's where it was going. I can't explain what I did. I just…I saw the singer on stage…just watching…I don't know…I am a sculptor and artist, Well, I went up and bought a stupid tape.

And the sales girl asked me, "Which one do you want?"

I said, "Give me any one."

So I gave her my twenty-dollar bill and she didn't have change. It crossed my mind to buy two tapes, but I said to myself, "No way, I need gas money." So she calls this singer over to the table, by looking at her face, I could tell she was feeling good because I bought a music tape. By this time my sister had come back to our table with her water and cookies.

She looked at me, and said, "You bought a tape."

"Yeah," I said.

On the way home she said, "Why did you buy a tape?"

I said, "I don't know."

My sister said, "She wasn't very good."

I said, "Yeah I know, but I am an artist, and I know how I would feel if I had an exhibit, and no one bought anything. I just felt sorry for her."

My sister is extremely watchful of her money and ten dollars for a tape was a lot of money for her. All I can say again is I don't know why I did it, I just did it.

Then the image stopped and the Holy Spirit said, "That's the third thing you did."

Sometimes it hurts me to say these things, for I relive the events. Though they were good things I did…and I felt good when I did them. I just did them for who knows why. Let's just leave it alone, and move on.

Anyway, during this experience of events I was seeing in my mind I was still crying through all the visions. Then the Holy Spirit said to me, through this communication, that I could have anything I wanted.

The Holy Spirit said, "I'll give you anything you want." It was beautiful. It was just so beautiful hearing that.

For I knew who was talking, and the Holy Spirit said it again, "I'll give you anything you want, **anything**," He said," I am telling you the **truth**."

I just knew I was sane, and that the Holy Spirit was going to give anything just for those three things. But this whole thing just didn't make sense to me, for my body could not accept it. It seemed unbelievable, I didn't say it, but that's what I felt. So I just started to cry, cry and cry, and I just cried some more. I felt so good inside, and I couldn't explain it.

I just cried and cried, but then, all of a sudden, my mind started working like a super fast machine, and I thought I needed this and that: I want my business to be successful; I want my house finished. All those things were running through my mind, and for some reason, I started to cry louder and louder and louder to the point I couldn't even say what I wanted if I could.

Then something just clicked and my mind just stopped. I said, "All I want is to be with you," and I cried and I cried. Man, I just cried. I said, "I just want to be with you." That's all I said, and cried…(Oh my mouth is dry)

Then the room became quiet. I don't know how it happened? How the Holy Spirit said it…? The Holy Spirit said, He wanted to hear my confession, and I was still crying, trying to think what I should confess. I thought of four or five things I guess, and I was still crying through this occurrence. I have to keep saying that because my body was in one world and my mind or spirit was in another world.

Well, I thought of these sinful things, I guess, and started to say them or think them. But before I ever started, I can't explain what happened…As I started to think of them, and to say them, they were erased from my mind, a very strange feeling. I…Like I had total amnesia as I started to say the next sin, and it was erased from my mind. I went through all of them, and to this day, I don't know what I confessed. Well, I just confessed everything and it felt good.

I remembered afterwards sweating so much in the fetal position that my mouth was dry and I had to go downstairs to get a drink.

So, I excused myself to get a drink and said to the Holy Spirit, "I have to go downstairs and get a drink, for I am thirsty. **Really, my throat is dry,**" I said that, not knowing if it was proper to leave. But I was so dehydrated my body could not take anymore.

So I got up and walked downstairs to the refrigerator. I got a drink, but I felt the Presence of the Holy Spirit with me the minute it entered the kitchen. I can't explain the feeling. I just knew that the Holy Spirit went down with me. I even saw my own face in the spirit making an unusual expression. I don't know how, but I was seeing my own face in my mind.

I froze, and I said, "Are you here?"

And the Holy Spirit said, "Yes, I am."

I said, "Oh."

So, I closed the refrigerator door and drank my drink and I felt…the word isn't strange, I felt good, but this whole thing of the Holy Spirit following me downstairs was bizarre, and unusual to me.

As I walked up the stairs, I said, "Are you here?"

And the Holy Spirit said, "Yes, I am."

I climbed back into bed. I felt peace, serenity, and good. I said to the Holy Spirit, "You know this is new, this is strange, but I'll do whatever I can, whatever you ask. Just don't give me anymore than I can take," and the Holy Spirit reassured me. I don't know, but I just felt good inside and I can't even explain it. I slept really well that night.

The following Wednesday night, I went to the Four Square church service, and I became nervous. I felt anxiety, light headed, and my knees felt weak. After the service, I had planned to talk to my special friend to see if she had read Chapter Eleven of the Book of John. I saw her walk into the church, but something influenced me not to talk to her, and to stay away from her. So after the service, I practically ran to my car and went home.

On the way home I started getting evil thoughts, like I hate this person, or that I hate my friend for hating me, or for giving me dirty looks. I had all kinds of stupid things running through my mind that I normally don't have. So, I started saying, "Satan leave me alone in the name of Jesus Christ," and they would stop, but they would stop for only a half-second, or a minute. Then they would come back and I would say, "Satan leave me alone in the name of Jesus Christ," again, then they would stop once more. This went on as I drove all the way home.

Then, when I drove up the driveway and walked up the steps, I had a sense to call my friend Susan. I have known Susan for maybe a year or so. I would talk to her sporadically. I had her phone number written down on the bottom of my singles directory with felt pen in large print. I had this sense to call her, but I didn't know why. Maybe it was to share this new experience. So, I walked up to my room to call her. I started to dial her phone number and I noticed that the last digit on her phone number was missing.

It didn't disappear before my eyes, but there was a digit missing, and since I was having these evil thoughts, on the way home, I said to myself, "Wait a minute, this is certainly not two plus two is four." I started pacing the floor and decided to go downstairs to my filing cabinet and look at my old phone bills, and see if I could find her phone number. It was a long distance call, and I knew it would be there. After I found the phone number, I went back upstairs and called her. Her mother said she was out for the evening.

This whole thing was beginning to make me nervous, so, I started pacing the floor again, saying to myself, "What is going on here?" Something has happened to Susan's phone number," I kept telling myself. So I called my friend Alice, my Christian Mormon friend, hoping she had enough Christian common sense to help me. I told Alice what had happened, and that I couldn't understand the reason for the phone number having a missing digit.

I told her about the evil thoughts, and She said, "You're ministering people Ray, and Satan doesn't want you ministering to people. That's why he is attacking you."

And I said, "**OH, REALLY.**" What she said scared and startled me.

She said, "Let me pray for the Holy Spirit to protect you."

Now, I was starting to get worried. It doesn't take much to worry me. So, she started to pray. This happened over the phone at 10:30 PM, after the Wednesday night church service, almost one week after the first appearance of the Holy Spirit. As Alice started to pray, her daughter started crying. For I could hear her in the background, but Alice just kept on praying and her daughter increased her crying.

I said, "Alice I can't hear what you are praying."

So Alice prayed louder into the phone. And at the same time her daughter increased her crying and she got louder and louder and louder. As her daughter started crying, louder and louder, that it got to a point, I couldn't hear a word Alice was saying.

I said, "Alice you're going to have to scream for I can't hear you."

And Alice just kept on praying and praying. She stopped for a second and yelled, "**DON'T WORRY**, the Holy Spirit can hear me, you don't have to hear me."

Alice just kept on praying and praying, and I just kept on listening to this entire racket and noise between Alice and her daughter. Then Alice's daughter got so loud in her cries that finally Alice said, "I can't take it anymore. I'll have to call you back," and she said, "I love you," and hung up.

I was really getting confused. I kept saying to myself, "What's going on here?" Then I had this sensation again, these crazy feelings that I had to go to minister to my son Steve and talk to him, or something. I didn't know what, and it was late. He was downstairs in his room, so, I went down to talk to him to explain why I was crying the week before, when I had returned from the Jack-in-the-Box restaurant. I wanted to explain to him what was going on.

I knocked on his bedroom door and he let me in. We have a little black dog, named Leroy. He kept jumping on me without ceasing. He always jumps on me, I think its normal for him, but he wouldn't leave me alone. So, I sat down on the edge of the bed and Leroy tried to lick my face and so forth, he has always been like that. But he wouldn't let me talk to my son about the Holy Spirit, and the occurrence that happened the week before.

I kept pulling him off and he kept coming back. I would throw him off, and he would come back. I thought it was normal for Leroy, because he is hyper. But I was very serious about telling my Son about the Holy Spirit, and I was trying to answer his questions, because he was into this L. Ron Hubberd scientology stuff. And I have been trying to reach him for the last year or so. I thought to myself, "I might as well try now, since he is willing to sit here and listen," so I went for it.

As I was talking to Steve, in my mind I said to Leroy, "Get away from me Satan in the name of Christ," and then, Man!, **I could never, never, never describe this energy source, this Power, this whatever label you want to put on it.** It filled the room with such energy or power that the intensity felt like I was playing with nuclear weapons. **Leroy just froze in his tracks and backed off.**

You know, when you scold a dog and their head goes down, and they give that sad look. That's the way Leroy behaved, and I didn't say a word to him. I only said it in my mind, but somehow Leroy read my mind, and backed off. My son wasn't aware of what was going on in the spirit, as I watched Leroy from the corner of my eye. I just kept on answering Steve's questions about the Holy Spirit. Leroy did back off, but for only a minute or two.

Then Leroy jumped onto the floor as I was sitting on the bed, and tried to lick my face again. I just kept on speaking to my son, and looked down at Leroy and I said, "Satan, calm down in the name of Christ", and I felt the incredible energy force. I will never forget that sensation of **Energy** and **Power**. It was just awesome, and Leroy just seemed to melt right there on the spot, and then he backed off. I believe, I could have killed our dog just by telling him to drop dead. That's how much Power was in that room.

My Son didn't sense any of it, but I sure did, and I am more than sure that Leroy did. The room stayed with this limitless Power Presence until I left. Like I said, "I'll never forget this Power experience. **IT WAS JUST UNBELIEVABLE!**" So, I finished ministering to my Son, and said to him, "If you ever want to talk some more let me know." I had told him to read the Bible, and gave him the chapters and verses that I had given my female friend. After this I went upstairs and laid down, afraid, and worried about the occurrences.

Before, it was in my dreams, and I was protected. Now, I sensed the protection was a little looser. This was totally new, maybe I was being exposed to something stronger now. The attacks were a little stronger but I only now understand they were actually attacks. I was really frightened, I didn't know, or understand what was going on. I just couldn't comprehend, and I have trouble putting it into words.

I called my sister, and told her what had happened. She became scared and called my brother in the State of Washington, and my parents in Vacaville. I have no idea what she told them, but I believe they thought I was going crazy. Remember all this occurred one-week after I prayed for my special female friend, and after the first appearance of the Holy Spirit.

I was so frightened that I took the singles mailing list and started calling everyone I could think of, from the top to bottom of the list, but it was eleven o'clock at night and I only got their answering machines. The things that were going on were terrifying me, and I didn't know how to protect myself. My Christianity was just out of control. I kept on dialing all the people I knew, and trying to get anybody to listen to me.

I needed instructions on how to protect myself, or prayer, or anything that would help, and I didn't care what it was. Finally I got to the last person on my list, and it was Jim; he didn't want to talk to me because it was late for him. I told him it was important, and I told him what happened.

So he started to pray for me, and I prayed for him. After we finished praying I hung up and I felt at peace. Then I went to bed and tried to sleep.

The next day I contacted Susan, the girl with the missing digit of her phone number. I shared with her the events that had happened. We have shared experiences in the past. We could tell each other anything, and on many occasions we spent time on the phone knocking down Christians, holy rollers, and tongue speakers. Susan has a friend who is involved in this area of Christianity. I don't believe Susan's friend is as serious a Christian as she tries to make people believe; but we always comment on some things she does.

Then Susan said to me, "Ray, you're not turning into one of them are you?"

I said, "I don't know, I can't explain this stuff, but for some reason, I had to call you, and tell what happened."

She said, "You're serious!"

And I said, "I am **SERIOUS!!** I can't explain what is going on, and for some reason, I had to call you."

Then Susan shared with me, and said, "You know Ray, I have been very depressed the last two or three days. I have been thinking about suicide, and no one knows, not even my parents." Then I became silent. She said, "This really means something, what you're telling me, all of this stuff."

I said, "You know Susan, I don't know why I was supposed to call you, and I don't know what I am supposed to say. I have no answers. You know this is totally new and strange to me. All I know is that I was supposed to call you, and tell you what happened to me."

Later that week we made a date to talk. Eventually she went to church with me.

A few days later, I was talking to my Mormon friend, Alice, who gives me Christian advice, and I was telling her that I was waking up every morning with my T-shirt completely wet from perspiration.

She said, "Well, why don't you pray about it, and see if you get an answer."

So I prayed that night, and I received an answer in a dream. The dream was...I mean, I even saw myself singing and praising God. I kept saying, "Oh God you're so beautiful, I love you. You're so great, you're the Greatest, all Glory to God." Just one saying after another, I was doing that all night, and Satan was attacking me, while I was praising God. I don't know for sure, but I was left with that feeling.

And I guess the Holy Spirit was protecting me, because the Holy Spirit assured me that I wouldn't be given anymore than I could take. So, He must have erased the memories of the attacks and praises to God in my dreams. The only thing for sure was that when I woke up my clothes were all wet with sweat from the warfare in my sleep.

This made me feel secure, for I sensed the Holy Spirit had kept His Word, and I was shown what was going on. Maybe the Holy Spirit knew I didn't have the spiritual strength to withstand the attacks. Now, in looking back, I could see that I was green; I didn't know anything at all about spiritual warfare, and I still don't know enough. I couldn't take the blows from Satan. I was vulnerable and the Holy Spirit just blanked out whatever happened in the night attacks.

I go to sleep late, and these early morning occurrences are hard on me. During one on Sunday morning, about 4 A.M., the Holy Spirit told me to call my special female friend.

The Holy Spirit said, "Tell her you love her, that you care for her, and tell her your deepest feelings."

Well, since we had an argument earlier, and weren't talking, and it was four o'clock in the morning, I said, "No!, No way am I going to call her, and tell her. I am not going to say such a thing." I felt strongly about this.

The Holy Spirit said, "Call her!"

I said, "**NO!**" "I will not do this! I will not do this! I will not do this!" I said it loudly, "**I WILL NOT DO THIS!!**" I fought it for an hour. Then I said, "It's five o'clock, it's too early."

The Holy Spirit wanted me to call her then, at five o'clock. "This has to be totally idiotic," I said to myself. I felt like a fool, and crazy, because

I had shared some things with her earlier, and had sent all her stuff back to her, tape recording, pictures; all with a very nice Dear John letter. Now a week later the Holy Spirit wanted me to call her, tell her my innermost, deepest feelings, and tell her that I loved her.

I said, **"You've got to be kidding!"**

So, I wrestled with this, and prayed about it. I said, "Maybe at six o'clock." I said, "Maybe at six o'clock."

I hoped I would fall asleep, and this whole thing would go away into the sunset, but the Holy Spirit would not leave me alone. I tossed and turned until a minute to six o'clock. I was still awake and praying about this. I didn't want to do it! **I REALLY DID NOT WANT TO DO IT!**

It got to the point where, I was going to be obedient, or not. I looked at the clock, it was 5:59 AM., and I kept saying, **"NO!, NO!, NO!, NO!, Please!**, I don't want to do this, I don't want to do this! No, Please! I don't want to do this!" I just kept saying this over and over, and then it was six o'clock, and I said, "Oh, what the heck!" So I called her, and her telephone answering machine went on, and I said, "Hello, it's Ray. We have to talk, but you don't have to talk to me, but if you want to, call me back, I will understand if you don't" and I hung up.

I felt so relieved, the pressure was off. I said, "Oh, I did my job, it's over and done, I was obedient. I tried, but she wasn't home, the recorder kicked on." I was so glad it was the recorder and not her. So I said to myself, "Oh gee, I did my job!" Well, I fell asleep, and the phone rang at seven o'clock, and I knew who it was.

I said, "Hello," and She gave me a piece of her mind.

She said, "You shouldn't call me at six o'clock in the morning!"

She was trying to act mad, but she wasn't. She was giving me a bunch of hot air, and I knew it. She didn't have to call me back, but, so she could keep her self-esteem, I just listened. We talked for about an hour about our relationship. I told her how awkward it was seeing her in church, with all the tension, and she said she was working on it. The time came when

I had to open up my heart, and tell her what the Holy Spirit had asked me to do. I still didn't want to do it. I was debating whether to do it.

Then I said, "I want to tell you something, and I feel very awkward telling you this."

She became very quiet.

I said, "I love you. I love you with all my heart, and I miss you, and it hurts me, when I see you in pain. It hurts me to see you making jokes, and clowning around trying to be funny and cute, because all you want is attention. I know all you want is love, and for someone to put their arms around you, hug you, and tell you they care and love you. It really hurts me to see you that way," and I said other personal stuff.

I remember telling her again how awkward it was, saying these things. I said, "It's very hard for me to make myself vulnerable about this. It's very hard," I said. "I am trying to make peace between you and I, but I am doing what I have to do."

Then there was another moment of silence, and she says, "Ray, for the last three days I have been praying that you would call."

I said, "**WHAT?**"

She said, "For the last three days, I have been praying that we would talk. But I can't call you, something stops me from calling you. I can't call you."

Then, I was silent. I knew then why the Holy Spirit wanted me to call her. This was a lesson in obedience for me. The Holy Spirit works in unusual ways, no one can see the whole picture. Well, that was Sunday morning, and I saw her in church, everything went well that day, and for the next few days, but within a week things were back the way they were, with all the tension, and so fourth. I fought my obedience that Sunday morning, and my reward was friendship for a few days. It's a shame it didn't last, but those few days were beautiful. To this day she still calls me, listens to my voice, and hangs up without saying a word.

A few weeks later I woke up with a dream of going to the Four Square Church. The problem was that the Holy Spirit had told me not to go to this particular church three weeks earlier.

The Holy Spirit said to me, "I would like you to stop going to this church."

So I told all my friends at that church I wasn't going there anymore. Now, three weeks later the Holy Spirit tells me to go back. I was so annoyed, I felt like I was being played for a fool. I was having a hard time dealing with this, yes go, and no don't go to church stuff. I guess the Holy Spirit is trying to teach me obedience. I had a definite feeling of rebelliousness, but when Friday morning came and the Holy Spirit said to go back, I said to myself, "Something startling is going to happen, maybe I will talk to my special female friend, or see something unexpected."

But I didn't talk to anybody. My special friend didn't go, and nothing happened; however the sermon was on obedience. Maybe I was supposed to listen to that sermon, I don't really know. I wish I could understand these things, and put the pieces together. I wish…I could put my mind to work, and see what was ahead. (I am kind of frustrated at the present time, it's about 9:45 AM., and I really haven't started my day, but I don't know…)

Comments:

(It's strange even now as I type this occurrence three years after the fact, I feel like I am under attack, and I really have no one to turn to, I feel so **alone.** I feel like I am going to explode from the inside out. Satan is really doing a job on me this minute. Maybe its because I am almost finished with the first draft of this book. For I am typing the beginning of the book last. I wish…I could explain the spiritual attacks, but there is nothing I can do, but trust in Christ to deliver me. Boy…**It really hurts right now,** "Please help me Lord, for I can't take much more of this.")

Back to the recording tape:

I haven't been feeling strong these last two or three weeks. I have been dating a little more, doing more things and having a good time putting this stuff in the back of my mind. I don't know whether that's good. I went to a dance with a friend, and she's has been a great help. Just being able to talk to someone about this stuff has been a great help.

These attacks, visions, or whatever you want to call them are beginning to wear me down; I feel I am losing it at times. The intensity of the occurrences and the visits from the dark spirits are just unbelievable. I don't know, something is going on here in the spirit, and I just can't put my finger on it. I definitely believe its the Holy Spirit, the Father, and the Son; all three of them, but I know in all rationality Satan is there also.

I am awake right now. I feel strained, but I don't feel bad about my mental stability. I feel perfectly in tact, but I can't explain this stuff. All I can say is that there is another world out there, and I think most people are blind about the devil and things of this nature. You know they are so wrapped up in their lives, and things of society, trying to make a living that they don't really see the spirit world. I can even say Christians don't know this stuff. I ask pastors and other members of the body questions and they either get afraid or they think I am crazy for asking questions about the spirit world. Because things like this just don't happen. People read about them in newspapers, or see them in movies and that's where these type of occurrences are supposed to stay.

I don't know why I am rattling on, I just…I don't even know why I am recording this, but maybe something is going to happen to these tapes, maybe people are going to use them, I don't know. At times the spiritual things are so intense and nerve racking, but definitely real; I just can't see the whole picture. But I know I am being guided, being shown certain things. I see these things just as I am seeing the light bulb in the ceiling right now.

It's so real, but these things are of another world. For a while, I denied it, because I thought I was losing my mind. Now, I know the serious side. The Universe is put together in such an extreme and complex way, but yet so simple. Simply stated: Jesus Christ, the Father, and the Holy Spirit, and don't forget Satan. It is basically simple, I believe we are running out of time, for I have had visions about it, and I really have never experienced this kind of stuff before.

I have told people about it, but all that happens is I lose so called friends, and pastors tell me to keep my mouth shut. The physical attacks are really intense at times, I believe I am in some kind of spiritual war. I have begun reading the Bible more, and other books, trying to read as much as I can and as fast as I can. No one seems to have any answers for me. I started seeing things and experiencing events I cannot explain, and I am having a hard time trying to stay balanced.

The following Sunday morning I woke up with a vision of Jesus Christ hanging on the Cross, and somehow I was able to see through Christ's Eyes, and I can't explain it. There is this young man named Charles that goes to my church. He has some sort of birth defect. He is small, with a great personality, and a very sharp mind. I believe he has more brains than a lot of people I know, and in this vision, I saw Charles singing and praising God with his hands up in the air, and he was putting his whole heart and soul into his praises.

I was seeing Charles from above and looking down through Jesus Christ's Eyes. I could even see the tears in Charles's eyes as he prayed, sung, and praised with his whole heart. This vision touched me and moved me, I could feel it in my heart, the intensity of his prayers. I felt like Jesus removed my spirit from my body, and placed it inside His own Body. I was sensing what Christ was sensing, seeing what He was seeing, and I cried. I just cried, I can't explain it, I just cried because I could sense His love for Charles.

Christ said to me, *"Ray,"* not in words, but through the mind, *"Go tell Charles that I love him. That I love him with all of My Heart, and when his time comes he's going to be with Me in Heaven. Tell him that I love his singing, and that I listen to his prayers, and that I am taking care of him, and watching over him. Now go, and tell him!"*

Hey, you have to understand, Ray Aguilera believes two plus two equals four. And going up to someone and saying, "Hey, I have a message from God," didn't hit me very well, but I had this strong urge to be obedient.

Somehow, I had to do it, and I didn't know how I was going to do it, or what I was going to say. I didn't want people to think I was crazy. I mean, I felt like that, anyway, with all of these experiences, but I knew they were real. I went to a Covenant Church that Sunday, then from there, I went to the Four Square Church that Charles was attending. I saw him out front talking to two men.

I said, "Charles, I have a message for you."

He says, "Hey, Ray, what's the message?"

I looked at the two men, and I said, "Can we talk privately?" I didn't know what I was going to say, or what I was going to do.

He said, "Okay."

So we walked away from the others, and I said, "Charles, you don't think I am crazy do you?"

The people in the Four Square Church were beginning to look at me funny, I was starting to behave differently.

He says, "Na-a-a-h."

Then I said, "Well, what I am going to tell you is going to sound crazy, and I don't want you to think I am weird, but I have a message from Jesus Christ."

Then he started to look at me funny, and I didn't know how to tell him. So, I just took a deep breath, and I said, "Charles, I had a vision this morning, and it was from Christ."

And Charles said, "Amen brother, are you born again?"

I said, "No, its not like that Charles. It's not like that. In my vision, I saw Jesus Christ and you, Charles," and I told Charles the whole story. He has small eyes, and he looked at me and checked me out cautiously.

I said, "Christ says He loves you and you're going to be with him in Heaven."

I knew it touched him, but he didn't believe the **source**. This was so hard for me, telling him this, then I started to cry, and his face changed.

I said, Charles, "I am not lying to you, from the bottom of my heart that's what happened." Then I saw a tear in his eye.

I said, "Well that's it, Charles," and I walked off and drove home crying. A day or so later, I called him, and he told me it was confirmed in church. I don't know how, they do this kind of stuff, this confirming. It was confusing to me.

Well, anyway, I went to church the following Wednesday night and I found myself giving prophecy in church. The pastor was asking for prophecy, and people started raising their hands, and to my surprise my hand went up. Now, here is this short little Mexican American that sits in the back, and says nothing, raising his hand; Generally you have the same people raising their hands, and having prophecies, and here I was with my hand up.

The sermon was on speaking in tongues, and my hand went up, and I said, "When you pray, pray from your heart not from your mouth." The pastor said, "How can you pray if you don't pray with your mouth." Then he went to the next person. I guess he didn't mean to be mean, but it didn't sound like he liked what I said, because his sermon was on tongues.

What struck my sister and I funny, was that when he got into his sermon about tongues, and so forth, he repeated what I had said twice and my sister and I just looked at each other, I guess the prophecy stuck to the pastor. I noticed the next Friday night the leader of the church singles group said, "Everyone should pray from the heart, and not the tongue," and my sister and I just looked at each other again, because she knew what was going on with me in the spirit.

I think I was having anxiety attacks when the next event occurred because I was told by the Holy Spirit to tell everyone. As a matter of fact, He told me to tell the single's group on Friday night. I approached the leader of the single's group and told him parts of what was happening. He was one of the individuals I had left a message on his answering machine the night that I experienced the Energy Force in my son's bedroom.

I said to the Holy Spirit, that I was going to drop it on the leader's lap because I had no authority in the group. If the leader of the group wanted me to share, I would share this occurrence, but I didn't want any responsibility if he didn't want me to share this unusual occurrence. I think the leader of the single's group thought I was crazy. He wanted to know if I was born again, and I guess if I said no, I wasn't part of this flock or something. I was Catholic and everyone knew it, and I have always been sort of an outsider, being Catholic and all. And here I am asking to speak to the group, because the Holy Spirit told me to.

During those times, when the Presence of the Holy Spirit came upon me, I would begin to cry, and it's hard to explain, but unless you experience it, you can't explain it.

The leader said, "Maybe you should take some time and get yourself together."

I said, "All I am trying to do is be obedient. I don't have any desire to speak to the group in the first place, but I told the Holy Spirit I would, and I am asking you to say yes, or no. If you say no, the responsibly is on you."

So he said, "No."

So, I didn't speak. Since that night the Holy Spirit has told me to tell anybody and everybody who wants to hear. Well, anyway, I don't know how I got side tracked.

A week or so later, I was in bed. This was one of those evenings that I will never forget as long as I live. I hope I can relate this story, without getting out of control. I was in bed, about three-thirty A.M., and I felt a presence that I thought was Christ; it approached me, as Christ. The voice sounded the same, but he spoke in a style or manner that felt different to me.

This voice told me that it was proud of me, that I was doing a good job in praising and so forth, and that everything was hunky-dory, that I was a good Christian.

But this voice said I had done enough, "It's time for you to come with us to Heaven."

I said, "WHAT?"

And this voice said, "Its time to go to Heaven,"

I thought to myself, "The only way I am going to Heaven is to die." I said, "Wait a minute, I have things to do here, I don't want to go. I have my business, and I have to finish building my house. I am not ready!"

And He said, "Well, you don't have a choice! You have done your duty, and you have your responsibility. It's time for you to go."

The next thing I knew, I guess it was my spirit, for to this day I don't really understand it, I was on the ceiling of my bedroom looking down at the parameters of the bedroom. I saw that the bed was made. Now, this was in the early part of the morning, about 3:30 AM, but what I saw was mid-day and the room was lit, and I felt the presence of my death. My house didn't have my presence in it. This is a feeling that's indescribable. I can't put the words to the feeling, for there are no words to describe the feeling of your own death, and not only sensing it, but also seeing it with your own eyes.

There was a void in my room, a void in my house, a void beyond my reality, a real, real, real strange feeling knowing that I was dead. The next thing I knew, I was back in my bed, and I started getting chest pains. I said, "Oh, my God, I am having a heart attack." I felt the pain in my chest, I said, "What am I going to do, as my mind began to race a mile a minute." I threw the covers off the bed, and I said, "I am not going! I am not going! I am not ready!" and I started pacing the floor. I turned on the light. I didn't know where to go, or what to do!

I was terrified, the realization of dying, and not having any control over it, and not wanting to die was just so intense. I paced the floor like a lion in a cage. I kept feeling the pain in my chest getting stronger and stronger.

I kept saying, "Go away pain, go away pain. I am not going to die, go away! I am not ready! I don't want to go!" Then I said, "Christ...I have never felt this from you before! I have never felt this kind of feeling before." So I ran to the phone, picked it up, and I dialed my sister, and I cried, and I cried, and I cried like I never cried before.

I said to Cristina, on the phone, "I am going to die tonight. I am going to die tonight!"

She started getting hysterical. She said, "What's going on?"

I said, "I don't know, I don't know!" Christ said I am going to die tonight, and I don't want to. I cried into the phone, "I don't know what to do," and I feel this pain in my chest. I am fighting it, but I don't want to go."

She said, "Let's pray, let's pray."

I truly believe Cristina helped in saving my life that night!

She started praying and singing, and she said to me, "Sing, sing Ray, sing. Ray, sing, sing with all of your heart!"

So, I started singing and singing, and praising God. Then this other Presence appeared, and it wasn't the same as the one, which said I had to die. This was a different Presence. (I even feel dizzy now, as I am telling you this!) I felt the Presence of God. Christ appeared, as my sister and I were singing and praising on the phone.

Christ said to me in my mind, *"Ray, Satan is going to attack you tonight."*

And I was just bewildered, can you imagine what was going on in my mind, and I said, **"Satan is going to attack me tonight! YOU'RE TELLING ME, SATAN IS GOING TO ATTACK ME TONIGHT!"**

And here I was singing out of control, and questioning Christ all at the same time, but I knew it was Christ. I can't explain how, I just knew....I hope it is clear, my nose was running and getting plugged up, and my eyes were watering, the intensity of just retelling this occurrence is just overwhelming. My sister was still singing on the phone, and I was singing with her. Somehow my spirit left and went into this spiritual world, and my physical body was still in bed…(I am going to turn off the recorder to blow my nose…). I hope this event is clearer now.

I said to my sister, "Can you hear me?" She said she could.

I said to Christ, "Satan is here!"

Christ says, *"I know,"* in a quiet voice.

I remember, I kept saying, "Satan leave me alone in the name of Christ, leave me alone in the name of Christ." I kept saying it over and over, but this evil presence was still coming toward me. I remember running in this spiritual world as fast as I could. I was running, looking for a place to hide.

While this is going on, my body is still lying on its back in bed with the light on praying, singing with my sister, on the phone, and at the same time, I am speaking in this spiritual world, saying, "Satan leave me alone." I could see myself running, but there wasn't a real place to hide. I can still remember that I found what I believe was a closet. I opened the door and rolled myself into a ball, with my hands over my head, hoping Satan wouldn't find me, maybe I wasn't saying, "Satan leave me alone in the name of Christ," with enough faith.

For Satan kept coming, and somehow I understood that Satan knew where I was. So, as fast as I could, I got up and ran out of this spiritual closet. I was running for my spiritual life. I was running, and I was running, and I remember he mowed me down like a blade of grass. When Satan hit me in the back, I went down, screaming at the top of my lungs. I landed flat on my face, screaming and yelling to Christ.

I yelled, "I am down!" "I am down!" "Get me up!" "Get me up! I AM DOWN," "I AM DOWN" "GET ME UP!! "GET ME UP!!" "I AM DOWN CHRIST, GET ME UP!" "I AM DOWN!"

I was crying, oh, was I crying. As Christ came to me, I screamed, "What's going on? Help me! Help me! I am down! Then Christ helps me up!

Then Christ says, *"Ray, make yourself strong! Make yourself strong."*

All I could say is, "Satan leave me alone! Leave me alone…"

On the phone, I could hear my sister singing at the top of her lungs, and at times she would start reading scripture from the Bible when her voice gave out. I was in a battle for my spiritual life! My soul was fighting one on one with Satan, for its life, and I didn't know how to protect myself.

All I could say was, "Satan leave me alone!!," but my sister was singing like an Angel, or reading the Bible, and she **didn't stop for a second.** She wouldn't stop, I could hear her and somehow I was singing too in the physical world, but I could see Christ standing on my left side in the spiritual world.

I was on his right, and I said to Christ, "Satan's Back!! He's Back!!"

Christ said in a soft voice, *"I know, I know."*

The feeling of Satan was like sand running through an hourglass, nibbling at my soul. My sister described it later to me, as the "Pac Man" video game eating at your soul, but I saw it as sand going through an hourglass. I was just so afraid, I was so **afraid.** I mean, I was afraid! I felt Satan eating at my soul. I ran, and I ran, and I ran in this spiritual world, and he hit me again, a second time, but this time it was behind my knees, and he knocked me down. I fell on top of my knees **screaming** but Christ caught me by my left elbow as I was falling.

I kept screaming, "I am down again!! I am down again!! I am down, help me!! **Please help me!!** I am down!! I don't know what to do. Leave me alone Satan! Leave me alone! Leave me alone in the name of Christ," is all I could say in terror.

I didn't feel pain. This was a different sort of pain. It was…It wasn't an earthly pain. It was spiritual pain. It was a pain, I don't know…Like not having the **Presence of God.** That's the only way I can describe it, but it hurt. It hurt my soul that jerk was after my soul, and I was fighting him the best I could. I didn't know what to do. (I am losing control again, let me turn off this recorder.)

Well, I am back. I hope it is understandable why I turned off the recorder. When I repeat this experience, it isn't with the same intensity it was that night. It's not as bad, but I still relive it. Its the kind of feeling no one wants to go through, as I was telling a pastor friend, earlier this week in the church parking lot meeting we had. I was telling him what was going on and that something had changed in my spiritual walk. He gave me a term called spiritual warfare.

These are words that Christians use, like interceding, and words like that. I think ninety-five percent of the Christians of today don't even know what they mean. I mean, really, really mean. It's like that Word from God about praying from the heart, and not just speaking it with your mouth. All these terms seem to go in one ear and out the other for me. This was so intense, the terms were of no value to me in this spiritual world.

I never heard about spiritual gifts and stuff like that before. I wonder if half the Christians that talk about them even know what they're saying, or if they really know what is out there in the evil dark spiritual world. Sometimes, I wonder if ninety-five per cent of the Christians even know what Christianity really is. I am certainly looking at it differently.

Here I am in this physical world, and in this spiritual battle in another world, and even that sounds crazy, but oh my God, I don't want to lose. I don't want to lose. Satan, this jerk, was after my soul. And I didn't know exactly what to do except I knew the Presence of Christ was there, but the battle was between Satan and me. It helped me to know that my sister was there singing on the phone, and that Christ was there, but this was a battle, a personal, intimate battle between Satan and me. I had Christ's protection, but when you're new at this, like I was, it was **sure terror**.

You're fighting a mad dog which possesses pure evil, and the words, "Pure Evil" do not do him justice. He's like a mad dog pulling on a rag. You pull on this rag and he pulls back. You pull and he pulls harder. You kick him in the teeth, and he rolls over. You can turn and run, and within a split second he jumps on your back. Then you throw that sucker off your back, and throw him on the ground. You can jump on him, and you can jump on him, and you can kick him, and you can jump on him, and you can kick him, and he gets up, and jumps on your back again. He barely gives you enough time to breathe and catch a second breath.

This sucker is **pure evil**. People think they can say, in the name of Christ, back off Satan, and that he walks off into the sunset. That's not the way it is out there people. No way! I have seen it. I have experienced it. You say it, and he backs off for a half-second, or two minutes, an hour, but he comes back. He does back off sometimes, but it's just enough time for you to catch your breath, and the sucker is back at your throat. I find myself saying hundreds of times, "Satan leave me alone in the name of Christ," everyday now.

He doesn't let off, twenty-four hours a day. For a while he was wearing me down. I couldn't get any sleep, and then he would hit me in my sleep. He would hit me while I was driving, the brakes on my car would fail for some unknown reason, and when I would pray, in the name of Christ, they would come back. Every time I hop in my car, I have to say, "Lord put a shield of protection around my car. I ask you, in the name of Jesus Christ of Nazareth, get me there safe, and get me back." This is a spiritual battle that is so real, and I have told only the part I have experienced, but I am sure there is a lot more out there I have not experienced.

Well, I am going to go on, just to give a little background, on what was going on, and words cannot accurately describe what I am going to tell. What I am going to say doesn't describe the whole picture, so beware of Satan. He is out there. They are out there right now, right next to everyone. The spiritual war is invisible, but it is there also. It's in another world somewhere, but at the same time it is right next to everyone. Sounds crazy, but it is true, Satan or his demons are there twenty-four hours a day. He's helping people do things, and making them think of things that are not of Jesus Christ. People are doing these sinful things, and are not aware that Satan is behind it all, and helping the way…So beware! Pray! Pray to Jesus Christ, the Holy Spirit, and the Father, and pray.

Back to the story:

During this intense battle, in the early morning hours, with my sister on the phone, I was running for my spiritual life, and Satan knocked me to my knees, and I was screaming, "I am down!" I couldn't scream it loud enough, and I knew that my skylight in my bedroom was open. I knew the neighbors heard me. I was screaming at the top of my lungs. I mean, I was screaming to the point where I had no more wind in my lungs. And it was between Satan and me.

Christ was there, in this spiritual world, and my sister was there, on the phone, in the physical world, so I guess I had both worlds covered with Love. Christ was with me as I was knocked down. I fell on my knees screaming. I mean, this little guy was screaming and yelling as Christ caught him.

I kept saying, "Help me up! Help me up! **HELP ME UP, I AM DOWN!** I am down. I am down!!"

And Christ said, *"Make yourself strong, Ray, make yourself strong."*

By this time in the battle Satan had beat me down to nothing, and I knew there wasn't anything in either world I could do.

So I said, "Christ, you're going to have to do it for me. You have to do it, because I don't know what to do. **Help Me!**"

Then I felt this sensation in my chest, I can't explain this at all, because it sounds weird, people are going to think I am nuts, if they don't think that already. My chest physically grew in this spiritual world, but I was still lying in bed singing and crying with my sister on the phone. But in this spiritual world my chest just grew. I mean, I felt it grow a foot and a half to two feet out, and I grew two to three feet taller, and I stood up like a statue made of stainless steel, Like a soldier on guard duty.

The sensation of immeasurable Power was in me, it was enormous. Then I felt the presence of Satan coming at me. He came at me like a speeding bullet. This was a feeling I'll never forget. It felt like I was made into a cast iron wall, and he came at me like a bullet, and I mean like a bullet, and he bounded off me, like a marble. He just ricocheted off me. I was **screaming with joy**, and started yelling and telling him off.

I said, "You can do anything you want to me, but I'll never forsake Christ. I am not going to leave Christ. You can give me your best shot, and I'll prove it to you. I am never going to leave Him, ever!" Then he came at me hard and straight, but it didn't matter, I didn't budge. He bounded off me, and I didn't move. I told him, "I told you, I wasn't going to leave Christ, and I am not going to."

All of a sudden, I was this big and bad guy shooting my big mouth off, as if I had done something great. I was so stupid for I really didn't do a thing. It was Jesus Christ that did the fighting, and here I was taking the Glory. I am sure one stupid dummy, and a fool, all at the same time. I wonder if I will ever learn who does the fighting and the protecting. I am the biggest idiot that was ever born!! For a few minutes earlier, I had my tail between my legs, and running as fast as I could trying to find a place to hide. It baffles me why we human beings are so self-centered, and I am right there leading the pack.

Well, I was still in bed singing, and praising God. Then my voice changed during this song. I am not much of a singer, my sister was really singing her heart out, and for some reason, my singing voice changed. I don't know how, some people might call it singing tongues, but I was singing and lying in bed, and following my sister's song. She wasn't singing any particular song just whatever came to her head, and I had my lungs filled with air like a balloon. I just can't describe it, other than that, and I started singing and praising God, but the last note just kept on going and going.

It sounded like Tarzan yelling in the jungle. Like Barbara Streisand holding that last note, it just went on and on; but this sound would have made Barbara Streisand sound like a babbling infant. I am not a singer, but my voice and the sound that came out just kept going on and on in a steady long….Sound.

The sound just kept on going and going and going. I mean, when it stopped, my sister said, "Wow! Wow! That sounded beautiful did that come out of you?"

I just said…"I don't know where the wind came from." My mouth just opened up, and I kept howling this musical note to God with **Praise**.

I remember rolling my eyes, trying to figure it out, as the sound was coming out of my mouth, and thinking when is this sound going to stop, my body was out of control. This note just kept going and going and going, it must have gone on for two to three minutes, without me catching a second breath. I don't even know where I got the air. I cannot to this day tell you where I got the air, the musical note just went on and on and on and on.

My mind was still conscious of what was going on, but I couldn't understand why it just kept going on.

When I ran out of air, and my sister kept saying, "Wow, Wow! What was that?"

And then I received another dose of air, and I started singing this note to Christ again. I don't know how to explain it. My mouth just started up again for another two to three minutes. I just made this sound again, then it went away.

Anyway, I was lying in bed and not much was going on during this battle at this particular time, and I had just finished singing. My sister and I started discussing what had happened earlier, because for some reason the battle just stopped. And as we were discussing it, Satan speared me through the heart, from under the bed, when I was talking to my sister. **The jerk!**

I was lying in bed, and without warning, I didn't even feel his presence, he speared me right through the heart, and I mean right in the heart of my soul. He hit so hard that it threw my physical body almost right out of the bed on top of the telephone, and I **SCREAMED** at the top of my lungs. I said, "**OH MY GOD!** He got me!! He got me!! He got me!!" and I screamed and I yelled, "The jerk got me, I had my guard down and he got me, he got me!"

I felt pain, but not physical pain, it was spiritual pain. I remember I started falling into this place, this…I can't describe it. I can't say it was a void, because this space, or area was not in the same level as the spiritual war I had been in earlier. It was…I had the sense it was a lower level, or dimension. I felt myself descending into it. As I descended, I felt my spirit floating down, then for some reason my spirit stopped. I looked around and saw, and felt this emptiness. I could sense empty space that went nowhere.

There seemed to be walls there, but not really walls. I remember putting my hands out and feeling something there, but there really wasn't anything there. There was some sort of force there that stopped me from leaving this particular area. I could scream, but the sound went nowhere. Like I said, they weren't walls. It was like a room with walls, without walls; it was some kind of hell. There wasn't any fire. No…, just like an enclosed room without walls, the agony and the pain was just indescribable.

I don't know if anyone else has ever felt…Being away from God, for this place, the Presence of God just did not exist. There was no hope. Hope didn't exist in this place. Stop, and think about it…Take a minute, and just think…a place without hope, those are just words, but try to feel it. Try to **feel**, and **sense it**, in your heart, and in your soul, a place like this. I am saying it like this to inform people, to give them an idea of how it was.

I was out of my mind down there, completely out of my mind. I was screaming, yelling, clawing the walls that weren't walls, and trying to get out. I remember pushing at them, but the walls pushed back. There wasn't any pain in pushing them; they were just there, but not there. It's hard to explain, but they were very real. The whole place seemed to absorb all sound. I could say it was a pit, but it wasn't a pit. All I can say, it was a lower level of the spiritual world.

Think seriously about what I am saying, for I believe it is very important. **Don't under estimate the importance of these words.** I was in a place with no doors, no way up, no way down, leading nowhere, and I was alone. I mean **TOTALLY ALONE.** I mean to the ultimate of loneliness. I was alone, no one was going to see me, no one is going to find me, and no one knew where I was. And all of this doesn't even describe the **terror.**

Well, I'm not sure my words are being understood. I really don't believe people could understand unless they were there, and yet it is **so important.** I don't know why I am spending so much time on this. But maybe the Holy Spirit wants me to tell people. Well, listen to my **WORDS.** Nobody will ever want to go down there. **I MEAN EVER!** Because they might never get out…and time has no meaning down there. **I MEAN, NO MEANING!** Listen to these words, there is no meaning of time, hope, there is no God down there.

I don't know how anyone could get out of that place. I saw no fire. I saw nothing but me, in a place that has walls, but no walls. Listen to me, for God's sake! Listen to what I am saying, watch your soul for that's all people have. Once it is lost, it's lost, and the abyss, this hole, or pit, or whatever it is called, it is real! It really is, nobody wants to go to that place. Listen to me, I have been there with all of my heart, and soul, I hope people are listening.

If anyone has a thread of Christianity, of faith, they must build on it. Because that's the only thread of life they'll have. For if they lose that thread of Christianity, they are lost. If they have a hair, a thread of faith in God, in the Holy Spirit they must reach for it, and run for it. Maybe God will use that thread to get them out of there, if they find themselves in there, they will have to get out as quick as possible. I believe that if this place has a door, and once that door closes, they might never get out.

I am not trying to scare people. I just want to be honest with them from the bottom of my heart. I hope I never see them fall into this place. For I don't know how they would get out. I have no idea if there is another pit below this one, but if there is, may God forgive us all, may God forgive us. For the little taste that I felt, I can't even describe it. If there is another pit of fire and brimstone below this one my heart will bleed for all humanity. For I have tasted a place I wouldn't want anyone to fall into.

Back to my story:

I was in this place going out of my mind screaming, yelling, and clawing at the walls, that were not walls, running around in circles, pacing, trying to jump, and trying to do whatever I could to get out; crying my soul out, and crying beyond crying, to the limits of my fear. I prayed to Christ, and I said, "Christ I am down, your servant is down again. Get me out of this place! Get me out of this place! Christ, get me out of this place! I am down!"

And I **screamed**. I don't know why the neighbors didn't call the police? I never knew I could scream like that. I had no idea what my sister thought, listening to this on the phone. I don't even know if she heard me. The walls and windows in the house were shaking with my yells. I could feel the intensity, and relief, when Christ pulled me out. I felt myself rising. I felt the Presence of God once again. I was placed back on a higher spiritual plane, or Spiritual world.

I don't know if these words can describe the feeling. Try to visualize, with an open mind, and listen to what I am saying. Maybe the Holy Spirit can place others there through my words, and help them feel the agony, torment, and testimony of what was happening to me in this Spiritual World.

Remember that my physical body was still lying in bed crying and singing my sister was still on the phone.

Then Christ said to me, *"Ray, the end of the world is coming. It is very, very, very close. I am putting together an army, and I have chosen you. I am going to give you a helmet. I am going to give you a shield. I am going to give you a spear."*

And He said something else, Christ said, implied or stated either, He always had an army through time, but I got the impression that he was putting together a new army. I am not really sure about this, but He was selecting people to do battle for him.

Christ said, *"You're going to do battle for Me."* He said, *"You are going to be on the front lines, and you are going to battle for Me."*

I saw a vision of many warriors charging down this dark battlefield into these clouds. I could see smoke, and we were running, and screaming just like people see in the movies. But I didn't see the enemy. I only saw the battle from our side, and I was saying, "Go there, and do this," and I was in front. I can still see them in my mind, just as if it happened a second ago. I saw this battle, it was like what people see in the old Roman days with Soldiers charging wearing helmets, carrying spears and shields. I kept saying, "Charge, Charge," or something like that. "Go over there, go over there, do this, and do that."

I don't know if this is true, or if it's my own ego, or pride; I had a commission of some sort. I was in charge of some people, or soldiers. I don't know what the term would be. I was giving orders too, "Do this, and do that." This felt strange, because there I was, in this Spiritual World, and God was showing me this in another World. So, I was in this spiritual world seeing in another world. I was seeing a vision, within a vision of the events that happened.

And then Christ showed me Himself on the Cross. All I could see was His Face, His Shoulders, and the agony He felt.

He said, *"Ray, what you experienced tonight was but a skirmish, a taste of what I went through on the Cross."* Then I felt His Agony for a second or two. He just gave me a sense of what He felt.

He said, *"It was just a taste of what I went through."*

My heart went out to Him. "How could He do this, how could He do this for us." I just broke down and cried for I couldn't take it, I mean....I started crying because I had not really realized what Christ went through.

He never really shared, in the Bible, to me anyway, what He experienced or felt on the Cross. He said a few words, "My God, My God, why have you forsaken Me," saying a few things like that. Now I have a sense of what He felt and went through. Boy, do I know! It was sure terror, but He did it for us. I hope whoever reads this journal remembers this. What

I went through was nothing, nothing, nothing at all compared to what Jesus Christ experienced.

Then the next image I saw was four apostles, and Christ said, *"Ray, see these apostles, they went through the same thing you did. They weren't great. They were just people like you. There wasn't anything special about them, outside of their faith. They were people that hurt, that had craving, lust, hunger, and were cold when it was cold. They were just ordinary people that followed Me, and did My Bidding. They went through the same thing you went through."*

Then I felt a little of their agony. Now, in talking to Christ, and not seeing anymore visions, I said, "Christ, I am not worthy, I am not a fighter, I am not a warrior, or a soldier. I don't have the faith to do this. You have made a mistake, you have made a **BAD MISTAKE**. I have a hard time going from day to day. You are asking the impossible." Christ was quiet, and didn't say a word....

I was so convicted by His silence that I found myself saying, "Okay, I will give it a shot. I'll try. I'll do the best I can, but that's all I can do. I am a sinner, and I am so weak, and you are asking me to do the impossible, this is the ultimate for me. But if I fall, you better be there to pick me up, because I am going to fall. I am going to say it again, you better pick me up, but please don't give me anymore than I can take. **PLEASE!** I will stick by you to the end of time, but if I do fall, or get wounded, please be there, for I am such an extremely weak person. I'll try to make myself strong, and I'll do my best, but remember what I just said. Because I know myself, I know Raymond," then the vision stopped.

As far as I could remember, my sister was still singing and praising, and by this time I was totally and completely exhausted, do to the warfare. I couldn't talk anymore, my body was totally worn out. My T-shirt was soaking wet.

I said to my sister Cristina, "I can't take it anymore, I have to get some sleep. I have to get some sleep, I am physically worn out."

She said, "No Ray, don't hang up! Please don't hang up! Hang in there!"

I said, "No Cristina, I'll be okay, I'll be okay."
She said, "No Ray, don't!"
"I'll be okay, trust me," I said.
So, she said, "Okay," and she hung up.

I fell asleep, then Satan came at me, once again in my sleep. He came in a dream, and in this dream I was downstairs in my Son's room. Now, this time I was on top of my Son's bedroom ceiling looking down, and saw the death of my Son. I felt...I didn't see him, it was during the day, and his bed was made, but the house reeked with his death. He didn't exist— he was gone. I cried, and I cried, and my heart just cried. I said to myself, "What am I getting into? What am I doing?" and I cried, and woke up.

So that was my first battle with Satan, with Christ at my side. I can still feel the tension, for I can't keep my words straight. Now I know what the words mean, **"Spiritual Warfare."** These words I don't take lightly; since then, I spend a lot of time praying and crying. I felt so green, inadequate, and insecure. My faith is being tested constantly, since I first prayed for my special female friend that Thursday morning.

The Mt. Diablo Prophecy.
December 2, 1990,

(It is 6:28 AM., April 10, 1993, tomorrow is Easter Sunday, and I am going to document the events of what happened on December 2, 1990. I thought I had recorded it on tape, but I can't seem to find the recording tape. So I am going to try to recall everything the best I can.)

I was asleep, and the Lord woke me up, and said, *"I want you to go to Mt. Diablo. I want you to anoint the Mountain with oil. There will be fifteen thousand Angels there, and do not to be afraid for He needed witnesses. "Announce it to the singles group on Friday night."*

My sister and I were going to a Four Square Church, which had a Friday night singles group. So I told my sister about the Prophecy; and the next Friday night the opportunity to speak developed.

I told the Prophecy to the Church singles.

But the Lord had said, *"Do not to tell them the whole story. Tell them I want people to go to the mountain, and pray, and that fifteen thousand Angels were going to be there. That's all. You will be led and protected by the Angels to Mt. Diablo, and do not explain anymore details until you get there."*

The details were that He was going to take Mt. Diablo away from the devil. That the devil had nine places on the planet he was allowed to use, or had been using for thousands of years. The places, I guess, were high places. I really don't know, but Satan would run his operations from them. I guess Mt. Diablo was one of those places.

He said, *"Do not worry who's going. For I know exactly who will be there." Don't worry if one, two, or a hundred people go with you." I need witnesses to witness what I am going to do."*

He was going to evict the devil from this mountain. Well, this mountain is located in Contra Costa County in California, on the East Bay of San Francisco.

A Christian friend and I discovered a plaque on top of Mt. Diablo in 1992, which said that Indians used to worship and sacrifice there for as far back as five thousand years. The mountain has always been associated with some sort of evil. It's my understanding that a priest, in the eighteen hundreds, saw the devil there on top of a rock, while he was praying, and since that day its been called Mt. Diablo (Devil Mountain). I am not really sure of all the history, but I gave my Prophecy to the singles group, and stated that we were going there that next Sunday, and if anybody wanted to go to meet us in the Church parking lot.

I asked the Lord, "Where on this mountain do we anoint it?"

He said, *"I am not going to tell you. The person that runs the soundboard at the Church, the person you talked to several weeks ago about Mt. Diablo, he knows exactly where to anoint the mountain. And anoint the ground wherever he tells you."*

During this particular time, I was getting all kinds of static from Church people. They were starting to look at me as if I was crazy. They thought I was getting weird. I was getting calls from people in the church telling me to shut up. That I was going to get reprimanded, and to keep my mouth shut about all this stuff. What was so funny, this was supposed to be a solid Charismatic Four Square Church. I was getting all kinds of static from friends, but I didn't care, I did whatever the Lord said.

Two days later on Sunday, December 2, 1990, my sister and I went to Church, not knowing who was going to be there, or if anybody was going to be there. The Lord said, *"There will be music. It's going to be a Day of Celebration in Heaven, and on the Earth. I am going to reclaim the nine places on earth that Satan occupies, and has been using for thousands of years. People are going to be healed on this Day, and there are going to be miracles all over the world, and I need witnesses for this event."*

So my sister and I drove to Church not really knowing if we were going, or if the soundman was going. I had not spoken to him in several weeks, and we didn't know where this special place was, that the Lord wanted anointed, because this young man was the only person that knew. I was afraid to talk to him about it because of all the commotion over the Mt. Diablo prayer trip. I knew there was a lot of talking going on in our inner circle of single friends in the Church, on what we were going to do at Mt. Diablo. It did cross my mind that the soundman might have heard all the commotion about Mt. Diablo, and would not show up. However, when my sister and I got to the Church he not only knew where we were going, but he had drawn a map, and had made copies for whoever wanted to go.

I called a few people before Sunday's trip, but no one seemed to be interested in going to the mountain. So my sister said, "Maybe its going to be only you and I." So we waited, and people started showing up, we wound up with ten people, five men, and five women. I believe there were five different Churches represented.

The Lord said, *"There's going to be music."*

But of the nine people there, no one had anything that represented any kind of music. There were only nine people at first so we waited as long as we could, and then left at the end of a caravan of cars. As we were driving out of the church parking lot, we saw Doug, from the singles group. My sister said, "Stop the car!, There's Doug." So we turned around and went back into the church parking lot.

We pulled next to Doug's Van and he approached us. He asked if everyone had left for the mountain. We said, "Yes," and that we had returned for him. He asked if he could go with us. We said, "Yes." Then He asked if it was all right if he took his guitar because the door on his Van wouldn't lock, and he thought someone might steal it. My sister and I just looked at each other, for we knew the Lord had said there would be music. We smiled at each other and said, "Why sure." I knew my sister was joyful because everything was happening just like the Lord had said; right down to the music, and all this was happening before our eyes.

So we rushed to catch up with the others that had left. We all got there at the same time, and the soundman led the ten of us up this mountain trail. I remember this one young lady that complained all the way up. She kept saying she wasn't going to go another step. She didn't want to go any farther, and complained about this and that, and she went on and on. She made such a stink about the distance that she almost talked the soundman into stopping and anointing any location on the mountain, other than the one, which the Lord had wanted.

I said to the soundman to go wherever the Lord told him even if it was higher up the trail, no matter what. It got so bad with this young lady's complaining, pouting, and making a stink, that one of the other women stopped, and walked slowly with her as the rest of us proceeded ahead. She was complaining because originally the sound man had stated that it was only going to be a quarter of a mile up a well defined trail, and it turned out to be about two miles of walking up this mountain trail.

On the way up some of us sang songs praising the Lord, and celebrated as we walked. Well, we got there, and I shared with them what the Lord had said about the Angels, and we all gave some sort of a testimony of why we had come up to the mountain. Then I told them the reasons the Lord had wanted us there. That He was going to reclaim this mountain. That there were going to be signs and wonders all over the earth on this date.

I explained how the Lord had said, *"Buy a bottle of olive oil, and do not to break the seal until the mountain is going to be anointed. The oil should be poured onto the ground in the shape of a large Cross in the direction that the sound man wanted.* "*He will know where to pour the oil onto the ground and its direction."*

So I asked the soundman, "Where do you want it?" And He said, "I believe it should be in this direction, and facing that way."

So after we prayed, and anointed each other on the forehead in the name of the Father, the Son, and the Holy Spirit. I took the bottle of oil and poured the rest onto the ground in the shape of a big Cross in the direction that the sound man wanted.

Then the Lord said, *"Turn the bottle upside down at the head of the Cross, and to leave it there upside down on the ground, and let all the oil soak into the ground."*

So I did it, and we started to sing songs. Then the soundman said, "I believed we should go to the edge of the embankment, and look toward the west and clap our hands, for the devil doesn't like the sound of hands clapping. So the ten of us moved to the edge of the embankment, and started clapping, facing toward the bay side of the mountain, and we clapped, cheered, and whistled. Then one of the young ladies said that the Lord was going to give everyone the desires of our hearts.

We were standing there clapping into the air, and my sister started screaming and yelling as we looked into the sky. She said there was a rainbow in the sky. This was about two o'clock, Sunday afternoon, December 2, 1990. I remember seeing nothing but dark clouds in the sky. It hadn't been raining, but there was a group of dark clouds in the western sky. But when my sister started screaming and jumping up and down everyone got excited, and started looking into the sky.

What appeared out of nowhere was a small rainbow. It wasn't a full rainbow, it was just a very small rainbow. Everyone looked, and looked, and no one could see it but her. Then someone else saw it. Then before long everyone saw it. Then everyone went crazy with screaming, yelling, and praising the Lord. Out of nowhere another small rainbow appeared, and we all **really** started yelling, screaming, and jumping. We were actually seeing wonders in the sky. Then a third one appeared. There was a total of three small rainbows near some clouds as we watched the larger dark clouds move away toward the south. These three little rainbows remained still in the western sky in the direction of the sun.

The ten of us just went crazy over this whole thing. It was just so unbelievable. We all could not believe what had appeared out of nowhere as we looked in the direction that the Cross was pointing, toward the west at the edge of the embankment. It was crazy, and fulfilling that afternoon on Mt. Diablo. We were all excited for we saw a miracle, and Doug, who brought the guitar, happened to bring his camera also. So he was able to photograph one of the small rainbows. This gave us proof that we didn't make it up, and a confirmation of what had happened. We also took pictures of all of us on the mountain. It was an amazing afternoon.

The Lord said to me, *"I needed witnesses,"* and *I am proud of this little group that came here. You have been obedient. I love you. You have touched My Heart. I needed witnesses to witness the eviction of the devil's forces from Mt. Diablo. The same thing will occur all over the planet at all nine locations. December 2, 1990, will be the beginning of the Great War in Heaven, and on Earth. The beginning of the end is at hand. Now Satan is the devil of the sky. For he now has nowhere to lay his head."*

I remember when the ten of us were walking back to our cars, there was a different atmosphere around us. We were all happy and joyful, but there was a silence, for we knew what we saw and had experienced. We really didn't know what was meant by the saying, *"Look at the sky."* And here years later, I still don't really know.

I didn't even know that the devil had nine territorial work places on the planet. About six months later one of the young ladies, that had gone with us up Mt. Diablo, found an article in a Christian magazine stating that there was a group of Christian people that back packed into the bush country of Australia, and anointed a large devil rock. It was done weeks after we had anointed Mt. Diablo. This article she found gave us another confirmation of what the Lord had said was true. It was maybe weeks later, but it took them awhile to get to this devil rock.

That was only two of the confirmations. We also heard on the radio news that the oceans tides were unusually high that Day, and they didn't know why. There were also announcements on the radio news that people were seeing unusual lights in the night sky for about a week. I was even lucky enough to see one of these night-lights in the sky.

I know we shared this experience with one pastor, but he never commented. I have shared it with other pastors since then, but they look at me like I am nuts. But we ten people who went to the mountain that afternoon know: "That something happened."

But all the Lord kept saying to me was, *"Look to the sky. Look to the sky."*

During this time I was really starting to get some strong pressure from this Protestant Four Square Church I was going to. I was being shown things I had never seen before, and basically the pastor kept saying to me, "Never mind what you're seeing or hearing; you're talking to demons. Listen only to me for I am your spiritual authority." It sounded like he kept saying "Listen to me only, don't listen to God," is how I took it. "Listen to us for we know what is best for you."

This mountain prayer trip happened on Sunday, December 2, 1990, after Church. Then on December 3, 1990, the following morning at nine o'clock, I was sleeping, and I was awakened, and the next thing I knew, my mouth starts speaking in strange tongues. Let me explain something here, (I) this fellow, at this time in his life, didn't believe in tongues, prayer language, or whatever you want to call it. I remember this one pastor kept telling me to ask for tongues because it would help me in whatever was happening to me, months before I'd received this gift of tongues.

I told him, I didn't believe in it, and that I didn't need it. But he said I did need it, and to record everything that happened because I would forget it. And now at nine o'clock in the morning December 3, 1990, my mouth starts making all kinds of weird sounds. I never asked for it. I never prayed for it. I didn't even believe in it, and for the next six hours, I just started speaking in different languages. I recorded it because this pastor told me to keep a journal, so I kept this pocket tape recorder next to my bed, because so many things were happening, and so fast, I didn't know what to expect next.

The Lord just woke me up, and I started speaking in tongues for two hours. Then He would let me sleep for two hours, then He would wake me up, and I would speak for another two hours. Then He would let me sleep for two hours. Then wake me up, and I would speak for another two hours. This went on for three days. I didn't go to work. I didn't get out of bed except to go to the rest room, I don't remember even if I ate. But for three days I spoke in all kinds of languages. I can't even remember how many languages there were.

But I did document some of the Prophecies that were given to me that day. This whole thing was bizarre, but real. My Christian walk took another step in a direction that I didn't want to go. I don't understand tongues. I know at times they lift my spirit up, when the enemy knocks me down. This stuff is just overwhelming, but now I find myself praying for hours, and hours in tongues. I pray more in tongues than I pray in English. I guess my spirit knows what it needs. I never was very good at prayer.

Then the pressure from the Church increased because of the Prophecies, and the Visions, and stuff like that.

Then the Lord said to me, *"Type and mail copies of this Prophecy out."*

After this request, things really got hot for me at the Four Square Church. For I did it, and mailed them where He requested.

The actual Prophecies in tongues started on December 3, 1990, the day after I went to Mt. Diablo, with five women and four other men to be a witness, and see our miracle of three little rainbows.

For me personally, I know what the truth is. That's for me, but others have to decide for themselves. I don't know when this stuff is going to stop. I remember a Pastor told me that sometimes it goes on for two or three days, maybe a week, but its been three years, and the Satanic attacks, the Visions, the Prophecies, and all kinds of personal miracles just seem to keep on going.

I remember, in the summer of 1992, when the Prophecies were coming two to four a day the spiritual warfare was so intense that I found myself in constant prayer due to the demonic attacks. I used to seal my house every night with a hedge of thrones soaked with the Blood of Jesus. And I prayed to the Lord to coat the walls and the ceilings with the Blood of Jesus. During this time I had rented a room to a man named John. One particular week we went to a midweek church service. John, my prayer partner, and I stopped at a restaurant to eat after church and John proceeded to tell us that he was having a hard time sleeping the last three days. He said he was afraid that I was going to get mad at him. He said that he kept seeing Blood come out of the walls and out of the new rug in his room. He would get towels and try to soak up the Blood, but could not because it filled the whole room. He would have to go outside and wait for hours until morning because he was afraid and thought I would make him pay damages for the new rug, but the Blood would be gone in the morning.

I remember looking at my prayer partner and thinking of my nightly opening prayer and by his look, I knew he was thinking the same thing. Later John shared with me that he had experienced other spiritual things in his past, once was when his wife almost died. I was amazed because this was the first time I had ever heard of someone seeing exactly this type of prayer appear before their eyes.

Examples of other things that have happened:
1. I was in an auto accident where my car was hit solid in the side and nothing happened to my car.

2. Praying for a water well and having the ground shake a week later without warning, and having water flood my backyard from some unknown water source, in the summer during a statewide drought, and the water company analyzing it and stating it wasn't theirs.
3. Money arriving at the right time, and at the right place.
4. People helping with equipment and knowledge.
5. Post Office workers paying for the postage, for the Prophecy mailings and so many other things have occurred that I am not recording that I cannot explain.

The attacks from Church leaders, from old friends, even my family members. Walking alone, and feeling alone, even though there are many people interceding for me, even people I don't even know, this whole thing feels very strange.

An added note: Of the ten people that went to the mountain, because of the Church's persecution and the Church's reaction to the Prophecies, five of the ten people that went up to the mountain disassociated themselves from me.

Without giving my name, the head pastor started to actually lie, saying things about me that were not true. One Sunday the assistant pastors surrounded me, and told me they weren't going to let me in church unless I submitted to the head pastors' authority, **and to keep my mouth shut.** The head pastor even tried to get me arrested at one point at a church member's home.

That's my story. Read the Prophecies, Discern, and Judge, and Pray, and Pray that the Lord will reveal to you the **Truth**, because it's not my Word. I haven't the brains to put it together because to much came to fast, and I really can't write very well. I guess that's all, God bless you.

Prophecies, Visions, Occurrences, and Dreams

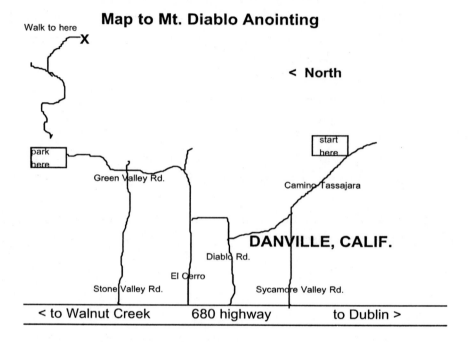

Part 2

Prophecies, Visions, Occurrences, and Dreams.

Prophecy Confirmations from readers can be found on <http://prophecy.org>. This web site has over 2000 Prophecies, Visions, Occurrences, and Dreams given to Raymond Aguilera.

Prophecies, Visions, Occurrences, and Dreams

876. Vision and Prophecy given to Raymond Aguilera on 14 March 1996 at 3 AM.

Vision:
The Lord showed me the map of Japan with a castle at the northern part of Japan.

Prophecy:
Then the Lord said, "Japan is one of the ten horns (kingdoms) of the Antichrist from the Book of Revelations. Japan will unite with the other nine and attack Babylon in one hour. (over)

877. Vision given to Raymond Aguilera on 16 March 1996 at 9:00 PM.

The Lord showed me a figure of a man wearing a long robe with long sleeves and a hood. I tried to look at his face, but all I saw was darkness and no head inside the hood. He was carrying a long black pole in his right hand that went from the ground to about one foot above his head. In his left hand he was carrying a lighted torch like the kind the Statue of Liberty is holding.

Vision:
The next vision was the same lit torch—except this time it had a glowing round ring around the base of the flame, but it encompassed the whole torch. I guess you would call it a halo.

878. Vision given to Raymond Aguilera on 17 March 1996 at 8:00 PM.

A vision of an automobile spark plug with the wire end pointing down (ceramic part). And on top of this automobile spark plug (the spark part), I saw a small Statue of Liberty. (over)

879. Vision:

The Lord in a vision took me back to the things I saw at the Airport Vineyard in Toronto, Canada a few years back.

Prophecy:
The Lord said, "My Spirit is all over the place, but I am ONE Spirit." (over)

880. Vision:

While we were laying hands on a brother—who had asked for prayer—the Lord gave me a vision. This vision was of an unlit oil lamp full of oil with its wick still in place—without the flame protecting glass cover. What was so unusual was that—on top of this wick (that WAS NOT lit) there was a White lighted Candle.

Meaning of Vision:
People are seeking for the Holy Spirit by trying to light an oil lamp, but the lighted Candle (Holy Spirit) is already there. The oil lamp has nothing to do with the Lit Candle. (One is man made and the other is God.)

881. Prophecy given to Raymond Aguilera on 20 March 1996 at 1:15 AM in Spanish.

It has arrived—it has arrived! It has arrived the flame from heaven. I don't understand why the people of the world don't want to hear Me. They are deaf and they are blind. They are so near the pit, but everything that I have said in the bible is going to happen—exactly! I am not going to lose a one, because I am God and what I say happens. Did you hear Me, Reymundo? What I say is going to happen. I told you that I was going to give you the money, and you know that I have given it to you. When I say it—it happens! I know that your brothers and sisters helped you, but they are going to have to help you more. For I have things that you have to do. And I don't want you to have worries about money.

For I am going to use you with Force, and the devil is going to get mad. Put it on your calendar. But he (devil) won't do a thing. He won't be able to do a thing. For I am going to protect you with My Angels, with My Word. For I am going to tell you things about the end, the things that are going to happen to the Body of My Son. And I want your mind to be Clear. There are many in the Body of My Son that are waiting for your Word that you're writing for your Father. When they read the Word of your God, the One who made the world, the sky, all that they touch, all that they see, all that they think, they are going to cry. They are going to cry because they are going to know it's their Father, with the Son, and with the Holy Spirit.

The ones who seek the devil—the people who have their ears stopped-up and their eyes closed. Yes! The ones who are blind; the ones who are deaf. For they want things; they want money; they want all the things that are not of God. They seek those things first, and at times, they don't even seek their God. They seek Me ONLY when things go bad and they get frightened. But the day of fright has arrived. They are going to seek Me, and I am not going to help them, and I am not going to hear them. For I told them, and I told them, and I told them. They turned their backs and they ran after their THINGS—the things that are god to them. Let's see if these THINGS can protect them.

Yes! There is coming a man—who is going to want to eat you with force. It's not going to be important to him—what you want to do, and what you don't want to do. For the foot of his shoe is going to be on top of your throat, until your eyes pop out of your head. Then lets see—if you seek your THINGS to help you. For this man is not going to care. He is not like your—Father; like the Son; like the Holy Spirit, that Loves you with all the Love that is. But you have to seek Me; you have to change your mind, your spirit. For I am not going to change to what you want. YOU have to CHANGE and SEEK ME! With tears—I tell you the truth. But I am going to correct you in the manner of God.

There are some who are reading this Word—this minute—they are thinking: "Oh—this man is crazy! He believes he's talking with God. And He believes that God is talking with him. He is really CRAZY! He has DEMONS in him." But hear Me—this minute! There is going to come a day that you are going to find out who this man—Reymundo—is talking to. I am going to put it in your mind, when the man puts his foot over your throat. Then you are going to think, and you are going to remember—that I told you. We are going to see—who is correct, your Father or your mind that has demons; that chases after gods of machines, of things; of the things that you want. We are going to see if this, Reymundo of Mine is Crazy.

If you want to seek the devil; he is going to give you a man, and he is going to show you the manner of the devil—to you, to your family, to your friends. Don't worry; the devil will protect you. He knows the manner to protect you. Don't worry! Hurry—keep doing the things you are doing. Everything is going to go very well with you. But I tell you the truth—there is going to come a day that I am going to place this prophecy in your mind—when you are kicking because you cannot catch your breath. For your eyes are going to be popping out of your face, with your crooked tongue, with your god, with your devils. EXACTLY! For you pointed your nose at your god, and I gave him to you.

But the rest—My Angels—the ones who seek Me with their heart, with the Communion, with tears, with prayers, and the ones who know how to repent their sins, those—I am going to protect. Those are MINE! You have to choose which God you want—and line yourself up in the direction of your God. What a shame! For I know this minute—that there are many, many, many—that are not going to believe Me. And they are going to line themselves with their devil. But that is their manner and I am going to let them go, but My Heart is going to CRY.

For they are going to believe that these Words are from a CRAZY MAN. But the CRAZY ONES are them. What a shame! Yes—My Little Ones—We have arrived at the point of the pit, of the war of the devils. Read the bible from the beginning to the end, and when you are finished, read it again! And when you are finished, read it again. You have to know the things that are in the bible, if you want to save yourself, your family, and your friends. For the day of suffering has arrived.

I tell you with Tears. I tell you with Love. I tell you with My Prophet, Reymundo, My Beloved. He has suffered for you. Now—for seven years—he has suffered for you. And still—there are many that don't believe him—for they are fighting with other brothers of the bible, with other brothers of the Body of My Son. They like to fight, but the day has arrived—that the devil is going to turn loose the man. You have to gather with the Love of God. You have to work together with Force! Did you hear, Me, Clearly and to the Point? The time where everything goes easy is finished. It has arrived—the time of the devil. (over)

882. Vision given to Raymond Aguilera on 21 March 1996 at 7 AM.

I saw the torch of the Statue of Liberty (the real one). What was hard to believe was—I saw someone climb up to it with a ladder. He climbed onto the rim of the torch and started planting some flowers around the flame part. (over)

883. Prophecy given to Raymond Aguilera on 25 March 1996 at 12:44 AM. in Spanish.

Get up! Get up, My son. I tell you the truth, exactly. You have to get up! You have to work, and you have to point your nose into the bible. I am going to show you the things of God. I tell you because what I said to the past Prophets is going to happen. I am going to tell you the same, with the Lips of God, with the Eyes of God. Yes, the things of the end are here now. You are going to know what have I told you is the Truth.

The earthquake is going to arrive—the earthquake of the world. Yes, the earthquake is going to arrive. Everything is going to fall, and the water is going to rise. The large cities are going to fall because the earthquake is going to be VERY BIG. The whole world is going to be frightened. They are going to be frightened because they are going to know the God of Heaven, the One who made everything, with His Word, with the Holy Spirit. That He is the God of God's. He is the King of Kings. ALL is in His Hands; all that is His; He is going to Clean. All that is NOT His; He is going to give to the devil, and the devil and his things are going to the pit for all the time, that there is time.

You have to write the Words of God in the manner of God. For it has arrived, exactly, to the letter, to the point, all that I have told you about the past Prophets is going to happen. You are the only one...(Not understandable), that can understand, if you read the bible, with the Eyes of God. Exactly, that's what I am telling you.

For the ones of the church turn everything up and down and they don't seek with clarity what the Father wants to say. What a shame—Reymundo! What a shame! For they twist all, they twist everything, every which way. And they don't read the Word with the eyes of God. They read the Word with the eyes of money, with the lips that are pure with the purity of lies. Oh. Oh. Oh. How hard is the head of man.

I am going to show you things, Reymundo, but I want you to have a clear head. I know that you have worries—for the things that I am going to tell you, are very big. They are the things people of the world have always wanted to know, for many, many years. But I chose you before you were born, to do what you are going to do. Did you hear Me Clearly, and to the Point? I am NOT telling you these things so you can elevate your face or head. I don't want you to think you are great because great things fall! I want you to seek the things of God in the manner of God, like a little child, with the eyes of a baby because babies seek Me, with clear eyes, and with a clear heart.

But the so-called great-seek with the eyes of the devil, pointed at the devil, pointed at the money. They like the power. But you know who you are speaking to. They don't know. They don't know the Word when they hear it, because they believe they are so great.

I tell you in the manner of God: Sometimes you are going to learn very easily, and sometimes it's going to be harder, but you are going to know the Truth. Study the bible, and I want you to pray, and I want you to study. I will help you. I could tell you all that I want in one minute, but I don't want to do that right now. I want to see your perspiration on top of your head, learning the things of God, in the manner of God. But the correct manner is there, but I want you to study. Did you hear Me, Reymundo? I want you to study! I will give you the money for your house, for the telephone, for your computer, for all the things that you are going to need. But the most important thing is to STUDY, with the Eyes of God, with the Ears of God, with the Heart of God, with the Heart of a little child. Did you hear Me Clearly, and to the Point?

All that I promised you, I am going to give you Clearly, and to the Point. I know that you are anxious. I know that you feel very lonely. I know that you are waiting for your wife, but everything will arrive at the time that I choose. It is close. You have to wait a little while longer, because everything that you have wanted, I am going to give you. I know it is hard, for there are people that don't believe you, but that problem is Mine. It's not yours, because the Word is Mine, not yours. Do you understand? All you have to do is write what I tell you, and to the Point. And I will protect you.

There are many people that don't like you. There are many people that are very mad for what you write for your Father. But I am going to correct them, whether you see it or not. I will correct them in one manner or another. For we have arrived at the time—there will be no time. Many people are going to ask you questions that you won't be able to answer. If you do not know, don't say a thing. They are going to get mad because you won't answer them, but like I said to you, "It's My Word not yours." I will correct them. For they believe they know it all, and I am going to show them that they don't know a thing. But I am going to show them in the manner of God. I tell you the Truth—Exactly.

I know its been very hard these past seven years, but everyone who has received My Word has suffered, in one manner or another. That's because the devil is strong in the hearts of the people of the world. People like to hear from the devil, and they don't like to hear from God. For the manner of the devil is very easy. And for the manner of God; you have to make yourself strong; you have to make yourself clean; and you have to seek Me with the Heart of God. And it's a lot of work for people. It's a lot of work for the people, for everyone wants it easy. The Road of God is NOT wide, but the road of the devil is VERY wide. You have to travel by the narrow Road. For you have to suffer, with the rest of the Body of My Son.

They (the unbelievers) do not want to hear that Word, for they want to find Me easily without suffering, but I tell you the truth! It is true that I have had some find Me without suffering, but I have some plans for them. The rest—it's because they don't know how to seek Me like a child. They want to tell Me how I can speak, what I can show, what I cannot show, what I can do—what I cannot do, like THEY are god; and I have to do what they say. That's not the manner of God. That's the manner of the devil. But Reymundo, you don't have to worry about such things. When I tell you something, you just write it and send it out. The rest—I will have to correct with My Word.

When you cry in the night, I know that you feel alone. And when your heart cries because it feels so alone—you believe that I don't hear you, but you are in My Hands. Do you remember the Words that I gave you years ago? When I told you—that you had to place your eyes on Me in all things. If it was bad or good, to stand on the Rock of My Son, Jesus, and not to move until I told you to do something—for things are going to go up and down? You just remember to stand or sit on the top of the Rock of My Son, Jesus. If it is bad or if it is good, all will go well. But there are things that I have to tell the Body, and your ears want to hear it all. I am going to give you the chance, but I want you to stand on top of the Rock. Did you hear Me Clearly, and to the Point? This is your Father, with the Son, Jesus, with the Holy Spirit, telling you the Wisdom from Heaven with Love, with the Lips of Jesus, with the Lips of the Holy Spirit, with the Lips of your Father.

I know that sometimes you believe that I don't Love you with the Love of God, but yes; I Love you. I Love you a lot, Reymundo, but I know that the devil hits you in the head and you feel alone. I know that there are many brothers and sisters that don't want to help you, because they have hard hearts. They think—but they don't do—what I tell them. I am going to correct them. There are many that want to get mad with the flame of the devil; they want to eat you. I am going to correct them also.

For when I say something, its going to happen. When people open up their hearts and they seek Me and they do what I tell them, I like it. Those are the ones that I am going to save, for they have the Ears of God, they have the Eyes of God, they have the Nose of God because they have the Love of God, the Love of the Children. This is all that I want to tell you on this night, Reymundo. You can now lay down now and go to sleep. I know that you are tired. I know that you are ill, but you have to trust Me. All will go well with your computer, with your house, with your wife (the one that you don't know yet). Rest and sleep. I will speak to you on another day and I will give you more wisdom about the end, and about your heart. Remember—I hear your Tears. You are not alone. I hear your Tears My son. Rest and sleep. This is your Father, with the Son, with the Holy Spirit, telling you—that We Three Love you with all of My Heart. Sleep and rest. (over)

884. Vision given to Raymond Aguilera on 25 March 1996 at 9 AM.

The Lord gave me a vision of an automobile transmission. As I looked closely at the auto transmission I noticed that it had Three Levers to change the gears. (over)

885. Vision given to Raymond Aguilera on 27 March 1996 at 8:30 PM.

The Lord showed me a vision of a lit White Candle sitting on top of a table and right next to the edge.

Vision:
Then He showed me the same White Candle on the ground. Then as I was watching this big wave of black water rose up and was going to fall on top of the White Candle, but for some reason the black wave STOPPED in mid air and went back to it's original position. I watched this happen two times and the vision changed.

Vision:
Then this big wind came toward the lit White Candle and just before it reached the Candle this large round metal looking shield appeared between the lit Candle and the wind. The Candle was not effected by the wind.

Vision:
Then I saw a thin flat machine that looked like a pole that is used to hang your clothes or hats on. I could see this machine moving and it had arms and carrying a sleeping woman.

Vision:
Then I saw something that looked like a boat, but it could fly like an airplane. Then I saw the Lord's Hands hold this strange looking boat/plane and break it in two pieces.

Vision:

Then I saw a helicopter in the Lord's Hands and it too was broken in two pieces.

Vision:

There was also a vision about a flower. I saw this flower that had a formed or shape like a high champagne glass. Then I saw the Lord's Hands pouring something into it.

Then the Lord said, "I am going to fill this flower with My Nectar." (over)

886. Vision given to Raymond Aguilera on 2 April 1996 at 9:42 AM.

I saw what looked like a small oval crystal perfume bottle with many cuts on the crystal and it was beautiful and in the bottle there was perfumed virgin olive oil. Then the top was taken off.

Vision:

I saw a vision of an enormous Coke Cola bottle (the old style shaped). I could see a left hand moving up and down the bottle surface. Then the Coke Cola bottle changed into an oil-drilling tower. Then this oil-drilling tower changed into the Space Needle tower in Washington State. (over)

887. Prophecy given to Raymond Aguilera on 2 April 1996 at in 9:58 AM. Spanish.

I am going to scratch your head. I am going to scratch your head. Yes! I am going to scratch your head so you can remember the things I have shown you in the Bible years past when you read it. You are not going to believe it because it is going to come rapidly and to the point. These are the things you read many years ago. I am going to scratch your head with My Finger. And you are going to recognize and you are going to know, that all of God is exact and to the point. That the Word of God does not change from one day to the other. When I say something "IT

HAPPENS," exactly like I told you the first time. Like I told the Prophets years ago. Exactly, everything is going to happen to the point, to the minute.

The people of the world believe they can change My Word. They want to place words in My Mouth that I didn't say. But I am going to hit them like I hit a fly. There are some who are going to laugh this minute, but I am going to hit them like I hit a fly. But there is going to be one point in time, when they are going to see My Hand and they are going to know! Who is the God, that made Heaven, the earth—that made everything with His Word.

We will see if they know it all, when they see My Hand directly and to the point. I am NOT PLAYING A GAME! I am telling you to your face, Eye to eye. I am going to CUT YOUR THROAT! And I am going to throw your throat, your face, your body in the pit filled with your friends; that believe they can blaspheme God who made the world, Heaven, all that you see, all that touch, with the Son, with the Holy Spirit. I don't PLAY AROUND! If I tell you that I am going to cut your throat! Put it on your calendar because it is going to happen. And I am NOT going to care if you cry or not. This is the TRUTH!

What I tell you to the point has arrived, the day that you are going to see My Eyes. And I am going to read your heart of all the filth, all the things of the devil that you have, in the mind, in the spirit. Many people believe that God is nothing but LOVE, LOVE, LOVE, AND LOVE. But I tell you exactly; exactly that I correct the things that are not mine. It doesn't hurt Me if I see your blood, if you belong to the devil. It doesn't hurt My Heart if I cut your throat, if you belong to the devil. It doesn't hurt or make My Heart cry, if you scream and cry because it hurts you.

You CHOSE the devil and I gave him to you and I am going to turn My Back and walk away to another place. For I told you CLEARLY, and I told you to the POINT! And you believe you are god, because you can tell Me what you want. For many, many years I have looked at you, the man of the world, and I have not said a thing. And I heard with My Ears all blasphemes that they said about God. They believe they are so great, but we are going to see how great you are when I place My Foot on top of your head. Like I told you, "I am NOT PLAYING AROUND."

The life of ALL, of all the world, of all the people, of all that you see, of all that you touch, is in My Hands. And, "I, I ALONE," am the only ONE that can do what I want with what is MINE. What is not Mine, I am going to give to the devil. And you and your devil; I am going to correct, with My Foot, with My Hand, like a fly, screaming for the death of the spirit. I am MAD! And I don't care if you get mad.

This minute, the people of the world are filthier than all the time that there has been time. And I am going to correct all in ONE DAY, IN ONE HOUR. We are going to find out who is the strongest when you see Me Eye to eye, Face to face. When you have your tongue hanging out, with your eyes popped out, when I whist your neck and I throw you into the pit, with all the rest that is filthy. There—you are going to have the company of your friends, the one who believe they know it all. Did you hear Me with your ears? Did you hear Me with your head, that has no head, that is kicking on the floor, like a chicken that doesn't have a head. I will see you! For here comes the day that I will see you Eye to eye. Put it on your calendar for I am waiting for you with the Force of God. (over)

888. Vision given to Raymond Aguilera on 2 April 1996 at 9:38 PM.

I had a vision of the Head of Jesus Christ. Then as I looked, I saw the Lord's Crown of thorns being removed by the Father and a Golden Crown with many Jewels was placed on Jesus Christ's Head. (over)

889. Prophecy given to Raymond Aguilera on 2 April 1996 at 9:40 PM. in Spanish.

Leviathan, here comes leviathan, with the moist meat, with everything that is filthy. Leviathan has arrived.

My sons and daughters of the world, I know that you are seeking Me. I know that you seek Me here and there. Where you work, with your friends, in the churches, with your husband and your wife, you seek Me everywhere, but I am there in front of your nose. You can reach out your hand, and you can touch Me.

Many that believe in God—want to hear the Word of God. They want to hear it directly, to see what God says, the One who made the world, the stars, all that you see, all that you touch. You have to pray. Yes! First you have to pray with all of your heart. You have to repent and you have to change the manner that you are living. You have to seek My Son, Jesus, with the Tears of God; I tell you the Truth. You have to seek Him and the Holy Spirit will help you.

Yes! You don't see Him, but He is there, telling you things; showing you the manner of God, the manner of the Son. Look! Here comes the point of this world, the time, that you are going to find Me. Sometimes it is going to be very rapidly. Sometimes it's going to be slowly, but it is Clear and Exact—that We are going to see each other, Eye to eye; Love with Love, because you sought Me with the Faith of God, with the Faith in Christ, Jesus, in the Faith of the Holy Spirit. This is your Father telling you the wisdom from heaven.

I know the tears, I know the things; that happened to you when you were a child. I know about the bad things that happened to you. The things that your father and mother did to you. I saw all and I am going to correct everything. This is Clear and to the Point, and I am going to seek you too. I am going to protect you with My Angels because you are seeking Me with your heart, with the heart of a little child. I know! The tears that you have cried because you don't believe I am there, but yes, I am there. I hear all; I see all; I correct all; the things you cannot do yourself. With the Holy Spirit, with the Angels, with the Word of My Son, with the Force of the Father—We will correct the things that you need to corrected.

For I now know that you Love Me with the Love of your heart. I know that you Love Me with ALL that you have. I know those places you cannot control because you don't have the power—but look—I have the Power of ALL! I can change everything, if you are sick; if you need something; if you want to change the mind of your mother or your father or brother or sister; if you want them to seek Me also. I will help you, but you have to pray. You have to eat the Communion. You have to gather with the other brothers and sisters that believe like you—that have a pure heart and are looking to My Son, Jesus with the Force of the Holy Spirit. All will go well.

I know the things that are going to happen before they happen. No one can fool Me. But look—I know your heart. You seek Me, and I will show you the things of God. I am going to give you dreams; I am going to give you pictures, pictures of the spirit. I am going to give you the visions of your male and female friends of the world, and you are going to hear the Word of God. For the Holy Spirit is going to call to you—He is going to touch you. And sometimes you are going to be frightened—for never, never in all of your life have you touched the Holy Spirit in the manner He is going to touch you, in the days that are coming. This is Clear and it is to the Point—ALL that I am telling you.

For there in front of Us, a day is going to come, that you are going to live with the Father in a manner that you have never ever lived before. Because you are going to be CLEAN and all that you see or touch is going to be clean too. I know it is very hard to understand these things because you have never felt things like this. For here comes the day that it is going to happen. But there are going to be in the future some days that are going to be very hard. And you are going to have to make yourself very strong.

For there is going to be a man who is going to want to eat you, I want you to make yourself strong, but don't worry about what happens. For everything is in My Hands. You are going to need the faith, that your Father, with the Son, Jesus, with the Holy Spirit—that THEY can correct ALL. They cannot take away anything, for ALL is MINE and I protect what is MINE. Yes! I tell you with Love. I tell you with Tears. I tell you the wisdom from Heaven.

For you BELONG to Me and I am yours, and no one in the whole world, in all the stars, can break that WORD! For the TWO of Us are ONE! And I am waiting for you in Heaven. It is very close. I know that some don't believe for they don't have the faith, but all you need is a little faith. And all will go well because day by day you will become stronger. And the Angels and the Holy Spirit are going to show you, so you can change. So you can change your wife, your sons and daughters, your friends, your female friends. I know it is hard for you have never walked like this.

You have to change what you see, what you touch, what you seek that isn't of God. For all the things of God are CLEAN and they are CLEAR. The things of the world are very easy and the devil likes to show you, and take you to places that are not good; where people drink; where people take drugs; the places where you seek men and women, in the places that are filthy. But I can correct all! You have to repent and you have to control what you can, and leave the rest for Me. But you have to pray, and you have to tell Me that you have repented, and you have to change the ways you are walking. I just don't want to hear your lips. I want to hear your heart. That's what is important. This is all I want to tell you on this minute, on this day with My Prophet, Reymundo.

Hurry! Seek Me, on your knees praying to your God with the tears of repentance! Eat the Communion—and I will show you the things of Heaven. This is your Father, with the Son, with the Holy Spirit, with all that is CLEAN and CORRECT and RIGHTEOUS. Hurry, My son and daughter with Love I tell you the TRUTH. I am there in front of your nose. Raise your hands and touch Me and I will KISS you on the LIPS and I will hug you, and We will have a party in Heaven. For you have found your God. With Love, I tell you this Word. (over)

890. Vision given to Raymond Aguilera on 3 April 1996 at 8:30 PM.

During praise and worship, I found myself in the spirit in a large outdoor stadium. At first I only saw a few empty seats, and the place seemed so quite and peaceful. The next thing I saw was the stadium again, but I was high in the air and looking directly down at it. As I looked down I saw all the seats filled with cheering people. The longer I looked, I noticed that they were worshipping the Lord. As I watch, this large bright White Light appeared high over the center of the stadium. And you could sense this immense Power coming from this bright White Light. (over)

Vision:

Then the next vision appeared. I saw a horizontal black rod about a foot long in the air, and on this black rod there were two almost round large yellow onions hanging upside down and side by side by their roots. Then twenty minutes later during praise and worship, I saw the rod being removed and the two onions fell to the ground. As they fell, they began to grow once they hit the ground. I could see the green stems growing from the onions as they laid on top of the ground. Then two white flowers grew from each onion. Then as I watched in the spirit, I saw the Lord's mouth open and with His tongue He began licking the two onion stems with the flowers. It looked very unusual seeing this, but it reminded me of what a mother cat does with her baby kittens. It looked Loving and gentle as He stroked each onion.

891. Occurrence and Prophecy given to Raymond Aguilera on 3 April 1996 8:30 PM. in English.

I felt a strong Presence of the Lord. My whole spirit was being revived. I felted so unusual and so tired, that I asked the Lord to take me. I asked the Lord to take me right now. I said to the Lord, "Lord I have seen to much. I have experienced to much. Take me right now!"

And the Lord said, "No, No My son! No! No!" (over)

892. Prophecy given to Raymond Aguilera on 3 April 1996 at 11 PM.

During prayer the Lord started speaking to me and telling me things. He said, "Blessed are those who are alive; are those who are dead, and those who are dead are dead in Christ." (over)

893. Prophecy given to Raymond Aguilera on 4 April 1996 at 1:30 AM in English.

The Power of God will manifest itself upon the people, on the righteous—upon the pure and the clean, at the allotted time. But the rest, the dragon will clean/ purify, through the trials and tribulations. For the dragon will be used as an instrument of God to purge the evil, the wickedness, from the ones that are not obeying the Lord or walking in His statutes (the Christians who are saved that are the prodigal sons of the Lord Jehovah). (over)

894. Vision given to Raymond Aguilera on 6 April 1996 at 1:00 PM. in English.

During worship, the Lord showed me the new high-rise Stratosphere Hotel and Gambling Casino in Las Vegas, the one with the roller coaster on top. I saw the Hotel with a small Bright Light that grew like an expanding White Ball of White Light. The Light started just below the saucer shape of the building. Then the Lord appeared as the Light diminished. He appeared taller than Stratosphere Hotel and Casino. Then I saw the Lord rip the saucer shape off the tall tower with His two Hands, and throw it to the ground.

Then the Lord said, "Stay away from this place. For as My Name is Jehovah, I will destroy it." (over)

895. Vision given to Raymond Aguilera on 10 April 1996 at 1:30 PM.

While I was laying down taking a break and listening to some praise music the Lord showed me, Three Lights moving in the air. Then they came together and formed ONE large Light.

It was the Father, Son Jesus Christ, and the Holy Spirit, and the Lord said, "Follow Me."

So I started following in the spirit down this path. It was a straight path for a while, then it took a sudden turn and I could not see around the curve. Then the vision stopped. (over)

896. Vision given to Raymond Aguilera on 10 April 1996 at 8:30 PM.

During prayer and worship the Lord showed me a bowl that was going to be carved with wide flat putty knife and I wondered how could the Lord carve this bowl with this wide putty knife?

So I asked the Lord, "How can this wide flat putty knife carve into this curved bowl?

Then before my eyes the Lord transformed the wide putty knife into a curved chisel that would be ideal for curving the curved surface of the bowl.

Vision:

Then the Lord showed me a vision of a bunch of small colorful flowers sticking out of this large and long braided flat basket that looked like a two-foot long flat purse.

Vision:

I saw a vision of a metal construction safety hard hat. Then I saw a hack saw cut it in two from the top across the width. (Above and across where the ears are located.)

Vision:

The next image was of a hangman's noose hanging from this horizontal brace. This brace and hangman's noose was on this pier next to the water. Then this fish with enormous teeth jumped out of the water and bit the noose and ripped it off the brace and took it into the water.

897. Vision given to Raymond Aguilera on 16 April 1996 at 1:30 PM.

A vision of a large sinking ship. I can see the tail end of the ship up in the air and sinking into the water. (over)

898. Occurrence and Visions given to Raymond Aguilera on 16 April 1996 at 10:30 PM.

During Communion prayer and just before having Communion with a few Christian brothers the Lord showed me a corner of a multi-story apartment building. As I watched it in the spirit, I saw it collapse floor by floor until it was totally destroyed by an earthquake.

Occurrence and Vision:

Then I saw a White Horse flying through the air. It was impressed on my spirit that it represented an Angel of the Lord, I don't know how I knew but it was an Angel in the figure of a White Horse. Then out of nowhere this enormous hand that looked like a gorilla's hand sneaked up and grabbed this White Horse out of the air like it was a small bird; crushed it, and smacked it to the ground. Then this hand somehow transformed its five fingers into two and went downward with an incredible force toward the crushed Angel. I don't know if it hit the Angel again, but it had great power in its two newly formed fingers.

Immediately my prayer language changed, and I felt like I was going to explode from within and I could feel my body and spirit jump into a warfare mode. I got up from my seat and wanted to stop the Communion prayer and get into the war. But something told me I had to finish

Communion and get a brother to anoint me with oil before I went into warfare. I had sensed the urgency to pray for two days, but I didn't know why. So for the next half-hour to forty-minutes I wailed and found myself flat on the floor. With my arms extended out and with my legs together (in the shape of a cross) with an unusual sounding prayer language that at times was quiet and at other times it was loud and fast. My prayer language was acting crazing during this time and I really lost track of time.

This large hairy black gorilla's hand reminded me of the gorilla movie, "King Kong," from the thirties or forties. But what was more interesting was the spiritual war I was seeing. This giant hairy black hand was fighting the Lord's Angelic Forces and was beating them. Then I saw what looked like a hole open up in the side of a mountain, and a tunnel extended out with hundreds upon hundreds of black horses (devils) shooting out, and began to help this large black hand fight the White Horses (Angels).

I was surprised by the speed of the battle, there wasn't a wasted movement by either of the parties involved, and I could sense that in the spirit the Angels were losing the battle. What was also startling was the gorilla's hand; this creature was enormous compared to the White Horses. I mean, his hand was so large it could place a White Horse in its palm, and these were life size White Horses or Angels or whatever you would like to call them.

Vision:

Then I was shown hundreds and hundreds of crucified people on crosses in this dark area with white smoke or fog in the background being ripped off from their crosses, and they began to run past me as I watched them in the spirit. I don't know where they went or how they got pulled off the crosses.

Vision:

Then I saw this dark place with all of these black creatures that had been slain in this battle with the White Horses looking like White melted

Puddles laying on top of these black creatures. They all looked like White Blobs on top of black masses. I believe they were all dead for there was no movement. But as I watched and tried to figure out what was happening I saw the White Blobs on the top of the dead looking creatures begin to move. They somehow reformed themselves into the images of White human looking Angels. They no longer looked like White Horses. I don't know why or how it happened, but they went back up into the battle.

Vision:

Then the next image was of hundreds upon hundreds of White Horses running from the right toward the left at lighting speeds with their manes blowing in the wind. When they got to the area of the battle they surrounded this large black creature. At this point the black creature looked about 5 or 6 miles high compared to the height of the White Horses, but they surrounded it and the battle immediately stopped. And somehow the small White Horses pounded him from the top as the others stayed around the perimeter and pounded him into this large hole in the ground. It looked like this enormous pit, then this enormous lid came over the large pit and they sealed it shut. Then the vision stopped.

What was placed in my spirit was that this large creature was a territorial demon with his demon helpers. Boy, I was amazed at how large and powerful it was. (over)

Comments:

There is more in the spirit than I ever realized. The spiritual war is for real with demons we don't see, and these battles are happening now; this minute. This is a reality that most people don't even believe, but it is still for real. As I watched the spiritual war I felt very helpless. I have been asking myself these questions:

1. How were the crucified saints sucked off their crosses like a vacuum?
2. Why did they run past me into this empty space?
3. Will they come back to their crosses?

4. Did this territorial Demon get larger because the saints were taken off their crosses?

People need to PRAY MORE, for in the spirit, there are some very bad demons out there. These things are beyond what our minds can understand, but yet they are very real. I learned something very startling tonight, we really don't know the extent of the dark forces. (over)

899. Prophecy given to Raymond Aguilera on 24 April 1996 at 8:15 AM

My Children, My Children, beware—for there is a war before you, a war you will not be able to comprehend. A war that will kill many; that will kill your husband, your wife, your son or your daughter. The tears of the world will flow like a mighty river through the land; through the mountains; through the air. These raindrops of tears will fall on My Beloved's. Beware My Children. Beware! For it will arrive very soon that these tear drops will run like a mighty river, but remember no matter what happens, your Father Jehovah, your King of Kings, Jesus Christ of Nazareth, and the Holy Spirit are there.

The prophecies that were given many, many, many years ago are going to be completed in the coming years. Many will see the completion of the river of tears, the flow of blood. For the wickedness of the world and the vengeance of God have reached a point in time, where God will implement His wrath through war; through pestilence. Everything will be cleanse that needs to be cleanse.

But My Children I love you, and I need you on your knees praying. Do you remember the verses in the book of Matthew where it said that the world would be wiped clean if it wasn't for the elect, but your God Jehovah remember the elect, the saints, and with His mighty Hand stopped the destruction of the world.

I want you to take a minute and I want you to pray. I want you to take some time out so you can look into the bible and study about the wars that have happened before. I want you to study the WORD, "WAR". I want it to become a reality in your spirit, in your mind; for that's where you are headed.

Though the devil has placed this bless me, bless me, bless me doctrine into the church to the point where it has blinded them to the reality of the wrath of God, the vengeance of God on the wicked. Look in the Old Testament of how the Lord corrected things through war; through pestilence; through disobedience.

The WORDS that I tell you are harsh. Some of you people don't want to hear it, but your Father from Heaven does not lie. He tells you the truth, all the time; straight, direct and to the point. If I tell you that I LOVE YOU, I mean I LOVE YOU! If I tell you, I will correct you, I WILL CORRECT YOU! If I tell you about the wrath of God; the WRATH OF GOD WILL HAPPEN! These Words are the Words of LOVE. These are the Words of Me protecting you through that same Word. Even though the Words are harsh and direct and to the point. Whether I am speaking to the leadership who has gone astray or whether I am telling you directly or personally, Eye to eye, Face to face. The things ahead are HARSH. You will see death. You will see famine. You will see things that you have never seen before and never want to see again. Like I mentioned in another prophecy; the wickedness of this world is the worse than it has ever been since the beginning of time, and it's steadily day by day getting worse and worse.

There are some that have not been born yet, that I am going to save. There are some who claim to be born again who are not; who speak with pride; who speak with deception, and there are those, the silent majority; who sit and listen and watch, and are prepared. Who pray; who repent; who do the simple things of God with the love of God; who's lips don't even say, "I am saved", because they are afraid that they might make a decision for God; that is ONLY THE DECISION for God. Do you remember the verses in the bible where one man said, "I fast and I fast—look at that man over there, he is a sinner, but I am a follower of the Lord.

Then the man who he was pointing at beat his chest and prayed and prayed, and said I am not worthy, I am a sinner, I am no good. But he was focused because he knew that the decisions of Heaven belong in Heaven. All I ask is obedience. Love thy Father—first. Love thy neighbor as thy self—second. Do the best you can with what you have, I will take care of the rest. But you have to repent your sins you have to repent.

This war, this catastrophe that is before you, is very real. Look in the dictionary look up the word, "WAR". Look in your encyclopedias the things that happen in war. The reason I asked you to look in the dictionary and in the encyclopedias is because more of you people believe secular books and writings than you do what is in the bible. So I am sending you there to study that word, "WAR", because some of you don't believe the bible. But what is in the bible is more true than what you read in newspapers; what you see on television.

For the Word of God is direct and to the point even though at times it is hard to understand, and you want to apply your worldly principals to the Word of God. But God is not democratic. God is a King, the King of Kings, with the Father, with the Power of the Holy Spirit. You cannot judge what you see in the bible with democratic principals. For I am the Boss and what I say goes whether you like it or not. Sounds hard; sounds harsh, but you have to remember Jehovah God who made that statement loves you beyond your comprehension of love, a limitless love.

That at times you don't understand, why certain bad things happen. You say, "God loves me why does this have to happen". Some things happen because it was prophesied, because of the wickedness of the world. I knew many, many, many thousands of years what was ahead. I have always warned the Body; the Body has always turned away and has listened to the things of the world, and many times they have paid the consequences for not obeying God.

So listen to these Words with the love of your heart, with the love in your spirit, for your Father Jehovah, Jesus Christ of Nazareth, your King of Kings, and the Holy Spirit; for WE are not your enemy. We are the Creator; We are the Maker the Breaker of the universe today, yesterday, tomorrow, forever. Remember that! We say these Words with the love of love.

Remember the river of tears that is going to flow through the planet from the highest mountain to the lowest valley. Heed My warning; study the Word, "WAR". For it is staring you in the face even if your brothers and sisters don't want to hear it—TELL THEM! That God Jehovah, Jesus Christ of Nazareth, and the Holy Spirit WARNED YOU THIS MINUTE, this day, about the Word, "WAR". Until We speak again with the LOVE and POWER of Jehovah, Jesus Christ, and the Holy Spirit telling you WE LOVE YOU beyond measure. Be good to each other; for you need each other in ALL THINGS, and pray and pray and pray, and have your daily Communion. So be it! So be it! So be it! (over)

Comments:

What a powerful prophecy for it left me drunk laying in bed with the room spinning. I could not move or I was afraid of getting out of bed for I felt I would fall and hurt myself. The power of the Holy Spirit has left me dizzy like I am in the middle of a whirlwind.

Something else strange happened this morning during this one hour of dizziness and fear. The telephone rang during the middle of this. I reached over the best I could and answered the phone. It was my brother Ted. He was calling from my parent's house my parents live in Vacaville, California which is about 50 miles from my house. What was so strange about the call was the story Ted was about to tell me. This happened approximately during the same time, I was receiving the last prophecy.

The story goes like this: My mother spoke on the telephone to my sister Christina who lives about 50 miles away in another city. After speaking to Christina my brother Gilbert called her who lives in Oakland, California which is about 70 miles away. Well, during my mother's conversation with Gilbert she heard my sister Christina calling her from outside her house and my brother Gilbert heard Christina too, but from the telephone and said to my mother what is Christina doing there. So my mother went to the door to let her in and no one was there. Then she remembered that she had just spoken to her ten minutes earlier and there was no way she could have reached her house in ten minutes. It was an audible voice for Gilbert heard Christina too, but from the telephone. My mother has told me several times that she has heard my voice and the voices of my brothers and sisters calling her before, but this is the first time someone else in the family heard them too. This has been a very strange day, and this dizziness lasted for about three hours after I got out of bed. (over)

900. Prophecy given to Raymond Aguilera on 25 April 1996 at 3:55 PM. in Spanish.

It has arrived. Yes, Reymundo, it has arrived. The White House is going to fall, with the force of the devil and to the point. The force, that is hitting your head now, is from the devil. It's because he doesn't want you to write what I am telling you; but it is the Truth. The White House is going to fall. You know that this is your Father, the One who made the world, the stars, all that you see, all that you touch. It has arrived, the day of the end of the White House. The President, of the United States, thinks a lot of himself. He believes he knows how to fix the things of God. But I tell you to the point He knows nothing. All the force, of the devil, is going to be placed on top of the head, of the President, of the United States, for the devil is going to push down the White House, with the force of the devils. The White House believes they can fix the things of the devil; but when you are walking with the devil, you cannot tell him what to do, for he will push you down. I know that the Word, that I am telling you, is hard; but it is the Truth.

Here comes the war that I told you about earlier. All the people are going to know that the things that I told you about are going to happen, like I said. There is a man with a vase; and inside, of this vase, are the plans of the devil; and the man has the vase hidden, yes—inside a very old house. But the bullet is going to come; and it is going to hit this man in the head. And, there are going to be others that are going come; and they are going to take the vase; and the people, who steal the vase, are going to know the President, of the United States. Yes! They are going to believe—that this vase is going to help them; but this vase is going to push them down, all of them, the president, and the government, for the force is in the hands of the devil. And the government of the United States won't be able to do a thing, for they have played with the devil, for many years; and the devil is the boss. Yes! It has arrived; the day that the White House falls. The things, that I have said, are from the Father, with the Son, with the Holy Spirit.

I know where the vase is—for I told the devil where he could hide it—for I got tired of all the evil that comes out of the United States. My Eyes see all; and all that they see, out of the United States, is evil, for hand by hand, they work with the devil. They don't believe I see, because they don't believe in God. They say they are going to pray; but they don't pray—they are just words. You can hear them when someone dies, or when something bad happens; there—they say the Word of God, and they tell the people to pray; but they don't pray, for they work for the devil. They believe they are strong. But, do you remember what I told you about the housefly? And how My Hand was going to kill the housefly? That's what's going to happen, for they cannot fool Me.

The climate, of the United States, is going to change, to the point, with water, with storms, with earthquakes, for We have arrived at the end; and the man, of the devil, has arrived. Remember when I told you to look at the sky, for there were coming—the things of the sky? The bomb is going to arrive; the infirmities are going to arrive; and the end has arrived, the end—of all that is good in the United States. They think a lot of themselves, even the ones who run the churches; but they don't seek Me with the Heart of God; they seek Me with the heart of money. They like the power. They like to tell people what to do, but they don't ask Me what I think. What a shame, for all of the world is going to be frightened!

The people, that you believe are great, are going to fall, rapidly and to the point. The greater, they think they are—the faster, they are going to fall. Like I told you earlier, your Father does not lie. All, that I have said, is direct and to the point. Here comes the man that is going to run the world, with the force of the devil. Remember what I have said about the word, "WAR." It is very important that you study that word, for that's going to be the life that is coming—war and war and war; then, the end will come, directly and to the point. All the war, in the Heavens, is getting larger, with the Angels and with the devils, and, day by day, you are getting closer to the end.

Those, who want to hear; are going to hear and the ones, who want to bury their heads under the ground—so they won't hear, I am going to help them, with the bullet. Yes! The day is going to come that you are not going to want to live. People are going to want to die, for everything is going to go very bad. And they are going to be sad because they were born; and they are going to cry, "why was I born?" "Why was I born, for I have to eat my son and daughter, like I eat the meat of a cow!" Did you hear what I have said? It has arrived, the day that you eat your son and daughter with the lips of the devil, for you are hungry. What a shame! What a shame, that you didn't seek your Father, the Son—Jesus, and the Holy Spirit.

You believed that you knew it all; and now you cannot even die. I have told you the Truth—you won't be able to hide yourself; then the day will come when you will see Me, Eye to eye, Face to face; then, I am going to ask you, "Why didn't you seek Me?" You believed you were so great; now you can show Me how great you are, when you are chewing on the leg of your son, for you are hungry. What a shame, the things of man, for he wants to be like God! It has arrived, the suffering of the world, with the force of the devil. It has arrived.

If you want to save yourself, eat the Communion. Seek My Son and repent of all the sins you have done, and I will save you. But, if you turn your back and walk away, I am going to let you walk away, for I have told you—and I have told you; and you did not want to hear, for you have a heart and a head of stone. This is all that I am going to tell you on this day, at this time, with My prophet, Reymundo. Exactly—all is going to happen, like I have said. This is your Father, with the Son, with the Holy Spirit, telling you the wisdom from Heaven. Yes! It has arrived. (over)

901. Prophecy given to Raymond Aguilera on 1 May 1996 at 1 AM. in Spanish.

Shoes. Yes, Reymundo, all the people of the world are going to need shoes, for they are going to have to run; they are going to have to hide themselves, if they want to live. The day of the shoes has arrived; the day of tears, the day that you have to hide. I know that the people that have read the prophecies are frightened; they are in tears; they are angry because they don't like to hear the Word of God, in the manner of God. They want to eat you, Reymundo, with the teeth of the devil, for many that get angry have demons inside of them. That's why they get angry, for their god is angry. That's why they want to eat you, and they want to use the Bible to eat you. But don't worry about things like this, for I have made a place for people like this, with these demons. I am going to send them to the pit.

I want you to point your nose into the Bible. I want you to study. For the day has arrived where people won't have the Bible to study. The man that I told you about earlier is going to want to burn, to throw away all the Bibles of the world, for he is angry at the Word of God too. He is going to join with the soldiers. And he is going run after all of the Body of My Son with the flame of the devil, with the heart of the devil. There are going to be many that are going to suffer. And there are going to be many that are going to see things with their eyes they never believed they would see. The things they are going to see, with their wives, with their husbands, with their sons and daughters. But everything is written in the

Bible; how it is going to happen in the days of the end. It is there CLEARLY. It is written; I am not telling you something NEW!

If people get angry, it is because they have not read the Bible, and they don't know a thing. Because if they had read the Bible from the beginning to the end; they would know that what I am saying is correct and to the point, but they all want things in the manner of man. And there are many of them who have demons inside of them and you cannot tell them a thing, for the devil has already won them. And I am also speaking about many who claim to be Christians. The ones who jump, and take the Bible in their hand and wave it in the air shouting the Word of God with the demons, with the lips of the devils. They believe they know it ALL, but they don't know a thing. They speak with the mouth of man, while they are holding the devil's hand. There—I am going to throw them, together, in the same pit, because they are friends, and friends have to live together.

But there are many Christians who say nothing. They are very silent, for My Word touches their hearts. Some are frightened. Others are joyous for they know the Word of God when they hear it. But everything is going to come out fine. If you see bodies in the middle of the street, if you see bodies where you live, if you see bodies where you sleep, if they are alive or dead—it is not important for I gave My Word many years ago. And when I give My Word—it happens!

I don't change My Mind because man doesn't like it. I am GOD! Man is only man, something I made with My Hands, with My Lips, with ALL that is CORRECT, with ALL that is PURE. The ones who chose the devil to be their god have joined themselves with the devil, and now they have to live with the devil. The rest who love Me, who seek Me with their hearts pointed, focused; those I am going to save with My Angels, with My Word. Everything that is Mine is Mine, and I am going to save it—ALL of it! This is CLEAR and it is to the POINT! All—who are hearing this Word can understand what I am saying, what is Mine—I will protect it. That's correct and to the point. That's not hard to understand!

But people like to twist and turn the Word of the Bible until it fits the word of man, and there are many words of man. All the churches have their words, and they all use the same Word of God in the Bible for they want to say their word. But My Word is Mine, and what I say—happens! This is EXACT and to the POINT! What a shame, that they are deaf and blind. What a shame, that they get angry with the force of the devil. But these things I don't worry about, if they get angry or not, for I know which ones belong to Me, and I know which ones belong to the devil. That's why I don't care if they get angry.

For the ones that belong to Me, seek Me in their heart, and they read the Bible from the beginning to the end. Those eat the Communion. Those repent their sins. Those seek theirs brothers and sisters, and THEY DON'T FIGHT! They don't seek out things to fight about, for they have the HEART of God. The ones who seek the fight—Oh, Oh, Oh! I am going to give them the fight, for the day has arrived that I am going to correct ALL with My Son, with the Angels. They are going to gather ALL that is bad, and they are going to correct it, and send them to the pit. That's not hard to understand, because I have already said it, many years ago. And on this day, and date, I am telling you again. What is not Mine, is going to the pit; the rest are going to Heaven with Me. With the Joy of My Heart, I tell you the TRUTH. This is CLEAR.

This is not hard to understand. But if you believe you can live in the World of God and in the world of the devil, you are fooling no one but yourself, for you cannot do it! If you belong to the devil—you belong to the devil. If you belong to Me—you belong to Me. You cannot live in the middle, for I will hit you like a housefly. And I don't like houseflies because houseflies have many diseases, and they are filthy. All that is filthy in the Eyes of God is going to the pit. And I don't care what you believe. For what is important is what the God that made Heaven, the world, the stars, with the Son, with the Holy Spirit—what He believes—is what is important; and that is ALL that is important. Do you understand Me?

There, I will leave you, Reymundo, so you can rest. Sleep. Until another day, on another date, then I will give you some more Wisdom from Heaven. I know the things that are in front of you. I know about your wife. It's almost here, Reymundo. Have patience it is almost here, for what I say—happens! She is going to call you with tears. With her heart pointed, she is going to call you. All that I have said, all that I have promised, I am going to give to you for you are My beloved, and with Force of the Son, with the Force of the Holy Spirit, with the Force of the Father, all will go well; for it has arrived—the Force of your Father to finish all that is filthy. Okay now, rest. Sleep, for you are My prophet. Hurry now, I will see you. (over)

902. Vision given to Raymond Aguilera on 2 May 1996.

I see the planet earth being covered with something purple or lavender in color. The color started at the North Pole and moved down toward the South Pole.

903. Prophecy given Raymond Aguilera on 5 May 1996 at 8:19 AM. in Spanish and English.

Spanish:
Hello Reymundo! How are you? How are you?

English:
I want you to pick a day. Any day that you want, and I want you to wear black, and I want all of your clothes to be black from the morning to the evening. Do you understand what I have said? All the clothes that you wear must be black for the day of darkness is here; the Day of Judgment; the day of wrath; the day of mourning. The day of vengeance is here clearly and to the point. The things that the world will see will be the cleansing of what is evil. For My Eyes and My Ears are seeing revolting things second by second. So I want you to wear black from the time

you wake up in the morning, I want you to go and put on some black clothes until evening. Then the next day, I want you to wear WHITE from the time you wake up until the time it gets dark. For that's the way it will be at the end times. It will be black then it will be white.

People of the world do not understand the ways of God, the manners of God, even though they are written plainly in the Bible. Like I said earlier, man twists and turns everything that the Lord says; everything that the Lord does to suit his purpose. Then he climbs on his own throne and claims to be god. He is going to have a chance to prove himself, when he faces the REAL God of the universe, Face to face, Eye to eye. The Creator of stars, of the heavens, of all that you see, of all that you don't see. For what you don't see is bigger and vaster than what you do see. You will see the Power and the Glory of Jehovah come upon this world rapidly without remorse.

For the Lord does not worry or feel bad about eliminating evil. For the evil things of the world don't belong to God. Do you understand the things of the Lord that are in the Bible? The basic things, the things that are right; the things that are wrong—the simple things—that you all understand that are written in the Bible; were written for everyone to understand with clear eyes. But the deeper things that are written in the Bible were made for a few chosen anointed ones that will guide and lead the Body of Jesus Christ of Nazareth. The problem is the ones that were NOT anointed, that were NOT chosen by God, Jehovah, Jesus Christ and the Holy Spirit, decided to take it upon themselves to guide and mislead the Body. This will be corrected immediately with the antichrist.

So the day of darkness, the day of Light is here! Remember what I told you, from the time you get up to the time of darkness wear black. The next day from the time you get up to the time the sun goes down, I want you to wear all WHITE. I want you to go and buy some new clean clothes, but they have to be WHITE. For that's the manner of God, Clean and Pure and Righteous. So be it. So be it. So be it. (over)

904. Vision given to Raymond Aguilera on 5 May 1996 at 10 AM.

During church service I saw a series of black arrows moving downward and at one point in there movement they changed into WHITE ARROWS. (over)

905. Vision given to Raymond Aguilera on 6 May 1996 at 10 PM.

The Lord showed me a city surrounded by high columns of natural rock. The rock columns were about a thousand feet into the air, and these rocks were side by side around the city almost like a fence. As I looked down from the sky I could see the city surrounded by these enormous rocks and there was only one way in and out through an opening between two rocks. (over)

906. Prophecy given to Raymond Aguilera on 7 May 1996 at 7:26 AM in Spanish.

How is it going? How is it going, My son? My Tears are going to run for the world, and they are going to fall like a storm for the things that are going to happen; for I have to clean up the world with My Hand, with My Son, with the Holy Spirit. I am going to clean up all the things that are filthy. I am going to gather, and I am going to save all the things that are clean with My Word—My Son, Jesus, and the Holy Spirit. We are together. Yes, We are going to CRY! Yes, the river of Tears of God is going to fall in the world, like a storm. The things of God are—all of the stars, all of the world, all there is and all that is going to be; and what is Mine, I will correct with the Love of Heaven.

The people of the world don't believe that I can correct the things of God. But, I AM God, the One who made ALL! They are going to be frightened, for everything that is in the Bible, is going to happen to the letter, to the point. What a shame, that they are deaf and blind. Oh, it HURTS My Heart—the things that they do; and the things they do, in the NAME of God. Those are the things of man, for there many people who seek God with the eyes of the devil. They believe they can change the things I made in the Old Testament; but I won't change the manner of God. I am the same, yesterday, today, and tomorrow.

For the people who have many sins, it is difficult—for they don't have the love of God, they have the love of the sin. But the ones who seek Me with the Heart of God. They know the Word of God for they read the Bible from the beginning to the end; they know My Word for they are seeking the God who made ALL—the stars, the world, the sky—all the things that you see, all the things that you don't see. I AM the First and the Last.

You know what? The ones who seek Me with the Heart of God, I am going to save. For here comes the day of the dead; the day that all that is alive, that is NOT Mine, is going to die with the force of the devil, with the Force of My Son, with the Force of the Holy Spirit, with the Force of ALL that there is. Don't get scared because I told you that the devil is going to HELP Me, for everything is MINE; and I use the devil like I want. He is nothing! He is just like the rest of the world, with the men that believe they can tell God what He can do. I will hit them all, like I hit a housefly.

I know that the world believes that they can do what they want, that God doesn't see a thing and He doesn't hear a thing; but mark it in your head, for I know you don't have a heart, I see ALL—I hear ALL! And here comes the point in time that you are going to see Me, Eye to eye, Face to face; and I am going to show you what I saw and what I have heard. You are going to be frightened, for you won't be able to move yourself. I tell you in seriousness, I tell you with Love, you have to correct yourself, this minute, for time is running out! And the minutes you have now, you won't have tomorrow. If you want to save yourself, you have to change the manner that you are walking. For some, it is going to be very difficult; for others, much easier; but you have to do it, for I am not PLAYING.

What I say is serious and it is EXACT, and it is to the POINT. If I tell you that I am going to kill you, I am going to kill you! If I tell you that I am going to save you, I am going to save you! This is CLEAR and this is to the POINT! You cannot change My Words, for what I say is EXACT! I know that there are many people in the world that they want to change. They want to change the things they are doing—that are evil. I know the heart, but you have to seek Me. You have to seek My Son—Jesus, first; and you have to do what you can to change yourself; and the Holy Spirit will help. Sometimes He will help you rapidly; sometimes He will help you slowly—but He WILL HELP YOU, for We know the manner We have to use to clean the things that are filthy.

You have to have patience; you have to have love, for the day that you choose, to change the way you are walking in your sins, is the day you will find Me. It is the day I will help you; it is the day I will save you. There are many ways in seeking Me. There is much love if you seek Me, but the things of God are clean—are straight.

I know the sin, and the sins you have done. I am speaking to you right now, Eye to eye, Face to face. All the people who are reading this prophecy, this minute, I am telling you—to your eyes, to your ears, that I know exactly what you have done, all to the point. My Tears cry if you don't seek Me, for I know the things of God. I know the things you have to do—the things that you have to seek—the things you have to change. I know it ALL!

But look My son, I AM, I AM, I AM, and it is nothing to Me to hit the world. It is nothing to Me to correct the things that you have to correct. But I want to save you with the Love of Heaven, with the Love of all that is. I AM, I AM, I AM. With the Son, with the Holy Spirit, I tell you the truth—it has arrived, the day, the date that My Son is coming with the Force of God to correct the things that THEY have to correct. Look My son, I know—that you know that this is your Father speaking with you, the Father that made all, with the Son, with the Holy Spirit.

You are Mine and I am yours, if you seek Me; but you have to seek Me in seriousness; you have to seek Me with the Heart of God. There are many who are hearing this Word that are using drugs, and there are many who are selling drugs. There are many who are drinking wine and there are many who want to correct the way they are living, and all of their sins that they are doing right now, this minute. You can change, sometimes it is going to be difficult—sometimes it is going to be rapidly; but you have to seek Me, yes—for the day has arrived of the Hand of God. Seek Me and I will help. Yes, it has arrived, the day of God, Exactly and to the Point. (over)

907. Vision and Prophecy given to Raymond Aguilera on 10 May 1996 at 10:00 AM.

The Lord showed me a reddish brown soft leather suitcase the kind you take on airplanes.

Then the Lord said, "Inside the suitcase there is a nuclear device."

Vision:

Then I saw a briefcase the kind businessmen carry on business trips. Except this one had a handcuff on it, and it was strapped to a man's wrist. (over)

908. Prophecy given to Raymond Aguilera on 16 May 1996 at 7:35 AM.

I have been praying to the Lord for an explanation, for the wearing of White and black clothes.

This is what the Lord told me, "Wearing White and black clothes Symbolizes, Witnesses, and Seals, what I have said is TRUE and is going to HAPPEN!" (over)

Note:
Yesterday, I spent some of my mortgage money and bought the White and black clothes I needed to accomplish this event. I will be wearing the black clothes on Friday, May 17, 1996, and the White clothes on Saturday, May 18, 1996. I was also instructed to burn the black clothes after I used them. May the Lord have mercy on us. (over)

909. Occurrences and a Vision given to Raymond Aguilera on 17–21 May 1996.

Note: A letter to the brothers and sisters on the e-mail list.

Hello brothers and sisters,

I have been getting e-mail from people on the e-mail list, wanting to know what happened during the White and black wearing of the Clothes from prophecy #903. Well, the day before, I removed all white marking and labels from the black clothes. Then the next day, Friday—May 17th, I wore the black clothes from daybreak until the sun went down. But at the break of first light on the 17th, the Lord told me to fast all day without water or food; and to remember to burn the black clothes that night. Everything went well, except for my hunger. I was so hungry, I felt like I could eat the furniture. I hadn't seen Ron all day, but luckily for me, he made a big dinner late that night.

The next day the same thing: from dawn to nightfall I wore the White Clothes; but not before removing all the colored labels and marking. Everything went well except for the Web Page photographs. I even went to my sister's house to help her pack, and repair, her rented house—wearing my White clothes, because she was permanently moving to Oregon. I did notice some strange looks from my brother and sister. Even Jim, my brother-in-law—her husband, tried to act like nothing was unusual. I did get the White clothes a little dirty, but the Lord did not say it was wrong.

The previous week during my sister's packing, she had found the photographs from the Mt. Diablo Anointing trip of December 2, 1990. Doug and I had been seeking these photos for about 5 years. Doug is the brother, in Christ, who photographed us on Mt. Diablo on December 2, 1990. Well, on Thursday the 16th, I had several of the photographs scanned onto diskettes. I received them back on Saturday. Then I started to upload them onto the Web Page site on Saturday afternoon and all day Sunday the 19th. This is when things started getting weird. It seemed like everything that I have ever learned about uploading files to my web page, left my mind. I worked on them for about 25 hours, until I finished them Monday evening. But Monday morning—the 20th, is when things got even weirder. I got up dizzy and had a hard time walking or thinking, let alone remembering the process for uploading the photographs on to the web page. I knew that I could only work on them until about noon, for I had to go and do a small job to earn some money for my mortgage payment.

Well, about noon, my head was so mixed up, I didn't know if I could drive the car, let alone do the repair work to this broken door jam. On the way to the job I knew I was late, so I had decided to tell the people at the job site that I had to go and get something to eat first, because I was so dizzy. So I told them; and I went to a Mexican restaurant around the corner and ordered some food.

While waiting for the food to be served, I felt like I was going to die right there in my seat. I am not saying this figuratively. I mean—I thought I was going to DIE right there. What kept going through my mind was, "After all I have gone through, I am are going to die in a Mexican restaurant that I have never been in before. What a place to finish my life!" But I did not die there; and I started to feel a little better.

So I went and finished the repair work and drove towards home. But when I got about four houses from my house, on top of a small hill above my house—my car coughed and died there. But it still had enough momentum that I was able to roll it down the hill and onto my driveway.

I got out of the car and walked over to Ron, who was outside working in the yard. I could tell he sensed something was wrong with me, so I told him the whole story. Then he proceeded to tell me that his computer crashed hours earlier. So I told Ron to tell anyone who came around to see me, that I was not available, for I was going to get some rest.

A few hours later, a friend from the Monday night Bible study picked me up, because my car was still broken. And during the worship time, the Lord said, "Ray, the devil wanted to kill you in the restaurant, but I told him NO! So he killed your car instead."

Vision:

Then the Lord showed me a vision of a large dragon that reminded me of a dragon's head you see on a Chinese New Year. The only difference was it had a man in it's mouth, from the head down to his waist. All I could see was the lower part of the man with the dragon trying to eat him headfirst.

After hearing this, I was left completely overwhelmed; and wondering what in the heck is going on, and what's next. Now this morning my computer is making funny noises.

Another Occurrence:

So this morning, after typing the above, I decided to take the rest of the, Dec. 2, photographic slides of Mt. Diablo to the photo finisher. I wanted to strike back at the devil, and have them transferred onto diskettes so I could upload them onto the Web site. And as Ron and I walked in the door of the photo store we are hit with a 4.8 earthquake from the San Jose area. This young office girl comes running out of her office asking loudly if anyone felt the earthquake. I was still so overwhelmed, that I didn't feel a thing. God bless you all. (over)

PS: Please forgive my construction of this letter for I cannot think very clearly yet. Oh, you can check out the two photo/slides on the Web page site: *http://prophecy.org*. The rest will be uploaded sometime this week.

910. Vision given to Raymond Aguilera on 21 May 1996 at 3:16 PM.

During prayer I asked the Lord to help me. And He gave me a vision of a man with a large upside down fish strapped to his back with some rope. (over)

911. Prophecy given to Raymond Aguilera on 23 May 1996 at 11:30 AM. in English.

Some of you, Christians who are submitting to your church authorities, are going to be facing a problem; for I am going strongly against some church leaders. And you are going to have to make a decision—whether to follow your church leadership, or follow Me—Jehovah, Jesus Christ of Nazareth, and the Holy Spirit; for I am going to clean-up the Body of My Son with Power. Remember, either you are with Me or you are against Me. I will not accept a middle ground. For some of you, it is going to be very hard; but you have to stop playing church, and seek your brothers and sisters in the streets. For the power of the antichrist is going to be strong, and your church leaders don't have any real power. We: Jehovah, Jesus Christ, and the Holy Spirit are the ONLY ONES Who can save you. REMEMBER THAT! Peace be with you—you hard-headed Christians. (over)

912. Vision given to Raymond Aguilera on 27 May 1996.

I saw a vision of an American eagle with its head turned and looking down at something. Then the next vision was the same eagle with its beak and neck tied with some string. The American eagle was in total bondage.

913. Vision given to Raymond Aguilera on 29 May 1996 at 8:30 PM.

During prayer the Lord showed me a long thin copper wires coming from Heaven, and these copper wires were connected to different people. Then I saw a tool that is used to cut copper pipe. This tool has a cutting wheel that applies pressure as it goes around the copper pipe until the pipe is cut into. Well, this copper cutting tool had this thin copper wire in its jaws and the cutting wheel was going around and around this one wire trying to cut it into. Well, as the circular wheel went around this thin wire all it did was make the wire thinner, but it could not cut it into, and it was just as strong as before the pipe cutter tried to cut it.

Prophecy:

Then the Lord said, "There are going to be many people who belong to Me and they are going to try to break away, but I won't let them go. No matter how hard they try or thin the wire gets. I will not let them go. For they belong to Me. For We are bonded for ever."

Vision:

Then later during prayer that evening, the Lord showed me a White scroll and it was being opened. There weren't any names on it yet, but it was being opened. (over)

914. Vision given to Raymond Aguilera on 6 June 1996 at 1:33 PM.

I had a vision of thousands of people walking. I noticed that the people in the front were wearing blue and black clothes, and these people were older, in there sixties and seventies. It was a march of some sort. (over)

915. Vision given to Raymond Aguilera on 11 June 1996 at 10:30 AM.

I was walking home with my dog, Loretta, from the Post Office with a smile, for a few hours earlier I had only a two dollars to my name, and praising the Lord on how He had come through again. For a brother or sister had sent me a few dollars and I felt the Lord hand raising me up again.

Well, during my walk down the street from the top of this hill that leads to my house, I noticed this man walking up the hill toward me. I had not noticed him until I was about half way down the hill. He was a very clean looking man and on the thin side wearing this heavy blue sweater. He had white hair and was in his fifties or sixties with a nicely trimmed short white beard. As he proceeded toward me I made sure I kept Loretta close to me on the leash because some people are afraid of dogs. Well, he walked steadily toward me without moving away and approached me with a smile. He first looked down at Loretta and smiled and then looked up at me and smiled again, but he didn't slow down or stop. I smiled back and said hello, but he didn't say a word. I kept wondering why he was wearing that heavy blue sweater. So I turned around to look at him again and he had vanished. He was nowhere to be seen. This was sure an exciting morning for me with a few dollars in my pocket and seeing an Angel of the Lord all in the same hour I felt my day was already complete. (over)

916. Prophecy given to Raymond Aguilera on the 16 June 1996.

During prayer and worship the Lord said, "Go to San Francisco and renew your passport. For your time has arrived and it is here. I am going to send you out like Moses because I love the people below the United States. For the match will strike there soon. I am going to send a man to you and he is going to tell you what to do. I also want you to go to the brother in San Francisco who is suppose to be doing the Spanish translation of the prophecy book, and take your computer away from him. I want you to do it tomorrow."

Comments:

So I went the next day and picked up the computer and the application for my passport. I guess, I am going to have to sit and wait for this man with my instructions. I would like state that during this prophecy the Lord showed me His Love for the defenseless people below the United States. It is very hard to explain an experience like this, but you can take my word for it, the Lord has an immeasurable Love for His people below the United States.

917. Vision given to Raymond Aguilera on 21 June 1996 at 8:30 PM.

During praise and worship, the Lord showed Me a vision of an elephant jumping through a hoop—with an explosion and fire behind him. Then…when the elephant was going through this hoop, I saw two rifles, side-by-side, shoot the elephant.

Vision:

Then, the next image I saw was of a big, heavy-set woman in this large clear tank, filled with water, being dunked into the water by her head—by this demon trying to drowned her. I could see the air coming out of her nostrils and mouth as she tried to gasp for air, from under the water.

Prophecy:

Then the Lord said that the big, fat woman was the United States.

Vision:

The next vision was one of those old, wide Champaign glasses; but inside the champagne glass—there was some pudding. Then the glass, with the pudding inside, was cut right down in the middle, like butter, and it separated in two pieces.

Vision:

Then, I saw a Lit White candle with some melted wax around the wick. And as I watched this Lit wick surrounded by this melted wax, another transparent fire appeared in the melted wax and it moved around the REAL LIT WICK like a shark swims around it's prey. I would like to state it wasn't a real flame, it just looked like one—an imitation flame, but it was mobile. (over)

918. Vision given to Raymond Aguilera on 23 June 1996 at 10:25 AM.

I had a vision of the planet earth, with a large vulture on top of the planet. The vulture had two bodies—but one head. (over)

919. Prophecy given to Raymond Aguilera on 23 June 1996 at 10:56 AM.

The Lord showed me the image of a Plumb Line, and the Lord said, "I control the direction of the Plumb Line. My Plumb Line can move horizontal; it can move vertical; it can move to the north, to the west and to the east. It can point straight up into the air. It could point directly to you. There is no limit to the direction of My Plumb Line because I am the Father—Jehovah, that created everything that you see; everything that you touch; everything that is; everything that will be. Be prepared. Be wise. Be in line with the Plumb Line of Jehovah.

For some of you, this is confusing. To those who are in the Word: to those who are focused on their God—Jehovah, Jesus Christ and the Holy Spirit—know exactly what I am saying; they are the mature Christians. What I have said is very simple; but to man—it is very complex. All Wisdom comes from God. All evil comes from Satan. To understand the ways of God, you have to be following God: Jesus Christ, the Holy Spirit and Me—Jehovah. To understand evil, you have to be following Satan.

It's not hard to understand which God you are following. Whether your god is Satan, whether your God is Jehovah, Jesus Christ and the Holy Spirit—they will give you a Plumb Line and that Plumb Line will direct you to the path of righteousness—or to the path of the pit of hell. The choice is yours. Whatever direction My Plumb Line points: whether it's vertical, whether it's horizontal, whether it's to the right or the left—it's always leads you to Heaven: to the throne of God. If you follow the plumb line of the devil—it's a one-directional plumb line; it leads you to damnation: to the pit of hell—to everlasting suffering.

Do you get the picture? Do you understand My Words? This is a short lesson on the Plumb Line. It's direct; it's clear; it's pointed, if you are on the right path. If you don't understand what I have said, you are in trouble—to say the least. You better open that Bible. You better read it from the beginning to the end; and when you are finished, you better read it again. And when you are finished, you better read again. You better find out where you are going, or let's say—which Plumb Line you are following—or which Plumb Line you are looking at. No matter what direction the Plumb Line of God is pointing: it's always towards the direction of Heaven. You have to follow the road that is narrow; but you have to find the road first—before you can follow it.

I hear the term: "name it and claim it." This man-made term comes from the unwise. It comes from people who don't understand the Bible. It comes from the lost. Are you following the Plumb Line? I just told you: you can claim what you want—I'll decide whether I listen. The authority belongs to God—Jehovah, Jesus Christ, and the Holy Spirit. You can claim all the blessing you want, but if you are not on My Plumb Line—I don't know you! You can claim all you want: and all that you will get is the back of My Hand.

And this goes for the leadership, the so-called wise men of Christ, who are so busy patting themselves on their behinds. Because the devil is ready to kick them into the pit of hell on their tender spots, do you get My Picture? It is CLEAR—it is DIRECT! There is a lot of false teaching in the Body of Christ, these days. Ninety-nine percent of it is wrong. The reason I say that is because people twist the Bible to suit their purposes. Secondly, they don't read the Bible from the beginning to end. They jump around: to justify their "name it and claim it;" to justify their doctrine; to justify their pocket books. The wise are HUMBLE. And the HUMBLE—I will take to Heaven.

The preachers and evangelists like to pump up people. They like to get them excited. They think they are doing them a favor. They think they are bringing them to God. If you believe—that you have to pump somebody up to bring them to God: you are following the WRONG Plumb Line. If you cannot go to a brother, humbly and meekly, with what is in your heart, and preach the Gospel of God—you have a problem. There is no theatrics in the Lord—Jesus Christ; there is no theatrics in the Lord—Jehovah; there is no theatrics in the Lord—Holy Spirit—for We are GOD! What We say gets DONE—CORRECTLY, CLEARLY, and to the POINT. We don't have to entertain people. We don't have to amuse people. We don't have to buy people. We don't have to CON people.

The Word of God is enough! Whether it is through signs and wonders—whether it is the breaking of the body, through the spirit, that was caused by hearing the Word of God, whatever the manner—whatever the shape: it's the Word of God! It is not how you pretend it to be; it's not how you want it to be either: IT is what IT is! It has always been what it was, before you even existed. You don't have to sugarcoat it. You don't have to fan it with a fan. You don't have to stand on one thumb. You don't have to wear big fancy hairdos'. You don't have to drive a big car. You don't have to wear jewelry. You don't have to wear neon lights. You don't have to pretend you are sexy. The Word of God has done, what the Word of God said—PLAINLY, SIMPLY, DIRECTLY, to the POINT.

If you are a preacher or an evangelist that is following that path, you will be visiting Satan very soon. Do you get My Word, Clearly, and Directly to the Point? If you are a follower of a preacher or evangelist—pastor who projects these mannerisms that are ungodly, I'll state it again:

they are ungodly, they are man-made, they are made of Satan; for I know My Sheep and they know Me—I don't have to entertain them. I do give them signs and wonders through the Power of the Holy Spirit; but when they see My Signs and Wonders, they know it is God—because they have read the Bible—because they have a personal relationship with Me—not their evangelist, not their meetings, not their organizations. Do you get My Picture? Do you understand My Words? The Power Presence of God is very Clear. It's very Direct.

A lot of you are following Satan and you think you are following God—but even Satan, himself, trembles at My Words. Do you get that Picture? Do you understand what I have said? EVEN SATAN TREMBLES AT MY WORDS! Now, make up your mind—who do you want to follow—Satan or Me: Jehovah, Jesus Christ and the Holy Spirit? A lot of pastors, a lot of evangelists are going to get mad at this Word; but do I care if they get mad? I'll do to them what I am going to do to the devil. Do you get My Picture? Do you understand My Words?

Read that Bible from the beginning to the end and you'll understand what I have just said, "The Power of God is infinite". The Power of God belongs to God. It doesn't belong to evangelists. It doesn't belong to anyone—though I do use people in mighty ways; but the Power is Mine. Do you get that Picture? So much for your lecture today on the Plumb Line.

I can see the red eyes of certain leaders right now. I can see their anger. Their day will come when they look at Me, eye-to-eye, and We will see how angry they will get when they are in My Presence. We will see! Are you listening to Me—you red eyed pastors and evangelists—did you hear what I have said Clearly and to the Point? We will see if you do a dance to My Face. We will see if you will prophesy to Me; and on how you can, "Name it and Claim it," when you are in My Presence and I have My Thumb on top of your head. So be it! So be it! So be it!" (over)

920. Occurrence given to Raymond Aguilera on 25 June 1996.

I am going to document this feeling of exhaustion that I have. It's been a few days since I received the last prophecy. My body was left totally exhausted after I sent out the last prophecy to our e-mail list (brothers and sisters) even with some spelling errors. I could not wait to send it out. I wish the Lord would give me a break, what I mean is—to go easy with His Holy Spirit's Power. My body can't take too much more. I am losing my hair; and what I have left is turning white. I get so exhausted after receiving and typing a prophecy like this. It doesn't sound like much work, but it leaves me totally wasted. Afterwards, I am left off unbalanced and I can't function.

I went to see a friend after I mailed out the prophecy; and I found myself driving all over the freeway—like a drunk. I could not perceive distance or speed. I was suppose to do a small job for Carl, but I was so sleepy that I had to come back home. Then, when I got home, I fell straight to sleep for over five and one-half hours. After, my long afternoon sleep, I got up and found out I still couldn't do a thing. So I went to the Monday night Bible study. My mind was awake, but it was not really there. The Holy Spirit's Touch, or wherever you want to call it, has my mind still in the Spirit. It is still not back—into the flesh yet.

And I can't explain this craving for fruit after a prophecy either; and it is hard for me to understand it. I feel...like I am going to die if I don't eat some fruit. After the Bible study, the sister where we had the bible study gave me most of the fruit she had in her house. And this morning, I still feel exhausted, and cannot get out of bed and I have a craving for fruit. Then later in the afternoon, I ate so much fruit—my stomach got upset.

Any of you who are reading this—please pray for me. Pray that the Lord gives me the physical strength to move on. I can't seem to do it on my own. I almost thought of asking the Lord not to give me anymore prophecies. For I am physically exhausted, I am still financially broke. I am $100 overdrawn in my checking account, and I can't buy fruit or even pay my bills. I don't know. I sure didn't think the Lord worked this way; but when you sense all of His Power—when you receive a prophecy and even when you type it—even days later; you know His authority over you. Sometimes I cry! Sometimes I can't believe the directness and the pointedness of His message. I don't how many prophets are experiencing this, but if the Lord doesn't slow down, I feel I am going to die. Maybe that won't be so bad! But you know—I don't think I am going to die. I think, I have to finish my job, but my joints, hands, and all my body parts hurt, and are saying—give me some rest…and some decent food!!!

Lord, if You are listening right now, I need a vacation. Not a long one—my body needs to be refreshed. You just gotta do something because I am dying. I don't have enough rest, time, brains, body or money. You have given me so much work and I am only one person. Though there are other people helping me—I have to do too much myself! I guess that's all. I hope You don't think I am naming and claiming this. Let Your will be done. (over)

921. Occurrence given to Raymond Aguilera on 27 June 1996 at 10:00 AM.

The Lord gave me the scripture, Mat 15:2, this morning, and after reading it I listed the rest of the scriptures that followed it.

From KJV Bible:
Mat 15:2 Why do thy disciples transgress the tradition of the elders? for they wash not their hands when they eat bread.
Mat 15:3 But he answered and said unto them, Why do ye also transgress the commandment of God by your tradition?
Mat 15:4 For God commanded, saying, Honour thy father and mother: and, He that curseth father or mother, let him die the death.
Mat 15:5 But ye say, Whosoever shall say to his father or his mother, It is a gift, by whatsoever thou mightest be profited by me;

Mat 15:6 And honour not his father or his mother, he shall be free. Thus have ye made the commandment of God of none effect by your tradition.
Mat 15:7 Ye hypocrites, well did Esaias prophesy of you, saying,
Mat 15:8 This people draweth nigh unto me with their mouth, and honoureth me with their lips; but their heart is far from me.
Mat 15:9 But in vain they do worship me, teaching for doctrines the commandments of men.
Mat 15:10 And he called the multitude, and said unto them, Hear, and understand:
Mat 15:11 Not that which goeth into the mouth defileth a man; but that which cometh out of the mouth, this defileth a man.
Mat 15:12 Then came his disciples, and said unto him, Knowest thou that the Pharisees were offended, after they heard this saying?
Mat 15:13 But he answered and said, Every plant, which my heavenly Father hath not planted, shall be rooted up.
Mat 15:14 Let them alone: they be blind leaders of the blind. And if the blind lead the blind, both shall fall into the ditch.
Mat 15:15 Then answered Peter and said unto him, Declare unto us this parable.
Mat 15:16 And Jesus said, Are ye also yet without understanding?
Mat 15:17 Do not ye yet understand, that whatsoever entereth in at the mouth goeth into the belly, and is cast out into the draught?
Mat 15:18 But those things which proceed out of the mouth come forth from the heart; and they defile the man.
Mat 15:19 For out of the heart proceed evil thoughts, murders, adulteries, fornications, thefts, false witness, blasphemies:
Mat 15:20 These are the things which defile a man: but to eat with unwashen hands defileth not a man.

922. Vision given to Raymond Aguilera on 28 June 1996.

The Lord showed me the letter, "M", and as I looked at this large letter, I saw an image of a mountain in the background behind the large letter. The large letter somehow disappeared and I could clearly see this large mountain with some kind of White Light on top of it. I also saw that it was dark all around the mountain, but I could not tell if it was night time or the darkness meant something else. But one thing that was clear; was this growing White Light on top of the mountain. There seem to be dark and white clouds in the sky too. (over)

923. Prophecy given to Raymond Aguilera on 3 July 1996 at 1:30 AM. in Spanish.

Simon. Yes the shell (cáscara = Spanish word for skin, shell…) of Simon. It has arrived—the shell of Simon. I know that you are ready; I know that you are pointed; I know—all is ready—the shell of Simon.

I told you about your lady years ago. You are going to come together in the manner of God. I know that you do not believe Me. I know the manner of love and the manner of God. Your lady thinks of you too—with tears, with her heart, with her spirit. She is going to call you; and the two of you are going to come together with Force of God: I tell you the Truth. I know that you do not believe Me because you have waited for so many years. But what I say is Exact and to the Point. I have not finished using you. There are things that I have not told you yet about your life with your wife. But look—all is going to happen to the point; for I do not say one thing and then do another. I know that your spirit is pointed in the direction of your God. I know that you are alone. I know that you believe that I do not hear you—the tears of the heart, the tears of the money, the tears of the work, the tears of your friends, the tears of your family. I hear all of it, Reymundo; I see all of it.

But the things that you do not see are the TEARS OF GOD of the things I see—that I CRY ABOUT. When I see the little ones that they kill—like they kill dogs. What a shame! How can they treat their children like they were animals? That's why, I am going to hit the world HARD, FAST, AND TO THE POINT! And there are men sleeping with men, women sleeping with women. And the men who sleep with women kill the babies that I give them. All that I say to you is FROM MY TEARS— from My Heart of My Spirit.

Here comes the day that they are going to kill the old people too. Mark it on your calendar, for here it comes: the day that the old people won't have a chance either—and the sick ones and the ones who study the Bible. All of them, they are going to gather and they are going to kill them, like they do animals. Remember that I told you—for the devil is going to become strong with the man. The man is going to believe that the world is his because he doesn't believe in God. He doesn't believe in the manner of God; but that's another story I will tell you on another day, on another date.

But I wanted to speak to you tonight because I knew that your heart is hurting all the way to Heaven—because I promised you your woman. And the day has arrived that you do not believe Me. The letter that you sent her is going to frighten her. Did you hear Me? The letter that you sent her is going to frighten her in the manner that you wouldn't believe. But everything is in My Hands, for when I say something—it happens. And I correct the things that need to be corrected. The bad is from the devil. The GOOD is from God, the One who made all: the world, the stars, your body, your wife, the stars.

What a shame that people are so indifferent about their sons and daughters that they kill them like animals. This is all that I want to tell you on this minute—that I have heard all that you have said to Me in your prayers. I hear you, but sometimes I don't tell you that I hear you—but I do HEAR YOU! This is Correct and to the Point. Hurry—go to sleep and rest for We have things to do. (over)

924. Vision given to Raymond Aguilera on 4 July 1996 at 4:00 PM.

A vision of the Statue of Liberty holding a limousine over her head, and throwing it to the ground. (over)

925. Occurrence given to Raymond Aguilera on 21 July 1996.

I went camping for two days with three brothers to see if I could get some rest. It was a good trip—I believe, I have to leave town more often before I burn myself up. But on the camping trip, the Lord gave me a vision of His coming.

Vision:
During prayer the vision started with a Large single White Lit Candle moving forward. Then two small-lit candles appeared side by side behind the Large White Candle; then three small-lit candles appeared side by side behind the row of two white candles; then four white lit candles appeared side by side behind the row of three candles. Row upon row of lit white candles appeared behind the proceeding row until a Large Triangle of lit Candles could be seen marching behind the Large White Candle (Jesus Christ). It looked like the point of an arrow, and it reminded me of the vision of the Trinity where the Lord showed me a triangle and said We have three points, but We are one triangle. (over)

926. Occurrence given to Raymond Aguilera on 10 July 1996 at 4:10 PM.

I would like to share something that happened a few minutes ago. I went to visit my friend Jerry Lukehart, who wrote the preface to the Prophecy Book. I sometimes go to visit him when I am feeling down and out. Remember I just got back from a two-day camping trip, and I was feeling rested and relaxed. Well, I typed the vision I received on the camping trip this morning and e-mailed it out to the people on our e-mail. Afterward, I started feeling depressed because my mortgage payment was over due again and I have no money to pay it again. I kept telling myself, "This is getting to be a very old story."

So I decided to run and hide at Jerry's house because he is always broke too, and I knew he would know how I felt. I am sorry to say, I have done this many, many times before. Well, Jerry took me to a movie, and I forgot all about my problems for the afternoon. Now Jerry lives about 35 minutes away, so on the way home on the freeway, I started thinking about the problems I had waiting at home. Then without warning my voice began to sing over and over: I love you Jesus. I love you Jesus. What felt so strange and unusual was it wasn't my voice. I have never been able to sing and now my voice was praising the Lord over and over. "I love you Jesus. I love you Jesus. Praise you Jesus. Praise you Jesus."

So I just drove home with my voice praising the Lord in English, with a voice that wasn't mine. This went on for about ten minutes, then the voice changed into and unknown singing tongue. I could sense the Lord's Presence too, but my mind kept thinking about the sound that was coming out of my body. And wondering, who is singing? It was so beautiful, but like I said earlier, it wasn't me (At least I don't think it was me?). It felt like my body was praising the Lord without me. I know the principals of speaking in tongues without your mind's involvement, but I felt MORE detached than usual.

Well, the unknown singing tongues lasted for about ten minutes, and then this prayer language I haven't heard in over six years began to speak. This was one of the first tongues I had when I first met the Lord on Dec 3, 1990. This whole occurrence brought me back to the beginning of my prophetic walk (speaking in tongues) six years ago. I wish words could explain this occurrence, but I am afraid most of you would not understand it unless you experienced it. How can you be inside your own body and hear it praise the Lord, and you have nothing to do with it? Does that kind of make sense. I was TOTALLY left out of it. Remember the scripture Luke 19:40.

From KJV Bible:
Luke 19:37 And when he was come nigh, even now at the descent of the mount of Olives, the whole multitude of the disciples began to rejoice and praise God with a loud voice for all the mighty works that they had seen;
Luke 19:38 Saying, Blessed be the King that cometh in the name of the Lord: peace in heaven, and glory in the highest.
Luke 19:39 And some of the Pharisees from among the multitude said unto him, Master, rebuke thy disciples.
Luke 19:40 And he answered and said unto them, *I tell you that, if these should hold their peace, the stones would immediately cry out.*

Well that's how I felt. I had no control over my body, and it just sang out over, and over. Maybe I have stones in MY HEAD (hard head) and body? All I can say now is, "Praise the Lord!!" (over)

PS: People on the e-mail, I am so excited I didn't take the time to really proof read this. God bless.

927. Occurrence, Vision, and Prophecy given to Raymond Aguilera on 12 July 1996 at 6:15 PM.

My hands are hurting BADLY and I have been thinking of stopping this Christian walk for a little while. For there isn't enough money to keep it going anyway, and the attacks from the enemy are wearing me out; I was feeling sorry for myself again; when the Lord in His usual wisdom lead me to the Book of Proverbs. He guided me through as I read the end of chapter eight, and then He told me to place it in the Prophecy Book for the OTHERS TO READ.

Vision:

The Lord gave me a vision of a cracked tree trunk. As I watched, I could see His Hands take this wide strap and wrap it around the broken trunk, and the cracked trunk came back to it's original position.

Prophecy:

Then the Lord said, "Seven plus one." (over)

928. Prophecy given to Raymond Aguilera on 15 July 1996 at 10:30 AM. in English.

Vengeance is My Mine, I have told you many, many times; so eat the fruit of your evil. Many people of the earth think I am a big joke. We will see who will laugh last. The last Train will leave at 7 AM. Did you hear what I have said? "The last Train will leave at 7 AM." Then—We will see who is laughing. For the curse of Jehovah will hit your eyes when you least expect it.

And you, my little son, hang on, for I am going to send you help from the back lines. The brothers and sisters, that I am going to send to help you will be STRONG and DEDICATED! For you will begin to see and hear from the brothers, who have never been at war with evil spirits try to give you advice. Do not listen to them, for they think and they mean well, but they will only hurt you. I know the pain that you are going through, but hang on! For the end is to close to stop now! Did you hear Me, Reymundo? "WE ARE TO CLOSE TO STOP NOW!" Remember the Blood of Jesus Christ. For everything in the universe will go to the cross.

The Art of Living is Loving Jesus Christ, and going to the Cross. The Wheels on the last Train are being oiled now. The Body of Christ will be fully protected, but they will see much blood, to the right, to the left, behind, and the hardest in front. Never forget that Jehovah, Jesus Christ, and the Holy Spirit, will ALWAYS be there. The planet will see the fruits of evil for the wickedness of the followers of Satan.

Remember the ground of Holiness is the ground that Jesus walks on, and the ground that His Holy Body on earth walks on. So be it. So be it. So be it, My little son. I hear your tears. Listen only to Us, for We are the only ONE who can help you. My beloved. (over)

929. Vision and Prophecy given to Raymond Aguilera on 17 July 1996 at 8:00 PM.

(Not typed up yet)

930. Vision given to Raymond Aguilera on 21 July 1996 at 7:52 AM.

I was reading the Book of Matthew, and I came to the Chapter and verses: 7:21-23. And the Lord gave me a vision of a black and white snake moving over the branches of a small tree. (over)

From the KJV Bible:
Mat 7:21 *Not every one that saith unto me, Lord, Lord, shall enter into the kingdom of heaven; but he that doeth the will of my Father which is in heaven.*
Mat 7:22 *Many will say to me in that day, Lord, Lord, have we not prophesied in thy name? and in thy name have cast out devils? and in thy name done many wonderful works?*
Mat 7:23 *And then will I profess unto them, I never knew you: depart from me, ye that work iniquity.*

931. Prophecy given to Raymond Aguilera on 21 July 1996 at 2:20 PM.

During the reading of the Book of Matthew, Chapter 13:34-35, the Lord said, "Study the Parables (Prophecy Book) and learn the wisdom of God directly from God; Himself, the Great I am, I am, I am."

From the KJV Bible:
Mat 13:34 All these things spake Jesus unto the multitude in parables; and without a parable spake he not unto them:
Mat 13:35 That it might be fulfilled which was spoken by the prophet, saying, I will open my mouth in parables; I will utter things which have been kept secret from the foundation of the world.

Psalm 78:2
Psa 78:2 I will open my mouth in a parable: I will utter dark sayings of old:

932. Occurrence given to Raymond Aguilera on 22 July 1996 at 4:30 PM.

I would like to share something that I was going to keep to myself. Monday, I was helping a brother work on his car. And in the process of adjusting his hand brake, I had to hold the brake cable with a pair of pliers, and the brother tried to tighten the set screw on the brake cable with a screwdriver. He was applying so much pressure to the set screw it broke, and he drove the FULL FORCE of the screwdriver into my right wrist on top of my vain. (My wrist was only about three inches away.) The first thing that came to my mind was BLOOD and hospital. I felt the full force, but I saw no blood or great pain. As I look at my wrist now, there isn't even a bruise, but why does the Lord let my wrist still hurt when I type. I pray to the Lord to heal my wrists and hands daily, but nothing happens. I guess, it will happen at HIS time. So pray for my faith again, and pray for my wrists and hands because He gave me two more prophecies and one is pretty long. I guess—I am asking you to pray and pray and pray for my hands and wrists. God bless you all.

933. Prophecy given to Raymond Aguilera on 23 July 1996 at 4:55 PM in English.

I am Jehovah: I am—I am—I am. I am Yahweh. I am Yahweh. I am Yahweh: I am—I am—I am. I am what you see; I am what you touch; I am what you want to be and many of you are trying to be—GOD. Many of you think highly of yourselves. We will see Who is the true God—Who is the Creator of the universe—Who is the Creator of what you see, of what you touch, of what you breathe. A bottle with a cork is standing before you. The cork will be removed very shortly; then we will see who is God. Remember the bottle; remember the cork; remember Who is Yahweh, Jehovah, the great I am—I am—I am. Remember the Train that leaves at seven o'clock. So be it. So be it. The world will see God before their eyes. So be it. So be it. (over)

934. Prophecy given to Raymond Aguilera on 23 July 1996 at 7:07 PM. in Spanish.

She-bear—the she-bear of the (Spanish word Mar = ocean or sea) ocean, the she-bear of the ocean. If you see under the water, you are going to see the she-bear of the ocean. If you want to seek the things of the devil, look under the ocean and you are going to find the she-bear. You believe you know it all, but you know nothing. I tell you to the point for the she-bear has begun to move. But you are blind and you are deaf and you don't see and you don't hear the things of God. I point you and I point you in the direction of God, with the Word of God, with the signs of God, but you take the Words and the signs and you turn them to say what you want. That's why you are deaf and blind and you are not pointed.

It hurts My Heart—all that don't see the manner of God with the eyes of God. I tell you exactly, that there are more Christians that are not going to believe Me, than are going to believe. What a shame—for they are seeking the god of man and they don't seek the God who made all, the stars, the world. He made all with LOVE, with the Love of Love. What a shame! I tell you what's going to happen and you don't believe Me. I point you in the Bible and you don't read it. I give you a picture and you don't see it. I give you the pieces of what's going to happen and what do you do? You seek the demons to show the signs of the devil. You seek the money so you can buy the things of the devil.

I know what's going to happen; I know everything is going to end, and I know My sheep. What a shame! What a shame! That there are so many that are so deaf, but the day is going to come I am going to have to correct you because you didn't believe Me in the manner of God. I know right now—this minute, that there are many that have read the Prophecies of this Book—that I have TOLD to read the Bible, and still haven't even opened the Book (Bible), and they are seeking and seeking God. How can you find God if you don't read the Word of God? How many times—how many ways do I have to tell you to read the Bible from the beginning to the end—and don't jump from here to there?

But I know that these Words, that I have given you this minute, have entered in one ear and have come out the other ear because you have nothing in the middle. You are DUMB! And what I have told you is VERY EASY; it is not hard to understand. Read the Bible from the beginning to the end. But I know again that this went in one ear and it has come out of the other, and it didn't stop in the middle because there is nothing in the middle. Everything that is in between your ears are the things of the world, and you don't understand the things of God. That's why you are blind; that's why you are deaf; that's why you don't find Me—for you seek the signs of the devil and you don't know the manner of God. You don't know how to pray. Oh My. Oh My. Oh My. What a shame!

That's why I tell you that there are many Christians that are not going to pass the things of God. For they don't know Me and I don't know them for they don't seek Me in the manner of God. They seek Me in the manner of the devil, and all the things of the devil are going to the pit. Do you remember about the wide road. There are many Christians on that road. I tell them and I tell them to change in the direction that they are going, and to turn onto the narrow road, but they don't even know what I am talking about—for they didn't read the Bible. I tell them to repent their sins and they don't hear Me—for they don't have any brains: they have the brains of the devil; they have the manner of the devil, and then they get frightened when God corrects things.

But I know My sheep, the ones who seek Me, and I am going to show them the Word of God Clearly and to the Point. It has arrived: the day of the road, the road that is not wide; for that road leads to My House where We are going to have a fiesta (party). This fiesta is on the other end of the road. If you read the Bible, it will show you the signs. It will give you the Map to the road that is not so wide, for the table is already; the food is already finished. All of My Angels are anxiously waiting, for We all are going to be a family. But I know that you don't know what I am saying—for you have never read the Bible.

You are seeking the stars; you are seeking the animals that come in the stars, that you believe are gods. You seek the male and female witches. You seek the things of the devil in the manner of the devil, for you are on the wide road. And you don't even know that there is a narrow road. You are having a lot of fun now for you are well planted in the world with the rest who are not Christians. But remember when you knock on the Door, I am not going to know you. For your door is on the road that is WIDE, but the devil is going to open that door. He is going to tell you enter, and say, "I know YOU VERY WELL—you are my friend." And he is going to hug you; and he is going to kiss you on the lips, for he is going to eat your tongue and ALL that you have inside with the hunger of the devil. That's the door that you are going to knock on.

Lets see, if what you have just read is clearer in that hole that you have in-between your ears. For right now I am looking in-between your ears, and I still don't see a thing. It is dark in there, like the things of the devil. What a shame! And you say you are a Christian. You don't seek your brothers in the street. You don't pray or repent what you do, and when someone tells you to repent, you get MAD! You know why you get mad? Because you are NOT Mine. You belong to the devil. What I tell you is clear and to the point. And I know you are going to get mad, but I don't care. You know why? For I have already made your house and for the devil. He is waiting for you. It has to be very large—for you have lots of male and female friends. You are going to have lots of fun with your eyes popped out, with your hair burned, with your skin on top of your bones—changing colors with the flame of the pit.

Oh what a shame! For you are throwing away the chance I am giving you. But the chance you have—you have to choose. How many times this year have you sought the sick ones, the friends, and the ones who are in the hospital that have no one, the old ones? How many times have you helped the ones who don't have food? How many times have you helped my prophet that has given you this Word, with prayers, with money, or just in thinking if what he is telling you is right or wrong? How many times have you read the Prophecies and you have done nothing? You have not changed in the manner you have walked. But there is going to come a day, when you won't be able to point your finger at Reymundo, or Me, or your male or female friend—because it is you, and you will have to point your finger at yourself.

It is very easy and simple—the things that I tell you. There are many other Prophets that I have sent to the world, but you don't hear them either because you have everything dark that is in-between your two ears. You want to seek God in the manner of the devil. Yes! The two of you are very close friends, hand and hand, and lip to lip. It has arrived the end of this Word. But don't tell Me that I didn't tell you—for the end of you has arrived in the manner of God, the One who made the world, the stars, with the Son and the Holy Spirit. I tell you the TRUTH, AND TO THE POINT, CLEARLY in the middle of your heart—for I know you don't have a head, for it is dark in-between your ears. I am, I am, I am. (over)

935. Occurrence given to Raymond Aguilera on 31 July 1996 at 11:18 PM

Special note:
This trip was a living parable for me, for the Lord revealed the meaning of some of the things that happened on this trip—the following week. You will have to read that material to understand this trip. God bless you all.

Camping trip with the Lord:
I was planning a trip to visit my sister in Eugene, Oregon, but really—I just wanted to get out of town because my hands were hurting me so much, and I was tired. Then on Monday morning, the Lord woke me up and said, "I want you to leave California and go north on Highway 5", and that was all. He didn't even elaborate. That was it! So, I called my sister and told her I might not see her on this trip because the Lord had given me other instructions.

So after having my car checked out, I found out that I need two tires and that all four motor mounts on the car were broken. This almost stopped me dead in my tracks for I was going to use the little money I had for the mortgage to pay for the trip, and I didn't even have half of that. So I began to really think this trip over, for after paying for the car repairs there wouldn't be much money left for gas and food, and I had no idea where I was going. But the Lord kept telling me not to worry; go north on Highway 5.

So I paid for the repairs and began to wonder where the rest of the money was going to come from. I emptied my checking account and I was up and ready for the road with two new tires and two broken motor mounts (I only had enough money to fix two motor mounts). I checked my PO Box to see if the Lord had mailed some last minute money. Guess what? The amount—I had spent on the repairs was waiting in the PO Box MINUTES before I left for Highway 5. With my car packed up, on

Wednesday, 31 July, I headed out. I didn't know where I was going, except I had to leave alone and get on Highway 5, go north and proceed out of the California.

I would like to say if any of you have ever done something like this, it sure tests you, doesn't it? Well, while driving north on highway 5, I was directed to go to Mt. Lassen. This was one of the places Ron and I didn't see on our Mt. Shasta volcano trip last year. I stopped at a small town before Mt. Lassen and I purchased some food. And for some unknown reason, I purchased a fly swatter. I camped at the first campsite inside the south entrance to Mt. Lassen National Park. After setting up my tent, I decided to take a walk. During this walk, I remembered what the Lord had said years ago, "Look at the sky." So during my walk, I looked toward the sky and wondered what the Lord had in mind.

Then the Lord said to me—or showed me, I don't know how to explain it, but a communication began with the Lord. He began to explain that when my wife and I split up years ago, I gave up getting remarried for my kids sake. And once I had raised my kids, that I had given up getting remarried again—but this time for Him (the Lord). I spent the next several hours that night watching the stars and praying to the Lord. I still didn't know exactly what I was suppose to be doing other than the instructions to leave the State of California.

It seemed that the Lord was showing me more volcanic areas or an extension of the Mt. Shasta trip. He didn't say it in words per se, but it was impressed on my spirit.

How many times can you see a volcano, or lava flows? I kept thinking to myself, "why am I here?"

I did sense the Lord testing me, to see if I would blindly go wherever He asked—at least I felt it in my spirit. I prayed some more to the Lord, and I went to bed wondering why the Lord had reminded me about my past marriage. The next morning I woke up...

It's strange as I speak into this tape recorder; I keep seeing this black creature and one of its large green eyes staring at me in the spirit. I don't know if it's good or bad—but I am being watched in the spirit…, but I am going to proceed and document the trip.

Well, I camped out and got up early that morning and repacked most of my camping equipment in my car for the next unknown direction. I sensed that I should read more Bible, so I went back to the campsite picnic table and started reading the Book of Matthew. As I was reading, I saw this young lady walking around the campgrounds. She walked by my campsite two or three times, and I glanced and she glanced, and that was about it. Since all of my camping gear was packed in the car, after I finished my reading, I headed for the parking lot hoping to get a Word from the Lord before I left.

Once I reached my car I checked the engine oil, and this young woman I had seen earlier came up to me and said, "Oh, you're not leaving are you?"

I said, "Yes."

I told her that I was on a camping trip hoping to give my hands a rest from the computer, and that I was leaving the State on a Christian retreat. We talked. And the next thing I find out was that she was a physical therapist and helped people with hands and shoulders types of problems. We started talking and she asked me if I wanted to hike with her on one of the trails. What crossed my mind was—maybe the Lord had sent her to help me with my hands, so I said, "Sure." I closed my car hood and followed her up this hiking trail. I didn't know where we were going, but I was curious. She started telling me about her profession; and I found out she lives only about 30 minutes from my house in El Sobrante (small world isn't it?)

This was another coincidence, which made me wonder what was going on with the Lord. On this 3-mile hike, she showed me how to exercise my hands before I type. She told me to soak them in cold water, and she mentioned that the problem might be the way I sit when I type, and that the problem might even be in my neck or elbows and not just my wrists. She explained about the surgery, and she told me to see a doctor that specializes in hands, and to have my hands checked out before they get worse. She proceeded to tell me all this stuff, and I am soaking all of it up and trying to remember everything. After our hike, we walked back to the campsite, and then went to the gift store and we sat around and talked about the park and our work. It was getting late and I had to leave. She went back to set up her campsite and to have a late lunch, and I drove off.

I saw some hot sulfur mud beds as I was driving through the park, so I stopped and hiked around them and later stopped and saw some snow, and things like that. By the time I finished walking around the park, it was late and I decided it was too late to leave that day, so I camped another 5 miles into the park. I got an early start the next day.

By this time the Lord had pretty much convinced me to go to the Lava Beds National Park near the California/Oregon border. So I headed in that direction and got to the park just in time for a tour of some lava tube caves. There were about 15 lava caves you could explore. I set up my tent quickly and joined the tour. We walked around the dark caves, and they showed us how the hot lava moved, and the extent of the volcano area. This area was basically desert with lava rocks all over the place.

Afterwards, I went back to my tent and found that the wind had blown my tent, leaving my stuff upside down, and had broken one of the tent bows from the dome tent. I reset my tent and strapped everything down, as I am trying to figure out what the Lord is trying to do—showing me these caves and stuff like that. That evening they had a lecture on bats and I went to that, but the Lord didn't say anything more.

The next morning, I headed out toward my sister's house in Oregon, wondering if the Lord would let me see her; but the Lord didn't say yes or no—the Lord didn't say anything. But as I headed out of the park, and the Lord pointed me in the direction of an area of the park where a famous battle took place—where Captain Jack, this Modoc Indian Chief, had a battle with the U.S. Army about a hundred years ago. Captain Jack and about 60 men with women and children left the Indian Reservation and went back to the lava beds, their homeland—when the army tried to make them return to the Indian Reservation.

This turned into a war, and 600 soldiers couldn't capture these 60 Indians. They held out for about six months.

I had read something about this battle many years ago, so I thought it would be good to tour this area. I was a little worried because I was alone in the middle of this rocky lava desert. When I got there, there was only one car in the parking lot, and no one to be seen. The guides had stated the park had many rattlesnakes everywhere, and to be careful where you walked or where you placed your hands. I could see how a person could fall into the lava rock and no one would know that you were there for a long time. So being by myself, I had to trust in the Lord.

But the Lord had said, "Go!"

So I went, and He showed me where the Indians lived and fought the U.S Army for about 6 months. It took a while to cover the battlefield area. I couldn't comprehend how the Modoc Indians could live in caves or what they would eat. I guess, they could eat rats and snakes. And they did say that the lake came to the edge of their lava rock fortress.

Prophecy:

As I was walking back toward the parking lot, the Lord said, "That's the way Christians are going to live. They are going to have to live in caves and hide themselves."

This was a very hard place, so I asked the Lord, "Why didn't you tell me in advance? Why do you wait until the last minute to tell me?" The Lord didn't respond.

Then the Lord gave me permission to go see my sister in Eugene, Oregon. So I decided to stop at Crater Lake National Park on the way, and stayed there for a few hours. Then I drove to Eugene and saw my sister, and spent two evenings there. During one of my quiet times during prayer, I heard an audible voice that didn't sound like the Lord. So I quickly jumped out of bed and ran into the kitchen and asked my sister to pray with me. After we prayed the blood of Jesus over the house, things seemed to quiet down. The rest of the day was pleasant, but I had a bad dream that evening, and my sister said she did also. Well, I rested up at my sister's house and left the next morning. I could tell she was worried for my safety, but I tried to act like it was nothing.

I headed out towards the northeastern part of Oregon, to Hell's Canyon National Recreational Park. I have always wanted to see it because it is supposed to be deeper than the Grand Canyon in Arizona; so I headed in that direction. Also, I felt the Lord leading me that way. After a long drive, I camped for the first time in Oregon. I don't know how many people go camping, but as you know—you can never find any firewood when you go camping, but to my surprise, I found this fairly good size campground mostly empty. I picked a campsite, and low and behold, there was a pile of firewood already there for a campfire. This is going to sound strange; this campground had outhouses (bathrooms without running water), and I used one when I got there, but I sensed I had to urinate in the campsite. I had to urinate 3 or 4 times at this campsite. I don't think the Lord was telling me too—but I just couldn't stop. This felt unusual and strange, but I camped, burned the firewood, read the Bible there, ate and got up well rested, and left the next morning.

Note: You will have to read the prophecies the Lord gave the following week to understand why I needed to urinate.

The next day I found myself at The Oregon Trail Museum. I toured the Museum for a few hours and left late that afternoon, and I kept heading northeast. A few hours later, the Lord sent me to John Day Fossil Beds National Monument off of Highway 26. I found myself driving on a dirt road in the back hills, which lead to the Painted Hills Unit. I took a quick left and went up this dirt county road, and I am thinking about my two broken motor mounts. I took it slow and steady and found this place where they have found many dinosaurs bones, and leaves frozen in rocks. I hiked a quarter of a mile to look at the painted hills that over looked this valley. These hills did look like they were actually painted.

This whole area was volcanic as far as the eye could see. At one time, this whole area was filled with nothing but volcanoes. Volcanic ash is what made the hills painted, and nothing was growing on them. I found this interesting to see, but in the back of my mind, I am wondering what I am doing here? What am I suppose to see? What am I suppose to learn? I walked through that whole area for 2 or 3 hours, but the place was pretty much deserted. There were very few people there, and I kept looking out for rattlesnakes because I was out in desert—like areas. As I was driving out, it dawned on me that the Lord was showing bits and pieces of the Book of Genesis. The things that I was being shown were from the beginning of the creation of the world. So now, I got excited and wondered what was next? And the Mt. Shasta trip was a possible end for this area.

So my next stop was this ghost town, called Whitney. This small ghost town only took a few minutes to drive through, and I was led to keep driving into the back hills on this dirt road that went 15 or 20 miles. All this time, I kept thinking about my two broken motor mounts, but I figured the Lord knew what He was doing.

As I drove on, I kept sensing I had to urinate on the ground there; and I am saying to myself, "Why am I doing this?"

This wasn't normal for me. I can't explain it; I really wish I could. I stopped at this place which had a running creek and I saw my second snake. It wasn't a rattlesnake, but a SNAKE. So I decided it was time to leave. So fifteen minutes later, I was on the road back to the highway, but guess what? I had to stop and urinate again. Now this urinating business is beginning to make me wonder if I am in my right mind. Then as I found the beginning of the paved road, I saw another snake crossing my path, so I stopped and let it cross—and I am thinking; "Why am I seeing all these snakes? So within 10 minutes, I am on the road again just like the Willie Nelson song; and headed toward Devil's Canyon National Recreation Area.

After several hours on the road, I decided to stop and get some ice cream; so I pulled over to the side of the road near a small store. I found out it wasn't a grocery store—it was a sculpture store. As some of you know, I used to be a sculptor. This young man was into selling his sculptures that he had made from plaster molds and things like that; and I was surprised because it looked like a regular country store. We started talking about my trip—and I told him how the Lord had instructed me to leave California. Then this young man told me he was a Christian; he gave me a short testimony, and I gave him a testimony about the Prophecy Book. He said that he wanted a copy of the prophecy book, and that he wanted to show it to his pastor.

This stopping here seemed too much of a coincidence to be a coincidence, and the pieces were coming together for me. So he gave me his address so I could mail him the short version of the Prophecy Book. He stated he was fairly new to the Lord. His face even looked strange, as if he needed to hear this. He was just in awe. And I was glowing and telling myself WOW another coincidence, like the physical therapist. I might say, I did feel really stupid—because as he was giving me directions to Hell's Canyon, I noticed he had a T-shirt that read "Fear God." I just never noticed it until I was climbing into my car to leave. So minutes later, I was on the road again.

Speaking about coincidences—when I reached my next campground four hours later, I found it mostly empty, so after going three times around the campground, I decided to stay at this one campsite. Guess why? There was a pile of firewood already for a campfire. I took this as a sign from God that I was suppose to stay here. Guess what? I sensed again I had to urinate three or four times in the campsite after I had gone to the outhouse. I was beginning to really sense the Lord in this. I stayed up most of the night reading the Book of Luke.

I got up early the next morning and hit the road again, and the next coincidence took place when I took the wrong turn, looking for this next ghost town near Hell's Canyon. I took a wrong left turn at the wrong city, and wound up 20 miles up another dirt road. I am creeping along at 5 miles per hour, and praying to the Lord, "Don't forget my broken motor mounts," every time I came across a big hole in the road. This next ghost town was nowhere to be found, and I was about to turn around and go back down the mountain, when a sign that read, Welcome to Wallowa-Whitman National Forest, together with another sign saying that there was a campground up the road.

This campground was way up in the mountains in the middle of nowhere, but there were two other campers there near this creek that looked like a river. So I drove around twice looking for the best campsite and decided on one when I found a fireplace with three large spilt fire logs, neatly stacked. All they needed was a bright red ribbon with a sign saying, "Camp here Ray!" This was really strange because when I drove around the other campers, they were trying to cut their firewood for the evening. All they had to do was to walk two campsites over and take the wood that was in the campsite I chose. This was unusual to me because in California camping, you never find any firewood—and if you do, the park rangers do not want you to burn it. They want you to buy it from them, or outside the park, for they don't want people cutting down trees for firewood.

I felt peace in this place, but guess what? I went to the outhouse and then I sensed I had to urinate in the campsite again. A very strange pattern has happened since I left my sister's house. I'm wondering—is it a coincidence again? Three campsites with three piles of firewood ready for the fire, and all that was needed for the last one was a match. I stood there looking at the two other filled campsites; and there were people hacking on wood with axes and saws, trying to get the wood ready for the evening.

I'm saying to myself again, "Why didn't they see and just come over and take this wood?"

It was sitting right here in a neat pile next to the fireplace. There was no reason why they couldn't have seen this firewood. Well—all I could say was, "I Praise you Jesus!" I then set up my campsite and ate. I started a fire and began to read the Bible, and really got in touch with the Lord. Finely I gave up trying to figure out these coincidences, and this peace came upon me. I can't explain how or what; but there was this peace all over this campsite; and I just felt like God Himself was there with me. I was camped right next to Eagle Creek and could hear the water moving peacefully.

I prayed, and I prayed, and I prayed that night, and I said to the Lord that when I got up that morning that I was going to build Him an Altar out of the stones from the creek. I don't even know why it came across my mind to build an Altar for Him. But that morning I woke up early and I went down to the creek bed and picked up a lot of stones, wrote a prayer and put it in a plastic soft drink bottle, and covered it up with a mound of rocks. This was my Altar to the Lord.

An hour later, one of the people from the corner campsite walked over and asked me if I had some jumper cables, for one of their cars had a dead battery. I told him I didn't have any, but I suggested maybe they could swap batteries with one of the other vehicles and get the dead one started with the exchanged battery, and once they had it started they could replace the original battery. About a half-hour went by and I saw nothing happening in the corner campsite.

So walked over to talk to them, and found out they didn't have any tools. So I told them, I had the tools if they wanted to try to exchange the batteries, but when they had taken off the first battery—an idea came to me. I remembered the fly swatter that I had purchased at the store. I told them to place the charged battery next to the dead one, and that I would make a battery connection using the wire from the fly swatter. So using my wire cutters, I cut the fly swatter in half and the two batteries were connected together, and the car started. It surprised everyone, including me. But I knew it was the Lord who told me to buy the fly swatter, for there wouldn't be any need for a fly swatter on a camping trip.

As the people from the campsite and I talked, I also found out that they went to Jubilee Christian Center in San Jose, and that they lived a little over than an hour away from my house in El Sobrante. What a coincidence! We started talking about the Lord and the prophecy book, and after we were finished the lady said, "It was no coincidence that you took the wrong road when you found this place. I don't believe in coincidences anymore." They asked me to send them the Prophecy Book when I got back to the Bay Area. This trip sure has a lot of coincidences doesn't it?

Well, after my camping friends left and headed for home, I tried to do some gold panning with a pot lid, and tried to keep my hands in the cold water most of that day. It was so peaceful there that I decided to stay an extra day. So I decided to look for some more firewood because I had burned most of what I had. Guess what? Right behind my car on the other side of the road there was one seasoned and precut fire log, just like the ones that were waiting for me next to the fireplace when I arrived. I had walked by there four or five times, and that wood was not there before.

So once I had decided to stay, I said to the Lord, "I did my job, and I am going to do what the therapist said; I am going to soak my hands in cold water, and the creek is the place to do it." So I walked in the middle of this creek, and sat down and soaked my most of my body—up to half of my body, for about 4 hours in the middle of this creek.

This Christian walk has me feeling like I am on a boat without any paddles, and the Lord is pulling the boat, for the use of my hands is getting less and less. So I prayed for healing, and I prayed for healing, and all I got—was cold and wet.

After the first few minutes in the water, I said to myself, "Maybe I should pan for more gold. Who knows, maybe the Lord will pay for this trip with real gold. I had seen a sign authorizing gold panning as I drove in. And I kept thinking—if the Lord can place some firewood at every campsite, He most certainly can place some gold in my cooking lid. So a lid from one of my cooking pots became my gold pan again, and I started panning for gold as I sat in the middle of the creek trying to keep my elbows, hands and wrists under the cold water as much as possible. After about 3 or 4 hours this man came by with his gold panning equipment, and we started talking about panning for gold.

He said, "Come follow me—I'll show you how to pan for gold."

In the back of my mind, I was thinking the Lord is going to pay for this trip with real GOLD!!! So I started using the same lid from one of my cooking pots; and this man was using his fancy equipment. All of sudden, I forgot all about God and started to have some fun and relax, and have a vacation, well—sort of…

This camper friend finally felt sorry for me and said, "You are not going to get anything with that. I have some extra pans. If you want to buy one for ten dollars, I'll sell you one."

I said, "Sure!"

When we came back to the creek where we first started panning for gold—I guess that I came back to reality in a hurry. For a big diamondback rattlesnake, about three feet long, was moving among the area where I got my rocks for the Altar, and where we had been gold panning earlier. The first thing that crossed my mind was, "Don't sleep in your tent tonight!!" Also, there were kids playing in the water—for new campers had come into the campgrounds. These children were playing only 50 yards or so from the rocks near the snake.

He said to me, "Well, what would like me to do here—for it could bite a kid or something?"

I said, "Do what you would like."

So he took his shovel, and went down and started battling this rattlesnake with his shovel. I might add, I was safely high on the bank watching all of this. He killed it, and was showing everybody.

This whole episode made me very uneasy. So I prayed to the Lord to see if I should sleep in my tent that night. I might say, I did not like His answer.

He said, "Sleep in the tent!"

So I took Ron's hunting knife and laid it next to me, in case another rattlesnake decided to crawl under my tent. I had a very hard time sleeping that night, and I did a lot of praying. I kept thinking how Paul in the Bible got bit by a deadly snake threw it into the fire, and he went about his business. So I decided—I better pray that the Lord doesn't test me this way, for I knew—I would freak out! I also remembered one of the prophecies where the Lord called me a wimp. He sure is a wise God, and knows us very well. My gold-mining, snake-killing friend wanted me to go gold panning the next day; and my whole attitude about campgrounds and gold panning changed drastically.

But then later, after he had killed the rattlesnake, when I had the official gold pan, we went back to the creek bed and he trained me how to get gold from the creek bed. But somehow my gold interest wasn't the same.

When it got dark, I went back to my camp, and he went back to his SAFE trailer; and I started reading the Bible nervously—with my lit lantern in the dark campground, and checking under my chair for snakes every ten minutes or so. I slept very uneasily. I decided not to stay a third day and not go panning for gold, but leave the next morning. I also decided not to go to Hell's Canyon. I felt this burden to get back home—fast! I felt very uneasy; because I didn't know if I was suppose to go to Hell's Canyon, or not. And I prayed, and I prayed.

Then the Lord said, "Go home."

So I headed out, and I knew I had to camp one more night on the road before I got home, for I was planning to go straight home without stopping any other place. I drove about 8 hours until I reached a campground south of Ben, Oregon, and I camped there. I was tired, and I sensed once again, I had to urinate in the campsite. I didn't understand this, but I was too tired to ponder over it. One other thing—there wasn't any firewood at this campsite, but I set up my tent anyway and laid down for the evening.

I said to myself, "This is the only place where there wasn't any firewood, and I don't know if I am suppose to be here."

But it was late and I was tired. I had not been there 2-3 hours when I became restless and I couldn't sleep. I did sleep for an hour or so, but when I had this nightmare about my daughter, a dream that didn't make any sense—it awoke me, and I could see a claw in the spirit. The next thing that happened, I felt like I was going to have a heart attack. My chest started to hurt, and the pain got worse and worse.

I was thinking to myself, "Boy if I die in this tent; no one is going to know that I am here. There was hardly anybody around. No one would ever think of checking in my tent."

Then the pain got worse and worse, and I kept praying, and praying, and I am trying to bind and rebuke what ever was causing it. I am just praying my guts out, and I really felt like I was going to die there. So I took my Bible and placed it over my chest; and I prayed, and I prayed, but the pain—it wouldn't go away.

I am praying to the Lord, "Did you send me here; and what's going on?"

I was really afraid for about a half-hour, then the pain in my chest went away. What was so strange: I felt Angels fighting in this battle all around my tent. I looked at my watch and it was twelve midnight, and I felt danger all around me.

So, I said to myself, "I am getting out of here."

In the middle of the night, I packed up my tent, trying not to wake up any of others in the campgrounds, and I hit the road at 12:45 AM. I drove all night until I reached my parents house. They live about an hour north of me. I had to stop there because I was falling asleep behind the wheel on the highway. I slept at my parents for a few hours; and then drove the rest of the way home.

A few hours later, my daughter borrowed the car for a job interview a few miles from my house. She came back and told me the car over-heated several blocks from the house. I lifted the car hood, and found out that the water pump went out. Another thing—during my driving on the trip something kept telling me NOT TO USE the air conditioner. Well, I praise the Lord, for He got me home safe. The car did break down, but it was only seven blocks from my house, and my daughter was able to drive the car into my driveway without any trouble. Praise the Lord again. So, I got back safe—still trying to figure out the trip. The Lord did tell me some personal stuff on the trip, things I cannot put in the book—because it's not something you could explain. He gave me a prophecy about the end times though, as I was driving home—which I did not record.

At the end of this prophecy, the Lord said, "Are you prepared?"

And I said to the Lord, "Am I prepared for what?"

And He never answered me; and I asked again, "Am I prepared for what? What's going to happen?"

And He never did answer me. It was the type of communication where the Lord speaks, so clearly—so plain, that you know He is speaking with AUTHORITY and POWER.

I would like to also state that my car's water pump went out when Ron and I returned from the Mt. Shasta trip last year. The car's water pump that went out this time was the new one that was installed then. It was only 10 months old.

Comments:

The impressions, that I can give you, are only spiritual impressions that were left on me.

The Lord was showing me basically, fossils, and prehistoric stuff. What was brought to my mind was Genesis (seven days that the Lord made the world). He was showing me the creation of the world, and at the same time, He was showing me the end of this particular area possibly by an explosion of Mt. Shasta which will destroy an area in 7 states. I guess—He is showing me the beginning and the end—The end of the dinosaurs, and maybe the end of a lot of people in this time frame. He didn't say it; but I sensed the pieces of the puzzle falling together.

I never did figure out why I had to urinate at all these campsites, but it was strange (that's all I can say, it was just strange,) but, I had to do it; and all the coincidences of the firewood, and things like that…During this whole trip, I didn't know what I was going to do, or where I was going to be—and I was afraid at times. The whole trip was amazing. And the car breaking down almost in my driveway. What a coincidence if it would have broken down in the middle of the mountains or desert, I would have been stuck. Well, with the Lord there—maybe not helpless.

The places that I was walking around were dangerous; and I was saying to myself as I walked there, "You got to be nuts being out here by yourself."

But, everything worked out fine, and I got home. The Mortgage Company called, and they are after me again; and I just have to sit and wait and have faith and trust, and let the Lord take care of it. This is a crazy Christian walk, and I will never understand why I do—what I do. I still remember the T-shirt this guy was wearing in the sculpture store, "FEAR GOD!" I guess—I'm afraid of God, and love Him too. Well I guess that's all...(over)

936. Vision given Raymond Aguilera 12 August 1996 at 10 PM.

During the closing prayer at the Portuguese Bible study, the Lord showed me Three Horses, One in the Front and Two Behind. Each Horse was pulling a large Wagon filled with over flowing Gold. It reminded me of one of those hay wagons carrying hay loosely but high. The Gold in the Three Wagons looked like sand, but in a mound.

Vision:

Then the next vision was of a branch from a tree. The branch had a long stem with no leaves except on the end. Then the Lord cut the branch off in the center of the stem, and the leaves fell to the ground. (over)

937. Prophecy given to Raymond Aguilera on the 13 August 1996 at 12:42 PM. in Spanish.

Shoe, shoe, put on your shoes for you have to run. You have to run and hide yourself. You believe that these Words are nothing, but put them on your calendar. For if you don't put on your shoes and run, you are going to have to run without shoes, and it's going to be harder.

Reymundo is going to tell you "**Things**" in the coming months. "Things" that you are not going to believe. I know, because even My Reymundo isn't going to believe them. But it is going to be the Truth and to the Point. The Things that I tell you are going to become clearer day by day. But—at first you are not going to understand what I am telling you, but what I tell you is the Truth.

My Son is going to come—and the Day that He is going to come is very close. And still most of the Body of My Son are asleep. They are playing CHURCH and they believe they are in My Hands, but I am going to frighten them, with the Word of My Son, with the Word of the Father, with the Word of the Holy Spirit. The day of playing church has to stop!

In all of the previous Prophecies, I have told you that you needed to read the Bible—YOU ALONE—with the Force of the Holy Spirit. But what do you do? You point your ears on the men who think they know what the Bible says. I don't want you to point your ears into what you believe—That these men believe. I want you to point your own nose into these pages YOURSELF, for the men who believe they know it all—are BLIND. They don't believe they are blind. But remember from the Bible, that I told you, "That the ones who believe that they know—are going to be blind and the ones who are blind are going to see; everything clearly. Remember that I DID tell you in the Bible. Remember that I DID tell you in this Prophecy.

Things are going to change rapidly. And if you haven't read the Bible from the first page to the last page, you are going to suffer more. And if you believe that these men who believe that they know the Word of God, are going to help you, you are going to suffer. It hurts My Heart, for it is very easy but you are LAZY! You want these men, from the church, to give you everything there in front of you. And all you have to do is hear it, and put it in your mind. That's not the manner of God.

When I left the Holy Spirit, I put "**It**" there in your chest so you could speak with Him, there—in your closet with your door closed. But what do you do? You don't pray in your closet. You don't read the Bible in your closet. You seek these men, who think that they know the Bible, and you run after them. Do you remember in the Bible when I told you that there are going to be the blind that run after the blind, and the two of them are going to fall into the pit. You believe that the Word is going to be hard when it is given to you. But I tell you, and I tell you, but you have a lot of laziness; and it is much easier to take the word of man and what he believes the Word of God says. But the fault is going to be yours, because I tell you this minute and I have told you in the Bible, and you don't do what I say to you. That's why you are going to suffer.

Here comes the man, who is going to run the world, with the hand of iron. And this hand is going to take you by the throat; and if it doesn't cut your head off, he is going to strangle you with the same hand—for he has the heart of the devil. Right now, these Words are only Words and you are going to want to play church with these Words, but everything is going to be different—the day that he has his hand of iron around your neck. Let's see if then you are going to want to play church. Oh, then—you are going to seek Me out.

But let's see if these men, who showed you the Bible in the manner of man, are going to help you. I tell you CLEARLY AND I TELL YOU TO THE POINT: get into your closet and READ THE BIBLE, and Pray until you cry with the Tears of God. It is much easier to cry in the closet—you alone with the Bible, than to cry with the hand of iron around your neck. But you have to choose the manner you want to cry. I am telling you Clearly and to the Point, Eye to eye: that is what's going to happen, if you do not hear Me.

I know where they are, My Prophecies—every letter, every page. I know who has read and who hasn't read the Word of God. I know the ones who are going to get mad; and what they want to do with My Reymundo. They are going to want to put their hands around his neck. But remember—if you believe you can beat (win) God, the one who made Heaven, the world,—give it a try, but I know who is going to win. I am putting Reymundo in a place he doesn't want to be, for there are many who are going to get mad at him. But I tell you the Truth: the Word is not his. The Word is Mine!

But everyone who has carried the Word of God in their heart and have walked in the manner of God, have suffered. But if you haven't read the Bible, you don't know this; and it is hard for My Reymundo to send the Words of God. There are many who believe he is just writing all night and seeking ways to write, but My little son doesn't have the brains. His fingers are wearing out, but you're not going stop him, for We still have work to do!

All the Christians believe that all of God is easy—that it is not going to cost you a thing. I am going to awaken you, for the Cross that you have to carry is going to become heavy; and you are going to have to carry it—running—because the man, with the hand of iron, is going to run after you. Remember—I protect what is Mine. Remember! I will tell you once more—I protect what is Mine! But if you don't read the Bible, HOW can you belong to Me—if you don't know your Father with your spirit, with the Word of God?

There are many who believe Me with their heart, and they don't have Bibles—with those, I am going to treat differently. And they are going to have a different chance than those who have Bibles, for I read the heart—the one you have in your spirit. But, if you have the Bible and if you read it—you know Me, for your spirit is going to burn with every Word that you read; for I am going to open your ears and your eyes with the Force of the Holy Spirit. But remember—if you don't know My Son, Jesus—you don't know Me and you cannot come with Me. If you have the key, put it in the lock—for the Lock is My Son. He opens all with the Force of God. The Lock and the key are of God. Remember, you cannot find Me if you don't know My Son, Jesus. But everything is in the Bible!

Here comes the time where many are going to leave the Body of My Son—for they are not strong. And the man, with the hand of iron, is going to frighten them; and he is going to change them. But, I tell you exactly that—if you have the faith and the heart of God, I will save you!

And it is not important what happens, for I can kill the spirit and the body. Remember those two things: the man can kill your body, but I can stop your spirit. I can place you in a pit with the Force of God. And I will tell you once more: These are only Words, but there is going to come a day, that it is going to happen. I want to frighten you with the Love of God, for I Love you with ALL that there is from Heaven. But you say to yourself: what kind of Love is this—that you frighten me? But the day that the man comes with the hand of iron, you are going to find out that your God Loved you. That's why I tell you before it happens—so you could make yourself strong. The Love of Love is your Father with the Son, Jesus, with the Force of the Holy Spirit. ALL that I tell you with My Prophet, Reymundo is the TRUTH!

How amusing, the things that are going to happen, for all of it is in the Bible and you did not read it. Remember the manner of God is not the manner of man. Sometimes, because you do not understand the Words, the manners: it isn't because it isn't God—it's because you are not Mine, you are of the devil—for all the things of the devil are blind. That's why? They fall into the pit—for they don't know where they are walking.

Hurry! Do what I have told you. Go into your closet and read your Bible with the Tears of God, with the Heart of God, with all that you have—and the Holy Spirit will give you the Force. He will give you the Love. He will show you My Son, Jesus; and in that way you will find Me, your Father—the One who made ALL with the Word, with the Holy Spirit. I am. I am. I am. (over)

938. Occurrence given to Raymond Aguilera on 13 August 1996 at 7:54 AM.

Since I got back from my camping trip, I am noticing something happening to me, even now—as I am speaking into this tape recorder. The Lord is changing something in my spirit. It's kind of scary. I don't understand, but I am beginning to see and understand some things that I never understood before. I believe it had to do with this last camping trip. Something is changing me and I don't really know what it is about? I woke up this morning and my prayer language began to sing, and sing and sing, to the Lord—and it would not stop. But it is more than just singing, He is giving me Bible Scripture verses. He gave me one on the trip; and He gave some other verses last night at the Portuguese Bible Study. He is impressing on my spirit, without saying any Words—that they are important; but only to study them if you have read the Bible from the beginning to the end, because they will have more of an impact.

The verses were:

Here the Key Word was **PSALMS**.

From KJV Bible:
Luke 24:44 And he said unto them, *These are the words which I spake unto you, while I was yet with you, that all things must be fulfilled, which were written in the law of Moses, and in the prophets, and in the psalms, concerning me.*

Later this week, I was reminded that the Lord's last Words, in Matt 27:46 and Mark 15:34, were from the PSALMS: Psalm 22:1
Psa 22:1 My God, my God, why have you forsaken me? Why are you so far from saving me, so far from the words of my groaning?

On my camping trip , I read all the Gospels; and now the Lord is placing it on my spirit to read the Book of Psalms. I don't know why, but I cannot seem to stop. Then He placed on me the Scriptures that He gave during the Bible Study last night.

The Key Word here was **TRUTH**.

From the KJV Bible:
John 8:31 Then said Jesus to those Jews which believed on him, *If ye continue in my word, then are ye my disciples indeed;*
John 8:32 *And ye shall know the truth, and the truth shall make you free.*
John 14:17 *Even the Spirit of truth; whom the world cannot receive, because it seeth him not, neither knoweth him: but ye know him; for he dwelleth with you, and shall be in you.*
John 15:26 *But when the Comforter is come, whom I will send unto you from the Father, even the Spirit of truth, which proceedeth from the Father, he shall testify of me:*
John 16:13 *Howbeit when he, the Spirit of truth, is come, he will guide you into all truth: for he shall not speak of himself; but whatsoever he shall hear, that shall he speak: and he will show you things to come.*
1 John 4:6 *We are of God: he that knoweth God heareth us; he that is not of God heareth not us. Hereby know we the spirit of truth, and the spirit of error.*

I don't have a clear picture yet of the camping trip, but on the way to the Bible Study the Lord revealed to me why He wanted me to urinate at the campsites.

Prophecy:
The Lord said, "You are My Witness, by urinating on the ground—that the West Coast of the United States is dirty and an abomination."

Several things came up in my mind.
I saw the smoke in the sky from a forest fire as I was driving home from Hells Canyon. Why—then when I got home, were there so many fires started by hundreds of lighting bolts in Fossil City and in the surrounding area, and now in California? I heard some of this on television today as I was typing this—that this is one of the worse fire seasons in

nine years, and they even called the United States Army to help. Is this another coincidence?

Why were these beautiful places that were non-populated so dirty?

Why reveal parts of it to me when I got back, and not when I was there?

What is going on in my spirit that is so…challenging?

My hands are really getting worse and worse. I called a doctor, a hand specialist, today and the doctor wants $150 just to look at my hands. I have no insurance or money. The money I did have, I spent for the trip. Why didn't the Lord fix my hands?

And this morning…and this is what is confusing to me in the flesh, the way the Lord operates—I sense He was watching me to see what I was going to do and I really don't know what to do…

Later that day, the Lord told me about the serpent (devil) in the Book of Genesis, and said, "I am going to crush the devil's head, like the camper that killed the rattlesnake (moving around the rocks) on your camping trip—did."

Note:

The Lord instructed me to add (moving around the rocks) just before I sent it out to the people on the e-mail list.

So, little by little, the Lord is showing me what some of the things that I saw and experienced meant—from the camping trip, but days later.

I received an e-mail from someone on the e-mail list asking me to reveal some of the personal things that the Lord had showed or said. I am at a lost at how to do this.

Prophecy:

So I asked the Lord for an answer, and this is what He said, "Can you explain how a rainbow smells? Can you explain how a rainbow feels when you touch it? Can you explain how to hear a rainbow? If you can explain these to your friends; then you can explain what happened on the camping trip, for the ways of God are not the ways of man. How many times do I have to say this? Not all things are for all, for some things are only for you and your spirit."

At this point in time, I sense myself walking toward the Light of Jesus Christ, but I stopped, and not being able to walk any farther toward this Light. I sensed the Lord watching to see if I would crawl toward the Light. It is hard to explain this because…it's like He is looking to see how far I will go to serve Him…or how far I would carry my cross? And the Scriptures that came to my mind as I spoke this into the tape recorder were:

KJV Bible:
Mat 10:39 He that findeth his life shall lose it: and he that loseth his life for my sake shall find it.

It's more than faith, maybe there is more to the Book of James than I really realized. Especially in this country…we have had it to easy. We get so rapped up into the blessing—trap. That we don't read about the suffering that the disciples, and those who were martyred that followed Christ, went through. We read it, but we don't digest it; we never place ourselves, really, in their place. It really doesn't have any impact or reality in our spirits.

Like I said, it's a little frightening. It feels like the Lord is going to make me a target—for the Satanists, for the people of the Body of Christ that have Him in a box, for the unbelievers. I feel very uncomfortable about being there, but I don't know if I can do anything about it—because I am seeking the Lord and He is moving me in that direction. Something is really happening, praise the Lord, but pray for me (big time!) (over)

939. Occurrence given to Raymond Aguilera on 8 August 1996 at 9 AM.

I found a copy of my first draft of the prayer, I placed in the soft drink bottle under a pile of rocks in the Altar I made for the Lord at

Wallowa-Whitman National Forest on the camping trip. I sense the Lord leading me to place it here. God bless you all.

Prayer:
8-8-96

I praise you Lord, (Jehovah, Jesus Christ, and the Holy Spirit) for showing me your righteousness and bringing me here to this place. Bless this place and protect it from all unrighteousness. I make you this altar because I love you always. Bless and protect everyone who is to hear your Word and follow your Light into salvation. I know that you are real. So help those who are not so sure for we cannot do it on our own. Heal the sick and broken hearted and give us peace and protection from the devil. We know you are coming soon to get your sheep and lambs.

I love you so much, yours always, your servant,
Reymundo Aguilera

940. Prophecy given to Raymond Aguilera on 13 August 1996.

The Lord said, "Watch Calais, France. Watch Calais, France." (over)

941. Vision given to Raymond Aguilera on 14 August 1996 at 2:02 PM.

I had a vision of Thousands of Clams and each was open—holding a pearl.

942. Prophecy given to Raymond Aguilera 18 August 1996 at 2:12 PM. in Spanish.

Yes—how is it going? How is it going My son? How is it going? I know—I know that people want to know what you know. But you know what? How can you show them, what you cannot! Yes, you cannot show them the things of Heaven with your nose—with what you touch. You cannot! Those things are yours and Mine. Yes Reymundo, write it down and tell them; that there are things for them and there are things for you—but I did not give you the manner to show them the things of you and I. You cannot! But you know the Things of God are different from the things of man, but people cannot comprehend what I have just told you.

Remember Who is the King of Kings—Who is your Father—Who is the Holy Spirit. We made ALL with the Word of God. There are many things that the mind of man could never understand; for they are not God—how can they understand the Things of God?

I am going to show you the world; I am going to show you Heaven; I am going to show you the Stars; I am going to show you the manner of God. Just write down what I tell you and those things will become more clear in the coming days. But close your ears to the people who want to push here and there—for what they want to do is push you into the pit with the devils. Do you remember what it says in the Bible about the ones who are blind that run after the ones who are blind? The both of them fall into the pit—with the devil laughing at them. You point your eyes, ears, nose, and your spirit—ALL, toward Heaven with the Father, with the Son, with the Holy Spirit and ALL will go well. Don't worry about these people, for the day is coming that I will correct them with the Angels, with My Word, with all that is Righteous. This is the Truth and to the Point!

How did you like it when We went camping, there—on the dirty ground? I am going to clean it up. Yes—remember the mountain of Shasta, for here comes the day. I know that there are still many people who don't believe what I am saying is the Truth. But Reymundo, don't worry about people; that's My Problem—not yours.

Remember that I told you that I was going to give you a wife. YES! Here comes the day, Reymundo. I know that you STILL don't believe Me—you have such a hard head! So many years I have been telling you that I was going to give her to you and you still don't believe Me, but that's the manner of man. But I am going to give her to you if you believe IT or NOT, for I have already given you My Word and what I say HAPPENS!

Hurry—I know that your hands hurt, but you have to finish the work of God. And I tell you with LOVE, for when I LOVE something—I LOVE it until the end of time, for all the days that there are days. My Love is My Love. Hurry—get up! You have work to do! (over)

943. Prophecy given to Raymond Aguilera on 19 August 1996 at 2:30 AM. in Spanish.

How are you My son, how are you? Yes, the blanket, the blanket of Shasta has arrived. Did you hear Me? The blanket is going to open over everything—like the Hand of God, for everything that is under the blanket is filthy. Did you hear Me with your ears, with all that you have? For everything that is in the United States, the devil is eating it and I am going to begin to clean-up all that is filthy.

Yes My son, all that is Clean, I am going to take to Heaven—the rest to the pit. Yes, it has arrived to the Point, the blanket, the Hand of God! Review (Mt. Shasta Data) yes, review with the Word of God and repent, and walk in the manner of God, for here comes the blanket to clean everything that is filthy. Yes, Yes, Yes. Don't say that I didn't tell you, for what comes out of My Lips is the Truth, and is Pointed. Yes! This is your Father, with the Son, with the Holy Spirit telling you the Wisdom from Heaven. Remember the Lips of God, for they do not lie—All is straight. (over)

944. Prophecy given to Raymond Aguilera on 19 August 1996 at 2:01 PM. in Spanish.

How is it going, how is it going My son, how is it going? The chorizo (Spanish word for sausage) is ready. Yes—the sausage is ready. How are you? How do you feel? How are your hands My son? Do they hurt you? I told you that you would be able to finish the Prophecy.

I know that you are suffering, but that is nothing compared to how the world is going to suffer. What you have is nothing, but the world is really going to suffer. It's going to cry with tears that are going to go up to Heaven, all the tears. But you know and I know that I tell them, and I tell them, and I tell them, and they do not want to hear Me. Then when they cry; they want Me to do something. But when I tell them to do something for Me, they laugh and they make jokes, for they do not need Me.

Look, Reymundo, I am going to heal your hands. I am not going to tell you when or how, but I am going to heal them. I told you to send her the letter. Why haven't you sent it? I am going to give you another chance. Send it today and everything will go well. Did you hear Me? I know that it hurts you to send it, but I know what is happening. I know the things of the heart.

Here comes the day that the bridge is going to fall. The bridge of San Francisco is going to fall with a Force that people are going to seek Me and you know what? I am not going to hear them, for there are men in San Francisco that want to get married with other men and there are women who want to get married with other women. How filthy is the mind of San Francisco. If you tell Me the name of San Francisco, it is revolting and nauseous to Me (Spanish: Me dar asco).

That's why I am not going to save anyone that has the mind of the devil—for it is nauseous to Me. They believe they are going to find wives and husbands in the manner of the devil, and all that they are going to find is the pit. I am not playing and I don't care if they get mad. How filthy are the spirits and minds of the City of San Francisco. They believe that they know a lot—We are going to find out how much they know when I bury them with the dirt, with My Hand. And I am going to hit them. If you have male and female friends in the regional area of San Francisco, in the city…oh, oh, oh, cry for them. Fall onto your knees and pray with tears, for I am going to hit them. For when I get Mad—something happens.

But what can I do? I have to clean up this world. I have to save My Sheep. I have to do what it says in the Bible, all the Words that were written for Me—are going to happen—because they are clear and to the point. And I don't want to speak anymore about San Francisco, for if I tell you more…I will get angry and I don't want to get angry right now.

I just wanted to speak to you to see how you are feeling. I know that you sense that I am changing you. I know that your mind is running like a computer. But have patience, for I am changing you little by little—for I don't want to burn you up. For when the Force of the Holy Spirit runs through the body, the body burns up—for the Holy Spirit is Clean and your flesh is filthy. Have patience, Reymundo, I am going to change you—for I have things to do and I want to use you. But I cannot use you like I want until I change you more. Did you hear Me?

Yes, I am going to send men and women to help you with the money that you need. But you know what? The things of the world are going to pass, and the things of the Spirit are going to grow until the point, until everything that I have made is going to STOP! But don't worry, for I have everything in My Hands.

I tell you exactly and to the point, it has arrived the day the bridge is going to fall in San Francisco. (over)

945. Prophecy given to Raymond Aguilera on 21 August 1996 at 2:00 PM.

The Lord led me to the Book of Romans Chapter 13, verse 1-7, and instructed me to read it.

From the KJV Bible:
Rom 13:1 Let every soul be subject unto the higher powers. For there is no power but of God: the powers that be are ordained of God.
Rom 13:2 Whosoever therefore resisteth the power, resisteth the ordinance of God: and they that resist shall receive to themselves damnation.

Rom 13:3 For rulers are not a terror to good works, but to the evil. Wilt thou then not be afraid of the power? do that which is good, and thou shalt have praise of the same:
Rom 13:4 For he is the minister of God to thee for good. But if thou do that which is evil, be afraid; for he beareth not the sword in vain: for he is the minister of God, a revenger to execute wrath upon him that doeth evil.
Rom 13:5 Wherefore ye must needs be subject, not only for wrath, but also for conscience sake.
Rom 13:6 For for this cause pay ye tribute also: for they are God's ministers, attending continually upon this very thing.
Rom 13:7 Render therefore to all their dues: tribute to whom tribute is due; custom to whom custom; fear to whom fear; honour to whom honour.

Then several hours later, the Lord said, "What will you do, when the antichrist is in power and instructs you to take the mark of the beast? What will you do? You better read the whole Bible from the first page until you have read the last page. Then listen only to the Holy Spirit. The Holy Spirit will tell you what to do, but if you hop around the Bible from here to there. You will be left confused."

So I will tell you again, "Read the Bible from the beginning to the end. Then you will understand the Word of God."

Don't let the devil and the antichrist use the Bible to get you. Read the WHOLE BIBLE from cover to cover, and listen only to the HOLY SPIRIT. (over)

946. Prophecy given to Raymond Aguilera on 21 August 1996 at 8:00 PM.

The Lord said, "Thomas, Thomas, doubting Thomas—cough it up. Cough it up, so says Jehovah." (over)

Vision:

Then the Lord showed me a beautiful woman, and She was putting on a golden necklace, and the Lord said, "She is the Body of Christ preparing for the Bridegroom. The time is here and now!" (over)

947. Prophecy and Vision given to Raymond Aguilera on 28 August 1996 at 8:00 PM.

The Lord showed me two pull switches with White Handles. Then the Lord pulled out the first one, and said, "This is a warning. Read the Book of Isaiah."

Then the Lord said, "Beware of the second switch. Read the Book of Daniel. Read the Book of Revelation."

Later the Lord said, "Why didn't you do it, didn't I tell you: Thomas, Thomas, doubting Thomas—cough it up. Cough it up." (over)

948. Vision given to Raymond Aguilera on 30 August 1996 at 6:48 PM.

The Lord showed me a windmill. Then I saw a large knife rise up and cut the windmill in two pieces.

Prophecy:

Then the Lord said, "The windmill represents Holland, and it will be split in two pieces" (over)

949. Vision given to Raymond Aguilera on 30 August 1996 at 6:48 PM.

I saw a colorful red and blue whirlwind moving in a counter clockwise direction. (over)

950. Vision given to Raymond Aguilera on 30 August 1996 at 6:48 PM.

I saw an image of the Eiffel Tower falling into a pit.

Prophecy:
Then the Lord said, "The Eiffel Tower is Paris."

951. Vision given to Raymond Aguilera on 30 August 1996 at 6:48 PM.

A vision of Three shooting Cannons covered with this White tarp.

952. Vision given to Raymond Aguilera on 30 August 1996 at 6:48 PM.

A vision of dark planet earth with a large black house rising into the heavens. Then this black river or black wave of oil brought down the black house back to the earth.

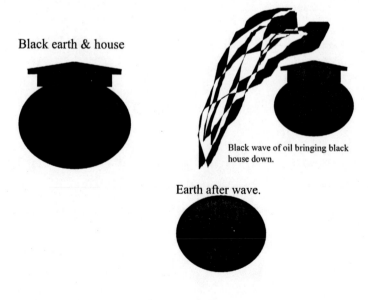

Black earth & house

Black wave of oil bringing black house down.

Earth after wave.

Prophecy:

Then the Lord said, "The black house is Babylon and the black river of oil is the antichrist. (over)

953. Vision given to Raymond Aguilera on 30 August 1996 at 6:48 PM.

I saw this moving White Lit Candle. Then somehow it was placed inside this burlap bag. Then this burlap bag was placed inside another burlap bag, but the White Candle burned its way out of the two bags. (over)

954. Prophecy given to Raymond Aguilera on 30 August 1996 at 6:48 PM.

The Lord said, "At this very moment the ax is at the Trunk of the Tree. (over)

955. Vision given to Raymond Aguilera on 30 August 1996 at 6:48 PM.

I saw an image of a seated Egyptian statue. Then it lost it's right hand and was left seated with only the left hand. (over)

956. Vision given to Raymond Aguilera on 31 August 1996 at 7:24 AM.

I saw an image of a large white house going over a great waterfall. The house had a black roof. (over)

957. Vision given to Raymond Aguilera on 31 August 1996 at 7:24 PM.

I had an image of the United States in the spirit, and I saw and heard air raid alarms going off all over the United States. (over)

958. Prophecy given to Raymond Aguilera on 1 September 1996 at 4:33 PM. in Spanish.

It is over there. The star of God is over there. It is over there, but you have to arm yourself. Arm yourself! Arm yourself with the Word of God, for the corral has arrived—the corral that the devil is going to use. I tell you the Truth and all to the Point—the corral of the devil is already here! The soldiers and all that is bad and filthy are going to arrive, but the star of God is going to arrive too. You believe it is the Star of Christ, but it is not—it is the star of the world—yes, the star of the world. Yes, it is the star of the devil! That's why, you have to read the Bible. That's why, you have to seek out your sons and daughters, and your brothers and sisters of Christ—for the devil has the corral READY!

He is going to seek you out, for he is angry. He is angry because the day has arrived—the day I am going to lock him up. Did you hear Me? Yes, look for the turned star. Yes, the turned star will tell you that it has arrived—the corral of the devil. That's all that I want to tell you.

Read the Bible from the first page through the last page. Yes! This is your Father with the Son, with the Holy Spirit, telling you the Wisdom from Heaven. Point your nose into the Bible. How many times do I have to tell you? You are going to suffer if you do not know the Bible—you are going to suffer! The world is going to fall with the force of the devil. And it is there in front of your nose, all that I have told you—but if you are not walking in the Spirit, you are not going to know the things of God. (over)

959. Vision given to Raymond Aguilera on 3 September 1996 at 4:30 PM.

During prayer time, the Lord led me to the Lord's Prayer. Then during the saying the of the Lord's prayer, I saw a dam filled with water—then the dam burst. The Lord led me to believe that it was going to happen in the southwestern part of the United States by showing me the word

"Colorado" and showing me a dam—and it looked like the Hoover Dam in Arizona.

Vision:
Then the Lord showed me a water faucet with only one drop coming out of it.

Occurrence:
Then—while I laid on the bed thinking about what I had seen, I felt this spirit sit on my chest. It startled me—as the weight got heavier and heavier. It was there for some time and I began to realize that this was for real. It wasn't painful, but I could feel the heavy weight. So in prayer I bound it and rebuked it, and it went away. (over)

960. Prophecy given to Raymond Aguilera on 3 September 1996 at 7:01 PM. in English.

Note:
While praying for a friend, the Lord gave me this prophecy, but I was left with the impression that it was a two-part prophecy—that it meant my friend and the Body of Christ.

Prophecy:
Yes, tell her that the Love of God is upon her—that day and night He watches her and protects her. Tell her that God Loves her, and when her time comes—she will see Jehovah, Jesus Christ, and the Holy Spirit. Tell her My son, for I know your love is the Love of Heaven. (over)

961. Prophecy given to Raymond Aguilera on 5 September 1996 at 6:19 PM. in Spanish.

Yes Reymundo, the pastor Alejandro (English word: pastor Alexander) has fallen. He has fallen. (over)

962. Prophecy given to Raymond Aguilera on 9 September 1996 at 8:12 PM. in Spanish.

The day has arrived—that your scalp is going to be very important. Yes, your scalp is going to be very important, for the man with the hand of iron is going to want your scalp. Yes, he is going to collect them. And your scalp is going to be money in the pockets of their soldiers. They are going to pay them—for every scalp they get with their knives. And they are going to place all of them on a wire so they will dry. The day of the scalp has arrived!

For speaking Words like this—you believe that these Words; are only Words from a crazy man that doesn't have any sense. But mark them on your calendar, for this is the Word of your God, the One who made the world, the stars, all that you see, all that you touch. These are not the Words of My Reymundo. The day of the hammer has arrived.

You believe that you can sit on your buttocks (Spanish word used: nalgas) and do nothing, and expect that everything will go well. I am going to awaken you and I am going to scare you with the hammer. You are still playing church. Still—you have not read the Bible. Still—you have not sought your brothers, and your brothers in the street. You believe that you have it easy, but everything is going to change very rapidly and you are not going to find the time to read the Bible.

I tell you the TRUTH! I know the manner of the man with the hand of iron. I know ALL that is going to happen—before it happens. But I am not going to help you if you don't read the Bible or seek out your brothers and sisters in the street for I gave you the Word and I told you what to do. All you did was sit on your buttocks—and you did nothing!

The day that the man with the hand of iron comes: you are going to seek Me OUT! And you are going to cry for yourself and your family—so I can help you, but I am not going to help you. I am going to let the man with the hand of iron take you by the hair, and let him cut your scalp—FOR YOU BELIEVED YOU KNEW SO MUCH, AND YOU

DID WHAT YOU WANTED. That's why I am going to leave you to do what you want—with the man with the hand of iron.

These WORDS are hard. These WORDS are EXACT! These WORDS are the manner of God, but how do you know the manner of God, if you don't read the Bible? You believe God is LOVE and LOVE, but do you remember that I correct things too—EXACT AND TO THE POINT? You have to read ALL of the Bible. You believe all will go well—if you only read the good things of the Bible. I AM GOING TO CHANGE YOU in one manner or another!!! If you have NO Fear of God; you don't know the manner of God.

I tell you and I tell you and I tell you, but you believe you know so much! That's why I am going to leave you alone with your friend, the devil—for you believe you know it ALL. Did you hear Me Clearly and to the Point? The devil will protect you—for you are not Mine. It has arrived, the day of the scalp. Yes, and to the POINT! Let's see if you get scared and begin to read the Bible in the manner of God, for it has arrived—the hand of the man of iron. (over)

963. Prophecy, Vision and Occurrence given to Raymond Aguilera on 11 September 1996 at 10:30 AM

Vision:
During prayer with a brother in Christ, the Lord showed me a small section of the planet earth. Then the Lord took an enormous Sword and He cut a line on the surface of the planet earth.

Prophecy:
Then He said, "Those on the left side of the Line are not Mine, and those on the right side of the Line are Mine."

Then the Lord said, "Make a choice! If you belong to Me, come over to My side."

Vision:
Then as I watched, I saw a White, almost transparent, mountain as it grew on the right side of the Line. By the way, this Sword made a Line that was large and wide like the Grand Canyon.

As we were praying, the Lord said to me, "If you Love Me, you will place your face to the floor." So my prayer partner and I laid on the floor with our hands outstretched, with our faces to the floor—and we prayed in tongues.

Then soon after the Lord said, "I am."

And the minute He said those Words; my body just went crazy, and I started to weep, weep and weep.

Then the Lord said, "I am," a second time.

Then my body went totally out of control. I just wept and wept, loudly.

Then a third time the Lord said, "I am."

My body, my tongue, my prayer language, was totally and completely out of control. The POWER of that Word was just so incredible. I cannot even describe it in words. Crying could not even describe the effect it had on you—but you knew Who was speaking.

And during the prayer, the Lord said, "I have read the branch."

Then my prayer language started up again. Then, just before it stopped, the Lord said the Words, "Esau, Esau, Esau. It is done! Ray do not worry about coyote. I will protect you." (over)

964. Occurrence given to Raymond Aguilera on 13 September 1996 at 1:02 PM.

Note: e-mail sent to people on the e-mail list.
Hello all,

If you receive this message within the next two hours, (it is 1:00 PM. PST) please pray to the Lord for me. Last night I watched a documentary on World War II and it frightened me so much that I could not sleep. All that was on my mind was the Antichrist and what was ahead in the coming years.

And then at 5 AM, I heard a crash in my computer room, and I found some of my backup diskettes of the Prophecy Book on the floor and my cat, or cats, had urinated on top of them. At first, I didn't think much about it—until I noticed that someone had turned on the fan on top of my computer. Then I realized that something else had turned it on for I have a difficult time turning it on myself—it has a tight slide switch, and there was no way the cats could of done this.

Now this morning, the Lord has instructed me to go back up to Mt. Diablo and anoint it with oil again. For those of you that have not read the beginning Testimony of the Prophecy Book, I was asked to anoint Mt. Diablo in 1990; and the next day, I received tongues, among other things that happened. I have no idea of what is going on in the spirit, but I could use some prayer cover—for I have to go back up Mt. Diablo as soon as I send this e-mail message out. All I can figure out is Satan struck my computer room, and now the Lord is sending me up Mt. Diablo to strike back with oil. I guess? I really do not know. God bless you all.

Yours in Christ,
Ray

965. Vision given to Raymond Aguilera on 18 September 1996 at 4:10 PM.

Vision:
A vision of a still wineglass full of some White liquid, but the liquid had turbulence. (over)

Vision:
A vision of a whirlwind looking at it's on reflection in a mirror. (over)

Vision:
I had a vision of a tall monument with four pools around it.

Prophecy:
Then the Lord said, "The four pools represent four invasions." The first will be fast and quick. The second will be to take control. The third one will be to organize. And the fourth one is to completely control the world with the power of Satan (the implementation of the power of devil.) (Non-understandable tongues)

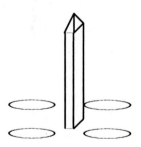

966. Visions given to Raymond Aguilera on 25 September 1996 at 7:37 AM.

Vision:
I see a large flat necklace made of gold.

Vision:

I saw a vision of a statue with one golden left eye.

Vision:

A vision of the Lord holding the earth in One Hand. (over)

967. Vision given to Raymond Aguilera on 19 September 1996 at 12:30 AM.

During prayer with two brothers this morning, the Lord showed me the land of Kuwait, and the devil, Satan, was there. During this prayer, the Lord showed me the warning, nuclear—radiation symbol. The Lord said that Satan was going to try to use something nuclear in that part of the world. I also was shown a very large fully-grown Tree fall from Heaven and plant Itself into the ground. (over)

968. Occurrence given to Raymond Aguilera on 25 September 1996 1:30 PM.

I would like to share something that happened last night or early this morning. I went to bed at 1:30 AM this morning and was praying, and I began to see visions and hear sounds. Somehow in the spirit, I was moving around this planet and seeing things as they were happening. It was very, very strange. I believe my spirit was in Africa at one point, and in different places around the United States. I could see and hear people in conversations, see animals in Africa, and events as they were happening around different parts of the world. I was actually there—I mean in the spirit, in hundreds of places during this occurrence. It was like speaking in tongues, but it was my spirit that went wherever the Lord wanted it to go.

969. Vision given to Raymond Aguilera on 25 September 1996 at 8 PM.

The Lord showed me a vision of the planet earth with an image of the Lord's finger nearby. And the planet earth opened up like the pac man, computer-game figure, and bit the Finger of God. Then God said, "I cannot be hurt."

Then the Lord gave me a prophecy:
We are in a time where the people who are wise and educated will be made blind and dumb. And the people who are lowly and humble—their eyes will be opened so they can see the true Word of God.

Then the Lord gave me the scriptures of the Book of John 18:5-6.
From KJV Bible:
John 18:5 They answered him, Jesus of Nazareth. Jesus saith unto them, I am he. And Judas also, which betrayed him, stood with them.
John 18:6 As soon then as he had said unto them, I am he, they went backward, and fell to the ground.

Then the Lord said, "If you cannot fall on your face before Me; you do not belong to Me. Remember—I am the King of Kings, and the Lord of Lords. I am Jesus Christ of Nazareth. (over)

970. Occurrence given to Raymond Aguilera on 26 September 1996 at 6 PM.

Note: Letter to the e-mail list.
I would like to thank those on the e-mail list who prayed for the Thursday night out reach meeting for the homeless. Brother Fritz called me Tuesday, and asked me to speak. He stated that he had seen the Prophecy Book on the web site and wanted me to speak at the out-reach

meeting. He said that he wanted to give the out-reach people a chance to hear the Word of God from a prophet, "For I know no church will invite you to speak," he said to me. His plan was to download the Prophecy Book, and to pass out a few of the prophecies during the meeting, before I spoke.

Well, those prayers from you brothers and sisters for the out-reach meeting might have saved brother Fritz' life. When I walked in the meeting hall, brother Rudy, Fritz's prayer partner and friend, informed me that brother Fritz had had a stroke yesterday. The message that was given to me by Rudy from brother Fritz was: "The devil attacked me while I was printing out the Prophecy Book. Please go on. I'll be OK."

I guess it was a mild stroke, but still a stroke. He didn't go to the hospital either, and is still at home. Parts of his face and body were affected though. Brother Rudy said it happened as the printer was printing, and he and brother Fritz were assembling the Prophecy Book. Rudy was upset; and a few of the homeless people cried and prayed for their stricken brother in the Lord. I would like to state: WE ARE AT "WAR!" The enemy will do whatever he can to stop the Word of God, but he has already LOST! What makes me feel so sad is that most people don't even know the reality of the dark forces, or what the term SPIRITUAL WARFARE really means. If it wasn't for the Lord, all of us would have been taken out along time ago. Well, the meeting went very well, and the message I was to give was given. Praise the Lord. Please keep brother Fritz in your daily prayers. It has been a very, very long week—God bless you all.

Yours in Christ,
ray

971. Occurrence given to Raymond Aguilera on 30 September 96 at 11:30 PM.

Note: e-mail sent to the people on the e-mail list.
Hello brothers and sisters,

A brother called me late last night. We had a prayer time and Communion over the telephone. During this prayer the Lord said to tell the brothers and sisters on the e-mail list to upload the Prophecies to wherever they can, and to give out hard copies to their church leaders, people on the streets, and finely to their relatives and friends. Tell them to be strong, brave, and bold—to pray daily and all will go well." (over)

God bless you all.
Yours in Christ,
ray

972. Prophecy given to Raymond Aguilera on 1 October 1996 at 8:40 AM in Spanish.

Defecated. Defecated. He defecated on the whole world with the word of the devil. Yes, Reymundo, he defecated on the whole world.

They do not want to repent. They want to seek out their god. That's why My Hand is going to hit the whole world. He (Jesus) is going to clean. For all that is filthy is going to the pit, and all that is clean is going to Heaven. This is My WORD, exact and to the point. It is simple. All that is filthy is going to the pit. All that is clean is going to Heaven.

You believe I am playing, but the day is coming that you are going to find out that what I have said, this very minute, on this hour, on this day, on this year, is the TRUTH and to the POINT!

Remember you have to repent. You have to eat the Communion. You have to look for your brothers and sisters in the street. You have to help the old people. You have to help the sick. You have to pray with tears to your God, telling Him that you want to repent. You have to help everyone of your family with money, with prayers, with what you can. And in that way you will clean yourself with all that is filthy in your body, in your life. And in that way you will find Me.

Here comes the day that My Son will come, and He is going to pick up the clean ones. Did you Hear Me? THE CLEAN ONES! There are many who are going to cry because they are not going to go. But I told them, and I told them, and I told them, and they did not hear Me, for they had things to do with the world, with the devil, with their friends, and they didn't have time for their God.

They were playing church. This is the TRUTH: playing church is not the manner of God. I tell you the TRUTH! I tell you Exact! I tell you to the Point! It is not important to Me if you are a pastor, or if you are the person who cleans the bathrooms of the church. If you are playing church; you do not know Me and I do not know you. You have to read the Bible from the first page until the last page…ALL OF IT—Completely! How many times do I have to tell you the manner of God? You have to pick up your Cross, and walk seeking Christ, your King of Kings. Hurry—get up. Do what I have told you, if you want to save yourself in the manner of God. With Love I tell you the TRUTH. (over)

973. Prophecy given to Raymond Aguilera 4 October 1996 at 8:53 AM.

The Lord gave me the scripture from the Book of Luke18:10—14, and said: The pride of the Pharisees which is the pride of the devil is upon many church members and church leaders, the self righteous, the pompous, the lover of Satan. (over)

From KJV Bible:
Luke 18:10 Two men went up into the temple to pray; the one a Pharisee, and the other a publican.

Luke 18:11 The Pharisee stood and prayed thus with himself, God, I thank thee, that I am not as other men are, extortioners, unjust, adulterers, or even as this publican.
Luke 18:12 I fast twice in the week, I give tithes of all that I possess.
Luke 18:13 And the publican, standing afar off, would not lift up so much as his eyes unto heaven, but smote upon his breast, saying, God be merciful to me a sinner.
Luke 18:14 I tell you, this man went down to his house justified rather than the other: for every one that exalteth himself shall be abased; and he that humbleth himself shall be exalted.

974. Prophecy given to Raymond Aguilera on 7 October 1996 at 8:45 PM.

During the Portuguese Bible study the Lord gave me 2 Timothy, Chapter 3, and told me to place it in the Prophecy Book.

From KJV Bible:
2 Tim 3:1 This know also, that in the last days perilous times shall come.
2 Tim 3:2 For men shall be lovers of their own selves, covetous, boasters, proud, blasphemers, disobedient to parents, unthankful, unholy,
2 Tim 3:3 Without natural affection, trucebreakers, false accusers, incontinent, fierce, despisers of those that are good,
2 Tim 3:4 Traitors, heady, highminded, lovers of pleasures more than lovers of God;
2 Tim 3:5 Having a form of godliness, but denying the power thereof: from such turn away.
2 Tim 3:6 For of this sort are they which creep into houses, and lead captive silly women laden with sins, led away with divers lusts,
2 Tim 3:7 Ever learning, and never able to come to the knowledge of the truth.
2 Tim 3:8 Now as Jannes and Jambres withstood Moses, so do these also resist the truth: men of corrupt minds, reprobate concerning the faith.

2 Tim 3:9 But they shall proceed no further: for their folly shall be manifest unto all men, as theirs also was.
2 Tim 3:10 But thou hast fully known my doctrine, manner of life, purpose, faith, longsuffering, charity, patience,
2 Tim 3:11 Persecutions, afflictions, which came unto me at Antioch, at Iconium, at Lystra; what persecutions I endured: but out of them all the Lord delivered me.
2 Tim 3:12 Yea, and all that will live godly in Christ Jesus shall suffer persecution.
2 Tim 3:13 But evil men and seducers shall wax worse and worse, deceiving, and being deceived.
2 Tim 3:14 But continue thou in the things which thou hast learned and hast been assured of, knowing of whom thou hast learned them;
2 Tim 3:15 And that from a child thou hast known the holy scriptures, which are able to make thee wise unto salvation through faith which is in Christ Jesus.
2 Tim 3:16 All scripture is given by inspiration of God, and is profitable for doctrine, for reproof, for correction, for instruction in righteousness:
2 Tim 3:17 That the man of God may be perfect, thoroughly furnished unto all good works.

975. Vision given to Raymond Aguilera on 9 October 1996 at 8:00 PM.

During praise and worship, the Lord gave me a vision of an automobile that the devil was ripping in two pieces. The automobile was being ripped lengthwise, like it was a piece of paper.

Vision:

Then I saw two circular saw blades, rotating side by side. They were as large as an automobile, and moving toward the side doors of the car. When they reached the automobile, they cut it in two pieces.

Vision:

Then there was an image of some kind of bomb.

Vision:

Then the Lord showed me the letters GM.

Vision:

Then the Lord showed me a shower head with water coming out. Then the water stopped.

Prophecy:

The Lord said, "People are going to be hurting for a shower."

Vision:

Then the Lord showed me a human tongue hanging out. Then the Lord showed me the inside of someone's throat. (over)

Vision:

Then the Lord gave me a vision of myself swing this sword on top of this hill. I did not know what I was swinging at, but I was in a spiritual war. These things kept coming at me and I kept swinging, and I kept swinging, and I kept swinging.

Prophecy:

Then the Lord said, "I know that you are tired, but stand on the Rock and keep swinging. I will be your strength. You are My warrior; just don't put down the sword." (over)

976. Prophecy given to Raymond Aguilera on 10 October 1996 at 12 AM.

Oh bear. There is the bear with his pointed teeth, seeking something to eat. Remember that I told you to read the Bible. Why didn't you pick it up? And why didn't you read it? I tell you about the bear with his pointed teeth, who is there in front of your face. And I tell you to read the Bible, and you just do the things you want to do, and you do not hear Me. Those teeth are going to eat you. For you didn't do what I have told you, in the manner of God.

How many times have I told you to pray? How many times have I told you to seek your brothers and sisters in the streets? How many times have I told you to repent your sins? How many times? How many times do I have to tell you? The bear is going to eat you, because you have your fingers in your ears. And the day is going to come, when you are going to cry, and you are going to seek Me. Then I will get your attention. But I am not going to hear you. I am going to do the same thing you are doing now. I am going to place My Fingers in My Ears.

You believe these Words are hard. You believe I am playing A GAME! This is your GOD, the One who is giving you these Words. I tell you with LOVE, and I will correct you with LOVE, but what I say will happen. And if you still don't pick up that Bible and seek the manner of God, you are going to find the manner of God when the bear cleans your face with his tongue, before he bites you. I know that I have gotten you attention now.

I tell you these things so you will open your eyes, and to awaken your spirit. If you could only see all the dark spirits around you—you would seek Me in a hurry and you wouldn't wait. But I can see them. But how can you see? You don't even believe in dark spirits, for you are walking with them hand and hand. They are your friends. And the ones who go to church, they believe they are so great! There they walk in church, hand and hand with the dark spirits. I know they also are not going to like this Word, for they believe they are so great. They do not believe they can do wrong. They like to look down at people with their eyes; like they are god. They're sitting in the middle of devils. Oh—Oh—Oh!

You have to read the Bible in the manner of God. You believe that the brothers and sisters (the disciples) that found Christ had parties and parties after I took Him up. Do you believe that they sought money? Do you believe they were playing a game? They killed them (the disciples) with the Lions; and they didn't eat because they were praying until tears came out of their eyes. And when they gathered, they prayed with the HEART of God. They didn't seek anything—ONLY the Father, the Son and the Holy Spirit. They weren't perfect, but they knew Me.

Well, I feel very sorry for you people. The ones who know Me seek God in the manner of man; and the ones who do not know Me—they do not care about the things of God. I know for I read their hearts. You have to stop playing church. And pray, and repent. Eat the Communion. Did you hear Me? This is your Father with the Son, with the Holy Spirit telling you the manner of God. (over)

977. Vision given to Raymond Aguilera on 10 October 1996 at 1:46 PM.

I saw a vision of a white house on the hill, and the house disappeared from the hill. (over)

978. Prophecy and Vision given to Raymond Aguilera on 17 October 1996 at 10 PM.

During prayer, the Lord showed me a large round light coming from the ground with people all around it, shoulder to shoulder, with their hands up praying and praising, as the light got brighter and brighter. As I kept looking at this circle of people, I noticed that there was something rising from the center of this 10-foot diameter light. As I waited patiently to see what it was; the people prayed more and more. Then this silver and gold Christmas tree began to rise slowly from the center of this white light. I could see that the Christmas tree had a silver and gold cross on top of it. Then this cross changed into a thin and dark cross.

Then the Lord gave me this Word:

Since you pray, worship, and praise this Christmas tree; so shall you die; by this same tree. (over)

979. Vision given to Raymond Aguilera on 17 October 1996 at 7:15 PM.

During praise and worship at the homeless outreach, the Lord gave me a vision of a rifle with someone pulling the trigger. Then a vision of a hand gun with someone pointing it. Then the Lord impressed on my spirit that someone well known was going to be shot.

Vision:

Then the vision quickly changed, and I saw a large sail boat or yacht on the ocean.

Vision:

Then the next vision, the Lord showed me four demons holding a body over their heads. This body was wrapped in white and was placed on some kind of high altar. (over)

980. Occurrence given to Raymond Aguilera on 21 October 1996 at 11:05 PM.

Hello Brothers and Sisters,

I could use some more prayer cover. I have no idea what is going on in the spirit world right now, but I was under a great attack from the enemy tonight. The attack was getting stronger and stronger as the clock ticked. It is 10 PM (PST) right now. It got so bad, I had to excuse myself, and leave the Portuguese Bible study. I sensed, I was going to be taken out by the devil. I prayed all the way home, but once I entered my house the spiritual attack left instantly. I can still sense the evil forces outside my house, but for some reason I am safe inside my house. This was a very strange occurrence. This ministry must be doing something right for such STRONG FORCE to hit. I can sense the battle outside with spiritual bombs landing all over the place, but in my house I sense safety. Very, very strange!

Praise you Lord, and THANK YOU! For I know, I would of fallen tonight if you had not come to my rescue, but please do not cut it so close next time. Thank you again, and don't forget the finances here, I hate to keep asking you, but the devil can still take this ministry out; if you do not supply very soon. And another thing, could you please take some of this pressure off me. For I am at the END of my physical and spiritual strength again. My body is telling me IT IS DYING from the pressure. And that Sword is so heavy! I told you; you should of picked a stronger person. Do you remember, when I said wasn't a strong person? I feel like I am down, but not out. And why do you push me so hard? Did you forget I am only your secretary? I do LOVE YOU, and forgive me for my negative thoughts; for I am—so tired. Amen.

981. Occurrence given to Raymond Aguilera on 22 October 1996 at 11:44 PM.

Hello again brothers and sisters,

I would like to take the time to thank those of you who wrote and are concerned for me. Since yesterday, I have been trying to figure out what "REALLY" is happening around me lately, with smoke alarms going off, my dog barking at locked doors and empty hallways. And here, it is exactly 24 hours later, and I am beginning to understand a little more, but I don't understand the whole picture yet.

But let me try to explain, what I do not know (sounds strange doesn't it):

Do you remember the thorn in Paul side (2Cor 12:7-9, A MESSENGER OF SATAN.), and from the book of Rev 9:3-11. Read and think about Rev 9:11 (They had as king over them THE ANGEL OF THE ABYSS, whose name in Hebrew is Abaddon, and in Greek, Apollyon.).

The first verse happened to Paul almost two thousand years ago, and the second is suppose to happen during the end times (to only those people who did not have the seal of God on their foreheads). I have been depressed before, but these attacks are supernatural in nature. All of us have been attacked in one way or another in times past. I do not know for sure, but the Lord seems to be showing me that these kinds of occurrences not only happened to Paul, but as we approach closer to the end, that these occurrences are going to be more common. Please pray about this, don't just take my word for it. These are not the everyday things that some of you are talking about. These things are somehow amplified in the spirit and in the flesh. Paul's words keep ringing in my spirit as I type this. (His pain!)

You actually feel like you are in a real war with these dark spirits. Where at times you have to run and jump into your spiritual fox hole or lose your head. This is for real, and I wish I had the words to explain what I am trying to say. I guess, we humans believe we thought up all these battle plans, and wars without Satan's help. Or maybe Satan, the teacher of war with his fellow demons, will show some people in person. Boy, I do not like—what I am writing tonight. God bless you all.

Yours in Christ, your little brother,
ray

From the KJV Bible:
2 Cor 12:7 And lest I should be exalted above measure through the abundance of the revelations, there was given to me a thorn in the flesh, the messenger of Satan to buffet me, lest I should be exalted above measure.
2 Cor 12:8 For this thing I besought the Lord thrice, that it might depart from me.

2 Cor 12:9 And he said unto me, My grace is sufficient for thee: for my strength is made perfect in weakness. Most gladly therefore will I rather glory in my infirmities, that the power of Christ may rest upon me.

Rev 9:3 And there came out of the smoke locusts upon the earth: and unto them was given power, as the scorpions of the earth have power.
Rev 9:4 And it was commanded them that they should not hurt the grass of the earth, neither any green thing, neither any tree; but only those men which have not the seal of God in their foreheads.
Rev 9:5 And to them it was given that they should not kill them, but that they should be tormented five months: and their torment was as the torment of a scorpion, when he striketh a man.
Rev 9:6 And in those days shall men seek death, and shall not find it; and shall desire to die, and death shall flee from them.
Rev 9:7 And the shapes of the locusts were like unto horses prepared unto battle; and on their heads were as it were crowns like gold, and their faces were as the faces of men.
Rev 9:8 And they had hair as the hair of women, and their teeth were as the teeth of lions.
Rev 9:9 And they had breastplates, as it were breastplates of iron; and the sound of their wings was as the sound of chariots of many horses running to battle.
Rev 9:10 And they had tails like unto scorpions, and there were stings in their tails: and their power was to hurt men five months.
Rev 9:11 And they had a king over them, which is the angel of the bottomless pit, whose name in the Hebrew tongue is Abaddon, but in the Greek tongue hath his name Apollyon.

982. Prophecy given to Raymond Aguilera 23 October 1996 at 9 AM.

Hello all again, this seems to be a daily thing.

Last night and early this morning the Lord gave me these scriptures. Then the Lord said this morning, "This is what My Angels did in the past. Do you believe the dark angels have no power. You better read the whole Bible, pray, repent, and take communion daily. So be it! So be it. So be it. (over)

I guess it is a post script (PS) to my last e-mail.

Your little brother,
ray

From the KJV Bible:
2 Sam 24:15 So the LORD sent a pestilence upon Israel from the morning even to the time appointed: and there died of the people from Dan even to Beersheba seventy thousand men.
2 Sam 24:16 And when the angel stretched out his hand upon Jerusalem to destroy it, the LORD repented him of the evil, and said to the angel that destroyed the people, It is enough: stay now thine hand. And the angel of the LORD was by the threshingplace of Araunah the Jebusite.
2 Sam 24:17 And David spake unto the LORD when he saw the angel that smote the people, and said, Lo, I have sinned, and I have done wickedly: but these sheep, what have they done? let thine hand, I pray thee, be against me, and against my father's house.

2 Ki 19:34 For I will defend this city, to save it, for mine own sake, and for my servant David's sake.
2 Ki 19:35 And it came to pass that night, that the angel of the LORD went out, and smote in the camp of the Assyrians an hundred fourscore and five thousand: and when they arose early in the morning, behold, they were all dead corpses.

983. Prophecy given to Raymond Aguilera on 24 October 1996 at 3:34 PM. in Spanish.

Costa Rica, Costa Rica, the things of Costa Rica are going to become hotter in the months and years that are coming. Point your eyes on Costa Rica, for the seed is already planted in the body of the devil. Did you hear Me? Point your eyes on Costa Rica, for the flame of the devil in going to hit there—for he is going to plant the seed in the manner of the devil.

These are the Words of your God, the One who made the world, the stars, all that you see, all that you touch. Tell the people of Costa Rica to arm themselves with the Word of God, for here comes the flame of the devil to the point. With Tears, I tell you the Truth. It has arrived,—the dead body of the people of Costa Rica. It has arrived. It has arrived. (over)

984. Occurrence and Prophecy given to Raymond Aguilera on 29 October 1996 at 9:06 AM. in Spanish.

Occurrence:

While laying in bed this morning, after prayer, I was looking at the my wrist braces firmly secured to my two wrists and wondered—when will the Lord heal my wrists? During this, I remembered how the Lord had moved a door knob hole that I had drilled wrong in a door, a few years ago—to show me His Power. I looked at my wrists again and said to myself, "If the Lord can move a wrongly drilled hole on a door, He surely can heal my hands. No sooner had I finished thinking this, when the Lord gave me this next prophecy. (within seconds.)

Prophecy:

He wiped. He wiped the past. George. George is the man who wiped the past. Yes, Reymundo—George. He likes the bullet. George has a very bad spirit in South America. You have to place your eyes and ears on the man named George, for he is one very bad man. Yes, watch him. Watch him, for here comes George with the finger of the devil. He is going to seek out all that is of God—with the pistol—with the knife—with the teeth of the devil. Here comes George to South America. Yes, it has arrived—the day of George in South America. (over)

Occurrence:

Right after this prophecy was given—maybe 30 seconds later, I got out of bed and walked into the bathroom. I had not walked 12 feet from my bed when I noticed my right wrist brace was GONE! I might add—this really surprised me—for 30 seconds ago, it was firmly secured to my right wrist. I quickly returned to my bed and tore my by bed apart, and it was nowhere to be found. Still perplexed, I went back to the bathroom then returned to my totally messed up bed, and then found my right wrist brace under my pillow. How it got there, I surely do not know! (over)

985. Vision given to Raymond Aguilera on 29 October 1996.

The Lord showed me the omega symbol, and showed me two men sitting side by side at this dinner table, with their neck ties hanging and laying over the table top. Then I saw a large cleverer knife come down and cut both ends of the two neck ties, at the same time on top of the table.

Prophecy:

Then the Lord said, "Because of your pride I am going to cut your tongues the same way." (over)

Vision:

Then I saw one of those objects with little cups that spins around to measure the wind velocity, but this instrument was going backwards. The wind was blowing toward it from behind and it was moving backwards in the wrong direction. (over)

986. Vision given to Raymond Aguilera on 29 November 1996 at 1:30 AM.

Vision:
A vision of a LARGE engagement ring setting upright with a lit candle placed on the inside (on the gold metal part) heating up the ring stone which was directly above the flame. (The lit candle was inside the ring band.)

987. Vision and Prophecy given to Raymond Aguilera on 4 December 1996.

During praise and worship the Lord showed me a White Candle in the middle of this circle of people bowing toward this White Candle.

Vision:
Then I saw a black bird that looked like a crow and it was hugging a bird from the tropics; the kind you would find in South America or Africa. (over)

Vision:
Then I had an image of a frog sitting on a rock. Then the frog jumped into the water and swan away, until it could not be seen. Then quickly another frog jumped into the water right behind the first frog.

Prophecy:
Then the Lord said, "Even frogs have the brains to go into hiding when they are in danger. (over)

988. Vision given to Raymond Aguilera on 1 December 1996 at 8:00 PM.

I saw some sort of radar disk with a strong beam of light hitting it in the center.

Vision:

I saw this plant or weed. I think it is called a dandelion. At the end of its' stem it has a round ball of white fluff or fuzz. As a child, I used to see children blowing this fuzz into the air. Well, I saw someone blow into this dandelion fuzz, and it went into the air. And this fuzz changed into little stars, and these stars flowed into the air as far as the eye could see. Then underneath of them, I saw the fins of sharks moving under them somehow. Then, I saw these little stars surround this lit torch with a bright flame. As I watched these little stars surround this torch, I saw this enormous Light like a sun appeared in the background. Then the image stopped. (over)

989. Vision given to Raymond Aguilera on 2 December 1996 at 2:30 AM.

The Lord showed me a dark tin can stained black and smoky full of soot, and it changed into a hour glass. And then I saw the Lord holding it on the palm of His Hand.

990. Vision given to Raymond Aguilera on 5 December 1996 at 2:37 PM.

I keep seeing a vision of a stretched piece of fabric or thin rubber blanket fasten to a pair of long poles in an upright position, with this round black ball that looked like a bowling ball repeatedly hitting this blanket material. And this blanket material repeatedly sends the ball back where it came from. (over)

991. Vision given to Raymond Aguilera on 7 December 1996 at 10:03 PM.

A vision of a sand hour glass and the sand was almost all gone. (over)

992. Vision given to Raymond Aguilera on 7 December 1996 at 11:30 PM.

During prayer the Lord showed me the planet earth from far out in outer space. As I watched, I saw all kinds of large worms coming out from the interior of the planet.

Vision:

I also saw a body of land that looked like Japan, and near the water I saw circular waves motions. The kind that resemble a pebble hitting a still pond and creating circular waves. It also reminded me of the circular light that goes around a radar screen, but it was coming from the water. I believe it was a hurricane.

993. Vision given to Raymond Aguilera on 8 December 1996 at 11:00 AM.

During church service the Lord showed me a skinny person with only skin and bones for arms and hands and reaching into the sky. And these hands were tied together at the wrists by some kind of rope, and the hands were holding a Communion Host. And as the Communion Host was brought down to be eaten, it changed into a White Lit Candle. The Lord left me with the impression the skin and bone person was the Body of Christ, and that it was staving and in bondage. (over)

994. Prophecy given to Raymond Aguilera on 9 December 1996 at 8:45 PM.

At the Monday night Bible study, during the praise and worship, the Lord stated that something dramatic, or something big was happening with the Prophecy Book somewhere in the world at this point in time. But He didn't say what. Then, when the next song began the Lord said, "I am telling you the truth." (over)

Comments:

After the Bible study, I found my right rear tire on my car flat. The next morning my daughter took the car tire down to get it fixed, and the tire repairman said the tire had been cut on the side with a knife. (over)

995. Vision given to Raymond Aguilera on 12 December 1996 at 7:15 PM.

During praise and worship the Lord showed me a room with people praising and worshipping the Lord. While they were praising the front door was kicked in; and policemen wearing head and riot gear surround the worshippers. Then the vision stopped. (over)

Vision:

Then I had a vision of an ugly creature holding a fish in it's mouth trying to chew it. (over)

Vision:

A vision of two kitchen faucets made into a cross with water coming out.

Vision:

During prayer time a brother anointed me and prayed for me. During this prayer time the Lord gave me a vision of myself over a deep gorge with a waterfall below. I could also see this narrow plank that crossed over both sides of the gorge. What startled me the most was, I was walking across this plank. (over)

996. Vision given to Raymond Aguilera on 16 December 1996 at 2 AM.

A vision of the moon in the shape of a banana, and it was red. (over)

997. Occurrence, Vision, Prophecy given to Raymond Aguilera on 18 December 1996 at 3:17 PM. in English.

Occurrence 10:30 AM:

I was driving in my car thinking of the money problems this ministry had; when a Strong Presence of the Lord filled me with peace. I felt like NOTHING in the world was going to stop His Words that had come through me—if the ministry had money or not. The Presence of the Lord just engulfed me with the reality that the end of the world was here; and nothing was going to stop it.

Vision 3:17 PM:

I saw a White Light that reminded me of the full moon, but it somehow looked or I sensed it was not the moon, but the Lord. Then this White Light appeared again with a Crown of Thorns around it. It was a breath taking experience. So I decided to record it. Then a few minutes later the Lord spoke.

Prophecy:

I am, I am, I am. I am what you see; I am what you touch; I am what you want to be. These things belong to God. These are God. Through the Prophecies you can see, and you can understand the ways and the manners of Jehovah. But there is only ONE Jehovah. You can wish all you want; you can play all the games you want, but there is only ONE Jehovah, ONE Jesus Christ, ONE Holy Spirit: ONE GOD. The ways of man are evil. The ways of man are filthy. I don't care if you call yourself a preacher. I don't care if you call yourself the President of the United States. The things of man are evil, are wicked, and are dirty.

If you want to become close to God, Jehovah, Jesus Christ, and the Holy Spirit; you have to read the Bible. You have to have Communion. You have to love one another, with the Love of Christ, the Love of the Holy Spirit, the Love of Jehovah.

The things on this planet are going to become very hard in the coming years, in ways you never thought were possible. But since you haven't gotten into the Bible, and read it, and studied it, and gotten to know your Father Jehovah, Jesus Christ, and the Holy Spirit. You are going to be surprised. For the power of the devil is going to fall upon you rapidly—fast—to the point. That you are going to wish, that you were never born. You are going to wish that you never wanted to be God. For that's the reason the devil fell, because he wanted to be God.

But the things of God belong to God, Jehovah, Jesus Christ, and the Holy Spirit. You will see, and you will hear, and you will hide. For the Power of God is going to fall upon the planet earth with the vengeance of God. But you are going to say to yourself: The vengeance of God—but God is Love, Love, Love, Love. Look at the other side of the coin, read the old Testament. For God will rebuke what is dirty, what is evil, what is not of Him. Did you understand what I just said? If you didn't—you better get into the Bible. For the devil is ready, the antichrist is ready, the power of evil is ready. For the cleansing of this planet has come to a point, where I will release the forces to cleanse what is dirty. To rebuke what needs to be rebuked. To save what needs to be saved.

I know the final outcome. I know the things of God, because I am God. Look and see at the things around you. Look and see how God has corrected things in the past, and look and see how God will correct things in the future. Read the Book of Revelations. Read the Words of God. Through Power, through the Directness of the Holy Spirit; you will see and understand that what I am saying is true.

The value system of this world has fallen to a point—that there isn't any value system. People are going, and doing what they want, when they want. They don't seek Me. They seek the idols, their possessions, their wants; they even seek their fears. But all of this is coming to an end. For I have placed a date and a time, and you have already have entered the first stages of the beginning of the end. Do you remember that date: December 2, 1990. Remember that I told you to tattoo it on your eye lids. That was the beginning, of the beginning, of the beginning of the end. Keep doing your wicked evil things, your sinful things, and We will be speaking soon with the Power of Jehovah falling upon this little planet of yours. For the things of the devil are the things of the pit.

Remember, if you want Me to save you—pray and pray, have Communion, repent, seek your brothers and your sisters with the Love and the Power of the Holy Spirit. That's all I am going to tell you now on this date on this time. For My Hand will fall upon this planet without mercy, without pity. For the things of the devil are coming to an end. So saith Jehovah. So saith the Holy Spirit. So saith Jesus Christ of Nazareth. (over)

998. Vision given to Raymond Aguilera on 19 December 1996 at 11:10 PM.

During prayer the Lord showed a cross section of a volcano with its moving lava. I could see this happening at night with all kinds of colors coming from the flames as the firewall moved across the landscape. The colors were what amazed me the most, and seeing it at night. (over)

999. Prophecy given to Raymond Aguilera 22 December 1996 at 5:28 PM.

The White House! Yes, the White House is going to fall with the peace. The White House is going to fall. For it is walking with it's chest sticking out with the flame of the devil. The peace is going to end. It radiates the eyes of the devil, with the heart of the devil, for the heart of the White House is the heart of the devil.

Watch yourself! See and hear the things of God. Read the Bible to the point. For it has arrived, the day, the hour, the minute, that the White House is going to fall to the point. They can say lies to all the people, but they cannot lie to God. For God knows the hearts of the all people, who run the White House, and all of it is filthy; the President, to the man who cleans the restroom. I am telling you the truth! I am telling you ALL to the point! It has arrived; all that I have told you in the Bible. For the chest of the White House is the chest of the devil. For the same reasons the devil fell. For they believed they were so great. They (White House) believed more in the man than in God.

Yes, these are the Words of your God, the Father, with the Son, with the Holy Spirit. The God who tells you things straight and to the point. For they are the things of God, and it is the truth. This is the Word of your Father, with tears I tell you the truth. Get ready! Place your eyes on your Father, the Son, and the Holy Spirit and all will go well. But don't say that I did not tell you. Yes! Yes! Yes! The end has arrived. (over)

1000. Prophecy given to Raymond Aguilera on 23 December 1996 at 6:47 AM. in English.

I am the God of Abraham. I am the God of Jacob. I am the God of Isaac. Listen to the Prophecies—study them; until you know them front wards and backwards. For you are very close to the end. Open your eyes. Open your ears. For it will happen suddenly without warning. Those of you who can save—put aside food—put aside food and water—the basics. Those of you who cannot—pray, and pray; bring the Body together so you can help each other. I will inform you; and I will guide you; and I will protect you. But you must read the Bible from the beginning to the end, and study the Prophecies.

You have to be strong, and be brave. For the antichrist will try to slaughter you, and destroy you; down to the every last one. Make yourself strong. Pray, pray, and pray, and pray. Take Communion everyday. The Holy Spirit will move among you; to lift you up; to encourage you; to guide you.

This is the Father of Abraham. This is the Father of Isaac. This the Father of Jacob. This is your Father—Jehovah, Yahweh, the I am, I am, I am—I am, with the Son, Jesus Christ of Nazareth, and the Holy Spirit.

The Peace and the Love of Heaven will befall on you; if you take, and follow my instructions to the LETTER! So be it. So be it. (over)

1001. Occurrence given to Raymond Aguilera on 7 January 1997 at 10:15 PM.

I was resting on top of my bed, when the Presence of the Lord filled my bedroom, and my prayer language began to speak with strange sounds that frightened me. Sounds that I had never heard before. What was so frightening was the intensity of the Power and the Presence of the Lord. My flesh could understand some of what was going on, but not all of it. And as I listened to these strange sounds the Lord placed the Word, "Curse," in my mind, and gave me the following scriptures.

From the KJV Bible:
2 Ki 2:23 And he went up from thence unto Bethel: and as he was going up by the way, there came forth little children out of the city, and mocked him, and said unto him, Go up, thou bald head; go up, thou bald head.
2 Ki 2:24 And he turned back, and looked on them, and cursed them in the name of the LORD. And there came forth two she bears out of the wood, and tare forty and two children of them.

1 Ki 17:1 And Elijah the Tishbite, who was of the inhabitants of Gilead, said unto Ahab, As the LORD God of Israel liveth, before whom I stand, there shall not be dew nor rain these years, but according to my word.

Rev 22:18 For I testify unto every man that heareth the words of the prophecy of this book, If any man shall add unto these things, God shall add unto him the plagues that are written in this book:
Rev 22:19 And if any man shall take away from the words of the book of this prophecy, God shall take away his part out of the book of life, and out of the holy city, and from the things which are written in this book.

Rev 22:20 He which testifieth these things saith, *Surely I come quickly.* Amen. Even so, come, Lord Jesus.
Rev 22:21 The grace of our Lord Jesus Christ be with you all. Amen.

Immediately, I went into prayer in my mind as my prayer language began to communicate with the Lord. My prayer began to test the Spirit asking if this was Jehovah, for the Power Presence was enormous!! But at the same time my prayer language began to speak to the Lord as if it was nothing.

Then my prayer language said the name, George, in Spanish a few times. Then the Lord said, I am, I am, I am.

Vision:
Then the Lord started to give me visions. The first vision was of a cone shape, and this cone was driven point first into the ground by the Lord's Hand.

Comment:
The impression that was left on my mind was a meteor.

Vision:
Then the Lord showed me the image of a Super Sonic Jet with its pointed front cone pointing down.

Vision:
Then I was shown two tubes 15 cm in diameter fused together at about 45 degrees

Vision:
Then I saw an image of Jesus Christ riding fast on this White Horse swinging this large sword that was in His right Hand, and the sword was on fire.

Vision:

I felt so strange—for it seemed that I was in two places at the same time. Part of me was in the world that we all know, and the other part of me was in this other spiritual world. The part that was in this world was praying with all it could trying to understand what was going on. And my spirit was in this spiritual world knowing exactly what was going on, and knowing what it was doing. It was like I was or had two separate entities. I could see myself in the spirit in this area or on top of this small mound holding this unusual very sharp and very deadly sword with both hands, and moving slowly in a counter clockwise direction, as if I were surrounded and protecting myself from as many angles as possible. For I was alone and surrounded. I felt so unusual in the flesh as I watched myself in this spiritual world move slowly, cautiously, without a wasted movement, and the Lord kept saying in my prayer language the name, George, in Spanish as I watched myself.

Then the Lord said, "I am I am I am," in a very Powerful and Authoritative Voice. "Curse this Planet, Ray. Curse this Planet, Ray." The Lord said.

Then my prayer Language Cursed the planet three times.

I have no idea of what was said in the prayer language, for I could not interpret the language, but it was Straight, Direct, and to the Point.

I can still sense this Power Presence in my bedroom, I wish I could put words to what I am sensing in the spirit right now. Like I said earlier, it is like I was in two different places at the same time with my conscious mind outside the spirit world, and my spirit surround by the Power of God in the spirit world. Incredible! Incredible! It's just incredible!! (over)

1002. Vision given to Raymond Aguilera on 13 January 1997 at 2:02 AM.

A vision of a computer monitor with railroad tracks extending in or coming out of the screen. (over)

1003. Vision given to Raymond Aguilera on 19 January 1997 at 10:54 AM.

A vision of a television screen or computer monitor with the reception going off and on. Then eventually it went off. (over)

1004. Vision given to Raymond Aguilera on 21 January 1997 at 2:30 AM.

The Lord gave me a vision of a fireman's hat, then a vision of the Space Needle in Seattle, Washington. As I watched, the Space Needle was driven into the ground like a screw. (over)

1005. Vision given to Raymond Aguilera on 25 January 1997 at 12:30 AM.

The Lord gave me a vision of a flying blimp, and this blimp changed into a fish. This blimp was moving from the right to the left. Then it's tail was cut-off. (over)

1006. Prophecy (story) given to Raymond Aguilera on 31 January 1997.

Once there was a man, who lived many, many, many years ago. His name was Cleavis. Cleavis had a wife and three kids. One day he was approached by the devil.

And the devil said to him, "Cleavis, if you do as I ask, I will make you wealthy. I will make you rich."

Cleavis said to the devil, "I cannot serve you. For I Love the Lord, my God, with all my heart, my soul, with all that there is in heaven and on earth."

This angered the devil and the devil cursed him, his wife, and children. And anytime Cleavis tried to do something; the devil would send his angels to harass him, to make things go wrong for Cleavis. But Cleavis knew that these things were from the devil and not from God. He did the best he could with what he had. Because he Loved the Lord so much, and he and his family suffered much.

Until the Lord said, "STOP DEVIL! Stop—you and your comrades, for Cleavis and his family belong to Me. For he is a righteous man. He, who had followed Me, and served Me, is a righteous man, I will bless him. I will bless him because he never wavered to right or to the left. Cleavis is a simple man, but yet he Loved Me with all of his heart, all of his soul. I will bless him and his family. So stand back! And let My Friend prosper for the Love of God is upon him, and the vengeance of God will fall upon you before your time if you harass him anymore."

So this man, named Cleavis was blessed for the rest of his days. Him and his family prospered; his children and his children's children, for the Hand of God was upon them. Everything he touched prospered, and he lived many years.

The Power of God can do many things, and Cleavis knew this, but it wasn't the Power (God's Power). It was the humbleness of Cleavis and the innocence of his Love for his God that protected him. For he knew that the Lord could raise and could pull down ANYTHING! This a lesson for all of you children, who don't know God. Remember all the Power, all the Might is in the Hands of the Father Jehovah, Jesus Christ, and the Holy Spirit. For no one knows the ways and the manners of God except the children of God. (over)

1007. Vision given to Raymond Aguilera on 3 February 1997 at 9 AM.

I had a vision of a man of dark complexion, of medium height, about 5'–7", with a mustache, and a short beard cut close to the skin with short dark hair. He appeared to be about 30–35 years of age, but what struck me unusual were his eyes. When I first saw him; they were dark brown or black. As I looked closer both eyes changed and looked like large cut diamonds the size of normal eyeballs. Both diamonds were embedded into the eye sockets of his head. It was very strange to see a person look like that. (over)

1008. Prophecy given to Raymond Aguilera on 7 February 1997 at 11:55 AM.

"Come, Reymundo, come! I will show you the world. I will show you, how I will direct those unattended matters; that have been left for many years—unresolved. I will open your eyes. I will show you the manners of the Lord, Jehovah, Jesus Christ, and the Holy Spirit. For this world is going to be drawn into a battle, where the nations will fall into the trap that has been planned for centuries. For the ways of man are finished." So saith, Jehovah. So saith, Jesus Christ of Nazareth. So saith, the Holy Spirit.

The things that were promised will be delivered; the things of judgement; the things of the Lord Jehovah will come to completion at the Valley of Jehoshaphat. Open your eyes, open your ears. For what was prophesied hundreds and hundreds of years ago; you will see with your eyes; you will hear with your ears. You will run and you will hide, but every Word that was said through the prophets will be fulfilled, to the Letter, to the Point.

Many of you think, that this is a game. That this is a puzzle. That this is a fantasy. You will see the Power of Jehovah. You will see the Wrath of God. You will see the Vengeance of God. For what was polluted in the Garden of Eden will be cleaned up. The devil will be locked up with his angels; and We will begin anew. A new ever lasting life; for those, who follow Jesus Christ; for those, who Love Jehovah; for those, who listen to the Holy Spirit. This is the Truth! It is correct; it is Clear; it is to the Point.

My Ways are not man's ways. My Time is not man's time. My Laws are not man's laws. For man corrupts, what he touches. Man thinks he is god, but We will see when they enter the Valley—who is God. The day of vengeance is approaching. The day of Vengeance will be complete as it was stated in the Bible, to the Letter, to the Point.

Come to the Valley and you will see the Power of God—The cleansing of God—of all that is evil. Open your eyes, open your ears. Read the Bible with the eyes of God. The Holy Spirit will show you through the Name of Jesus Christ of Nazareth. You will find the Father, Jehovah. So be it.! So be it! So be it!

Where can you hide? Where can you go? But the Love and the Peace of Jehovah is there for those who seek their God, with a pure heart, pure soul, pure mind. Remember to fast, to pray, to repent, to have communion, to seek your brothers and your sisters with Spirit of God. So be it! So be it! So be it!

Come all faithful servants. Come! The day is here that was promised through the prophets, Isaiah, Joel, Jeremiah, Amos, Daniel, John, all of them (prophets) will tell you, will direct you to the Valley of death. For the vengeance of God will be complete on that day, on that hour. But remember—My Timing is My Timing; My Word is My Word. Peace be with you, My son (Reymundo), My daughters, My children, My lambs. Peace be with you. (over)

1009. Occurrence given to Raymond Aguilera on 12 February 1997 at 7:45 AM.

During morning prayer, the Lord instructed me to place Chapter 13 from the Book of Ezekiel in the Prophecy Book.

From KJV Bible:
Ezek 13:1 And the word of the LORD came unto me, saying,
Ezek 13:2 Son of man, prophesy against the prophets of Israel that prophesy, and say thou unto them that prophesy out of their own hearts, Hear ye the word of the LORD;
Ezek 13:3 Thus saith the Lord GOD; Woe unto the foolish prophets, that follow their own spirit, and have seen nothing!
Ezek 13:4 O Israel, thy prophets are like the foxes in the deserts.
Ezek 13:5 Ye have not gone up into the gaps, neither made up the hedge for the house of Israel to stand in the battle in the day of the LORD.
Ezek 13:6 They have seen vanity and lying divination, saying, The LORD saith: and the LORD hath not sent them: and they have made others to hope that they would confirm the word.
Ezek 13:7 Have ye not seen a vain vision, and have ye not spoken a lying divination, whereas ye say, The LORD saith it; albeit I have not spoken?
Ezek 13:8 Therefore thus saith the Lord GOD; Because ye have spoken vanity, and seen lies, therefore, behold, I am against you, saith the Lord GOD.
Ezek 13:9 And mine hand shall be upon the prophets that see vanity, and that divine lies: they shall not be in the assembly of my people, neither shall they be written in the writing of the house of Israel, neither shall they enter into the land of Israel; and ye shall know that I am the Lord GOD.
Ezek 13:10 Because, even because they have seduced my people, saying, Peace; and there was no peace; and one built up a wall, and, lo, others daubed it with untempered mortar:
Ezek 13:11 Say unto them which daub it with untempered mortar, that it shall fall: there shall be an overflowing shower; and ye, O great hailstones, shall fall; and a stormy wind shall rend it.
Ezek 13:12 Lo, when the wall is fallen, shall it not be said unto you, Where is the daubing wherewith ye have daubed it?
Ezek 13:13 Therefore thus saith the Lord GOD; I will even rend it with a stormy wind in my fury; and there shall be an overflowing shower in mine anger, and great hailstones in my fury to consume it.

Ezek 13:14 So will I break down the wall that ye have daubed with untempered mortar, and bring it down to the ground, so that the foundation thereof shall be discovered, and it shall fall, and ye shall be consumed in the midst thereof: and ye shall know that I am the LORD.

Ezek 13:15 Thus will I accomplish my wrath upon the wall, and upon them that have daubed it with untempered mortar, and will say unto you, The wall is no more, neither they that daubed it;

Ezek 13:16 To wit, the prophets of Israel which prophesy concerning Jerusalem, and which see visions of peace for her, and there is no peace, saith the Lord GOD.

Ezek 13:17 Likewise, thou son of man, set thy face against the daughters of thy people, which prophesy out of their own heart; and prophesy thou against them,

Ezek 13:18 And say, Thus saith the Lord GOD; Woe to the women that sew pillows to all armholes, and make kerchiefs upon the head of every stature to hunt souls! Will ye hunt the souls of my people, and will ye save the souls alive that come unto you?

Ezek 13:19 And will ye pollute me among my people for handfuls of barley and for pieces of bread, to slay the souls that should not die, and to save the souls alive that should not live, by your lying to my people that hear your lies?

Ezek 13:20 Wherefore thus saith the Lord GOD; Behold, I am against your pillows, wherewith ye there hunt the souls to make them fly, and I will tear them from your arms, and will let the souls go, even the souls that ye hunt to make them fly.

Ezek 13:21 Your kerchiefs also will I tear, and deliver my people out of your hand, and they shall be no more in your hand to be hunted; and ye shall know that I am the LORD.

Ezek 13:22 Because with lies ye have made the heart of the righteous sad, whom I have not made sad; and strengthened the hands of the wicked, that he should not return from his wicked way, by promising him life:

Ezek 13:23 Therefore ye shall see no more vanity, nor divine divinations: for I will deliver my people out of your hand: and ye shall know that I am the LORD.

1010. Prophecy given to Raymond Aguilera on 16 February 1997 at 9:30 AM.

The Lord said, "To correctly measure the magnitude of an earthquake; you should use a three dimensional scale." (over)

1011. Vision given to Raymond Aguilera on 16 February 1997 at 9:52 AM.

The Lord showed me a bomb; the kind that cartoon characters use on television. The bomb looked like a black bowling ball with a fuse sticking out of the top. The only difference was that a beautiful ring surrounded the fuse with many colorful stones on it. It was the kind of ring a man would wear.

1012. Prophecy (Song) given to Raymond Aguilera on 18 February 1997

A Glorious day is here. Now and forever.
For our Lord, and Savior, our Redeemer is here.

Blessed be the Lord.
Blessed be the Lord.
For the Day of the Lord is here.
Blessed be Jesus Christ.
Blessed be Jesus Christ.

For Great are the Humble and the Meek on the Day of the Lord.
Blessed be the Lord Jesus Christ.

A Glorious Day.
How Glorious and Wonderful you are.
Our Redeemer. Our King.
How Great is the King Jesus Christ.
Glorious and Wonderful Father Jehovah.
Praise be the Holy Spirit.

1013. Prophecy given to Raymond Aguilera on 18 February 1997 at 3 PM.

Fly. Fly. I am going to hit the devil like a fly. Fly. (over)

1014. Dream given to Raymond Aguilera on 26 February 1997.

I had this dream where I worked in a fruit factory, and I had a female boss. I remembered she was a hard person to please. I was placed on this conveyor belt, where all these grapes were placed. My job was to remove all the spoiled and rotten grapes from the good bunches of grapes, and I guess, I was suppose to package them, but I wasn't instructed to do so. As I removed all the spoiled and rotten grapes from the moving conveyor belt, I noticed that all the grapes were going to fall on the floor for there wasn't anything there to catch these grapes. So I call my brother Ted standing near a doorway, and told him to find me a box to catch the grapes. So he threw me and old used box, but as he threw the box, I noticed a bunch of grapes had fallen onto the floor. I quickly picked them up and noticed that they were not damaged (at least they didn't look bruised). In no time, I had the used box full and began to place the other grapes onto a neighboring table full of grapes.

Then right behind the last bunch of grapes, I noticed some small purple pears already packaged nine per box. These purple pear boxes looked like square egg cartons without a cover.

Then someone called out and said, "Those are very delicate pears. Make sure they do not get bruised."

So I tried to move these pears, but I noticed that there were still a lot of grapes in the way of me moving these pears. The conveyor belt was stopped, and I was left with all this fruit that I didn't know what to do with. Then the dream stopped. (over)

1015. Prophecy given to Raymond Aguilera on 27 February 1997 at 7:00 AM.

The Lord said, "Cleavis, Cleavis, remember Cleavis." (*Cleavis from prophecy 1006). (over)

1016. Vision given to Raymond Aguilera on 28 February 1997 at 12:16 AM.

The Lord gave me a vision of a woman's Breast with Three Nipples. (over)

1017. Vision given to Raymond Aguilera on 5 March 1997 at 5 AM.

The Lord gave me a vision of myself praising and thanking Him as I danced through this thick dark forest. This forest was so thick and dark you could not see any light, but I knew that if I kept dancing and praising the Lord, I would get through it. So I just kept dancing and praising the Lord as I moved forward. Then all of sudden I reached this certain area of the forest, and a Horn Blasted a sound into the air. The sound was so loud that this large flame started to move across the forest and burned the forest down, and I was left standing unharmed. (over)

1018. Vision given to Raymond Aguilera on 5 March 1997

The Lord showed me this Large Light. It looked like a river of fire and it hit the Planet. (This was not a meteor.)

Then the Lord said, "Climb into the Light."

Vision:
Then the next thing I see is a universal bearing, the kind that is on the end of a automobile's drive shaft. The bearing that is in the shape of a cross with a small bearing on each of it's four ends. (over)

1019. Vision given to Raymond Aguilera on 6 March 1997 at 3:49 AM.

The Lord showed me a large black smoke stack with smoke rising into the sky. As I looked at the sky, I noticed the sky had red/orange clouds and these clouds were moving toward the smoke stack. (over)

1020. Vision given to Raymond Aguilera on 10 March 1997 at 1:26 AM.

The Lord gave me a vision of a parking meter, and at the base of the parking meter there was a rope tied to the base pipe of the meter. As my eyes followed the tied rope, it led to the other side of the sidewalk to a person bond with the rope like a mummy. (over)

1021. Prophecy given to Raymond Aguilera on 15 March 1997 at 8:02 AM. in Spanish.

Hear Me! Hear Me people of the world! Hear Me! I know that you have your eyes closed. I know that you cannot hear, but that is not going to change a thing. If you hear or not. What is going to happen; is going to happen to the Point. All that I have said in the Bible is going to happen. If you want a chance, read the Bible; seek the Lord of Heaven, of the world, the One who made everything with a Pure Heart. I know that you do not believe My Prophet, but that doesn't change a thing either. For years and years, and years, I have sent out My Word, and never have they believed until it happened.

What a shame—for I tell you with My Heart, the things that are going to come to past, but I know that the people of the world like the things of the world. They do not believe in God, Jesus, the Father, and the Holy Spirit, but they are going to be frightened. For I am going to turn My Back; I am not going to see them, and I am not going to help them. I know—that you think that this Prophet is stupid and dumb, but that doesn't change a thing. My Word is My Word, if you believe it or not!

I am going to send an Angel, and the Angel is going to point a star, a rock, from the sky. And when My Angel pushes the star, the rock, lets see where you are going to hide. For here comes the pit of the sky, and it is going to hit with a Force that is going to frightened all of the world. It has arrived the end of many of this world for they did not seek Me. For they liked more the world, the devil, than God, who made all—the stars, what see, what you touch.

But I have said My Word, and it is going to happen. For no one can change what I have said. No one has the Force of Jesus, of the Father, and of the Holy Spirit. Now that I have said it—it will happen; Exactly and to the Point. All that you have to do is wait for the rock of the sky. For here it comes, with the Force of God.

You are going to be frightened. Lets see if your brains can save you. Lets see if the devil can save you. Lets see if the President can save you. Lets see if your pistol can save you. Lets see! For here it comes Pointed and Direct, and to the Point with My Name Jesus, the Father and the Holy Spirit. I tell you the truth to the point. The rest—who believe in Me, and seek Jesus do not be frightened. For everything is in My Hands. Did you hear Me? Do not worry, but I want you to repent. I want you to seek Me. I want you to read the Bible. I want you to eat the communion. It has arrived the Word of God.

Note:
The Lord gave Me the Book of Luke Chapter 21. (over)

1022. Vision given to Raymond Aguilera on 15 March 1997 at 10:34 AM.

The Lord gave me a vision of a net that surrounded the whole world. It looked like a chain linked fence. It covered every square inch of the planet. (Over)

1023. Prophecy and Vision given to Raymond Aguilera on 19 March 1997 at 8:06 AM.

During prayer, the Lord gave me a vision of the Red Sea and how He parted the waters. The Lord showed me His finger as it went over the water and parted the Red Sea (where Moses crossed). Then beneath this area He showed me this enormous mouth with teeth, and the Lord said it was the mouth of Leviathan. How the mouth was ready to eat the soldiers that were after Moses. (over)

Vision:
Then the Lord gave me the vision of a white golf ball and a golf club. Then I saw the golf club hit the white golf ball.
Then Lord said, "That's how I am going to hit the planet earth." (over)

Vision:
Then the Lord gave me a vision of Three Lit Match Sticks all of them standing side by side. (over)

Vision:
Then the Lord showed me something that looked like fabric, but it wasn't fabric. It looked like a dam, and the dam was ripped down the middle like a piece of fabric. When water began to run down the Lord said, "My flood gates will be opened."

Prophecy:
Then the Lord said, "The circle is complete." (over)

1024. Prophecy given to Raymond Aguilera on 21 March 1997 at 11:49 PM.

The Lord gave me the scriptures of Isaiah Chapter 60:19-21, for the vision about the water flooding. (vision about the fabric looking dam.)

1025. Vision given to Raymond Aguilera on 23 March 1997 at 12:15 AM.

I had a vision of a man with no head wearing a baseball uniform. (over)

1026. Prophecy given to Raymond Aguilera on 26 March 1997 at 7:56 AM. in Spanish.

I am—I am the life; the life of all that you see, all that you touch, all that you know. I am, I am, I am. I am the life. I hear your tears to the point! You believe that I do not hear you, but I hear ALL. I am going to help you with My Hands. I am going to help you with all that you need. I know—that you have suffered. I hear your tears everyday to the point. It has arrived, Reymundo, the date that I told you years ago. All that I promised has arrived. I am going to send people; I am going to send what you need. And the other things you asked about from the Bible. I am going to open your eyes and ears to the Word, of the things that you do not know.

For We are arriving at the date, the date of the end. My Time is not the time of man. All is going to go to the Time of God (Christ, the Holy Spirit, and the Father). We Three are One with the Force of Force, with the Love of Love, with ALL that there is.

All the Words that you have written are going to scare the world, and they are going to cry. For they are going to know that the things they have studied in the Bible are the things of man, with the mind of man. For they did not have pure hearts and pointed toward My Son Jesus. They were not standing on top of the Rock of My Son. They were standing on top of rock of the devil. The word of man is the word of man, if you use the Bible or if do not use the Bible; this is the same thing. This is the word of man.

But if you stand on top of the Rock of My Son Jesus, and you pray to Me with the Heart of Love. I will open your eyes. I will open your ears, and the things of the Bible will begin to become clear, to the point. And when you hear them, and when they hit your heart; you are going to fall onto the floor, and on the floor you are going to cry. For you are going to know with those tears that these are the Words of your God. For the Words of God have Force. The word of man has the pit. Remember what I have told you. I am going to take what is pointed, directly, and to the point toward My Son. That is all that I want. The rest—is going to the pit. For what is Mine is Mine. The rest I do not want! It is worthless!

It is not important to Me if you are tall, short, fat or if you are intelligent or if you know nothing. What I see is the HEART. The Heart that seeks Me with all that you have, with all the Mind, with all the Heart, with all your spirit, with all that you have. People are going to be frightened because they believed they had Me, and they are going to find out they had nothing. For their hearts were dirty.

Hurry—Reymundo! We have to begin to write everything I have said to you. For the world is going to be frightened clearly and to the point with the Force of God. Did you hear Me Clearly? Did you hear Me to the Point? Do not worry about the people who believe they know it all. For I have a place for people like that. Oh, Oh, Oh! I tell them, and I tell them, and I tell them, but they do not want to hear. For their hearts are hard. But what is going to happen is going to happen at the Time of God. Hurry My son, We have to begin another Page of the Word of God. (over)

1027. Prophecy given to Raymond Aguilera on 26 March 1996 at 8:13 AM. in English.

I will use the bear with the Force and the Power of God. Here comes the bear, the willing instrument of destruction. Be prepared, be wise! Here comes the bear! The sleeping bear will awaken with force of the atom. Hide your face—do not look at the light! The light of the atom is the light of the power of the bomb. Run and hide! For here comes the bear, the mighty bear, the instrument of God; for the Wrath of God; for what is dirty; for what is filthy. Here comes the light of the bomb! (over)

Vision:

A vision of a kitchen faucet, and at the end of the faucet there was a baby bottle nipple. (over)

Vision:

Then I found myself out in outer space. It was dark and as I flowed in space, I noticed the stars were gone, and there was nothing there but complete blackness with everything in the universe gone. And as I flowed in this darkness, I noticed this single Light far in the distance, and it got bigger and bigger. As it approached me, I noticed it changed into some sort silver looking canister. I do not know what it was, but it looked Kingly. This was strange, but the Lord was telling me that inside the container contained the whole universe that we know. (over)

1028. Prophecy given to Raymond Aguilera on 10 April 1997 at 12:27 AM. in Spanish.

I am with you My son. I am with you with the tears—I hear you! I see your heart crying with the flame that wants to know the truth. You know that the world is going to end. You know more than people who believe they know. For you saw with your eyes the end. You saw with the eyes of God, what was going to happen. I know that the people of the world do not want to help you. For they love more the devil than the things of God, but do not worry about people not helping you. For I am going to help you, with My Hand, with My Lips.

Man seeks the things of man, but I am going to show you the things that no one else has ever seen or heard. For you have to write the things of the Spirit, what you see, what you dream. I told you about the star before it happened; I told you to look to the sky years before it happened. And people are now just beginning to see—what I showed you years ago. They got frightened—like you were frightened when I showed you the star that hit the world, and still to this day, they make fun of you.

They still have not read the Bible, and they still have not helped the people who are in the streets, the ones who are sick. They are still having parties, dancing and having fun. For they do not want to know the truth. I know that it has been hard all of these years that I have spoken to you. I know that you have suffered. I know all that has happened, and the things that are going to happen to you. You are My beloved, but look Reymundo the things that you know—and the things you are going to write; people want to know. There are not many, but there are people who want to know. They are seeking the things that you know.

I know—that your body is wearing out, with your hands, and mind. You are exhausted! I know—that you are hungry at times, and you have nothing to eat. I see these things, but you do not believe I see. You do not go to parties. I know—that you do not have joy. I know—that you do not have anyone to talk too. I know—that you are alone. I know—that you seek friends to help you with the things you do not know, but they cannot help you, Reymundo.

For I separated you with My Spirit. I am the ONLY One who can help you. For the things I have showed you in the years past are very heavy, and I know it hurts your heart. I know the dreams, and I know that the devil hits you. He hits you hard, but you are stronger now Reymundo and you can tell when he comes, but We have more things to do. I am going to help you with the money. For I know that the brothers and sisters are deaf;

they want everything EASY; they want everything FREE. I know—the computer costs you, and the things to live on.

But there is going to come one day, Reymundo, that all these things are going to become nothing. For people are going to eat rats, dogs, and cats. And they are going to eat everything that is filthy. I have sent out My Word for many years, and no one helps My Prophets that I send out into this world. They suffer and they suffer, but they send out My Word for that is their job. I hear their tears, and it hurts Me, when I see the tears coming from the people I choose. For when they suffer—I SUFFER! For they know—and I know that the Word is not theirs. It is Mine!

The Word that I send through your hand, through your computer hits people very HARD to the point. And they do not like you, Reymundo! For if they liked you; they would like Me. All of them want everything easy. They like the Love, and the Love; they do not like to suffer like My Son Jesus. That's why they do not help you, Reymundo. For they want it easy! They want everything free! But do not worry My son, for I Love you. You are My beloved, and your steps are My Steps, and your lips are My Lips, and your heart is My Heart. I tell you direct. I tell you to the point.

I know that you are waiting for your wife, but I know what going to happen. You are going to have to wait for Me for there going to come a day, that you are going to need her, but I know who it is. For she is going to be of the same mind as you. The two of you are going to work, with the same spirit, with the same mind, with the same Love for Me, My Son, and the Holy Spirit. I know that you believe you are crazy at times, for the things that you know. You cannot tell anyone for they would not believe you. They believe you are crazy, but you are crazy for your God.

But things are going to become hotter, Reymundo, My son. I am going to show you more things, and you are going to get frightened—and you are going to cry some more. But look—you are in My Hands, and don't have any worries with who gets mad at you, if it is the President, the Government, the world, or the devil. For I know where you are going to go when your time comes. And I know—and you know what is going to happen to the people that come after you. Read the Bible—you know and I know, what happened to the people who hit the people (prophets) who carried My Word.

There are not many people who can do; what you are doing Reymundo. I know that you believe that you are not doing much. There are people who are telling you to do this, and do that, but they do not have the nerve to do it themselves. They tell you, but they do not have the nerve to do it, and they do not even have the nerve to help you. But look—point your eyes toward Jesus. Point your heart toward the Holy Spirit, and point everything that you have to your Father. No one can push you down for you are in Our Hands. I tell you with Love. I tell you the Word of God, but I know there are times when you do not want to hear the Word of God; when you are hungry, thirsty, and cold, but I am there every minute of everyday.

But here comes the war that is going to frighten the world. The devil is now ready. Everyone believes they can make the world the way they want, but the world is Mine, and I can do what I want with what is Mine. When it happens they are going to seek you out, the ones who believe, and the ones who do not believe. Nothing has changed with man. Something bad has to happen before they will seek Me out, but look—I want you only to seek Me, and I will tell you the truth. If you like it or not, I will tell you the truth for you are My beloved. I am going to place an Angel on one side of you, so he can help you every minute of everyday. I know that you are going to look for him, and sometimes you are going to see him, but if you see him or not—he is going to be there to open the doors and shut doors for the end is coming. The end of everything that you see; of all the you touch.

What a shame, that people are so blind, but nothing has changed. The church of the world is going on the same road as the Jews that believed they knew it all. I see nothing that is different in their hearts, in their minds. It is like they put on the same pants, shoes, hats, and coats, of the

Jews. They look like twins. They look like twins. They look like twins. These are the people who are going to get mad with you, Reymundo.

We are going to start over, but there are many who are going to die, families, little ones, mothers, and fathers. What a shame! But the SIN is getting larger and larger, and the only thing that is different is that they SIN in the Name of My Son. What a shame! They do not eat the Communion; they do not repent, they do not do what My Son told them to do. They make and write laws, and when they want people to obey them, they place the Name of My Son on them, and they do them. And they believe I am going to help them because they said the Name of My Son when they do their sins. But I have patience, I can wait, for time is nothing to Me, and I do not forget a thing.

But I know, for I read your heart, that you are very sad; for you do not know who to speak to. For they do not know what you know, and you do not know how to tell them; what you feel in your heart. But look My son, make yourself strong for the end has arrived. For all the joy that they are having, they are going to suffer, and I am not going to protect them like I am going to protect you and your family. I know your heart; I know that you love Me with all that you have, but all will go well My son, all to the point, all the Words, all that you saw, all that you dreamed, all that has happened. Rest My son, I know that your hands hurt. I know that your heart is crying. Sleep and rest. Tomorrow I will give you money so you can eat for I know that you are hungry. Rest tomorrow, My son, I do not want you to work. Did you hear Me? I do not want you to work tomorrow, but I—with My Hands will give you the money that you need so you can eat. Rest! Did you hear Me? Rest My son, My beloved. (Over)

1029. Occurrence given to Raymond Aguilera on 14 April 1997 at 5:30 PM.

I sent the last prophecy a few hours ago to the people on our e-mail list. Afterwards I felt so exhausted, I felt I had worked 20 hours straight without resting. So I decided to lay down and rest. During my nap, I felt this powerful demonic attack, and I awoke more exhausted than before I had laid down. Then my daughter yells up to me and told me that the patio double pane glass door was slowly shattering. So I went downstairs and looked at the slowly shattering patio door and realized the devil attacked the house, and only broke the outside pane. I photographed the glass patio door, and I will place the photo on the web site. As you will be able to see from the photograph; the glass door is in the shade not in direct sun light. Here is another expense I do not have the money to fix.

1030. Vision given to Raymond Aguilera on 14 April 1997 at 9 PM.

During the Bible study, the Lord gave me a vision of an open grave, with an open coffin inside. I could see a skeleton of a man inside the coffin. (over)

1031. Vision given to Raymond Aguilera on 18 April 1997 at 9:30 AM.

The Lord gave me two visions of a figure of a woman.

The first image looked like the Statue of Liberty, and she was leaning on a dark wooden stick with both hands.

The second image was the Statue of Liberty that I am used to seeing. She looked like she was covering herself as if she had been undressed. (over)

1032. Vision given to Raymond Aguilera on 19 April 1997 at 9:30 PM.

During prayer the Lord gave me a vision of a large Brandy Wine Glass that was as large as a oval fish bowl. And as I watched this Large Wine Glass, I saw a smaller wine glass come up, and tap the side of the Larger Wine Glass, and it made a sound. As I kept watching, many, many other wine glasses came up, and tapped the Larger Wine Glass on the side. These tapping sounds, made these many sounds that radiated into the Heavens. (over)

1033. Vision given to Raymond Aguilera on 24 April 1997 at 6:00 PM.

During prayer, I saw this five pointed star, and in the center of this star was the image of the planet earth.

Vision: 6:30 PM
I had a vision of a wine glass, but the *full wine glass* was floating in a horizontal position.

1034. Prophecy given to Raymond Aguilera on 25 April 1997 at 11:30 PM.

I am, I am, I am. Stay awake, be alert. The horse and the hound dog are ready for the hunt. Watch the fox. He is fast, and he is swift. The hunt will avail nothing; for the fox is too clever for the horse and the hound. Mark My Words, the day of the fox is here. If you look closely; you will see the fox. The fox will make himself known within the next three years. Look for the fox; for the horse and the hound are right behind. (over)

1035. Vision given to Raymond Aguilera on 25 April 1997 at 5:00 PM.

I saw a vision of a candle about one inch in diameter and four inches high. And on top of this candle, I saw a small blue birthday candle; and it was lit. (over)

Vision:
I saw a clear glass mug with an emblem of an eagle on the surface, but on the inside of this clear mug there was some sort of whirlwind. (over)

1036. Vision given to Raymond Aguilera on 29 April 1997 at 6:00 AM.

A vision of a burnt out church with no roof with only partial walls standing up. On this partial opening of this one wall, I saw two ravens; one was White, one was black. Then I saw the White raven give something to the black raven. (I think it was food.) Then the vision stopped.

Vision: 8:42 AM

I saw a vision of a White Horse with a Rider. I can see the Horse moving in Water up to its' Eyes. Slowly the Horse submerged with it's Rider, but I was not allowed to see the Face of the Rider. The Rider was dressed in White and the Horse was White. (over)

1037. Prophecy given to Raymond Aguilera on 29 April 1997 at 9:01 AM in English.

I am the Lord, All Mighty, the One you saw riding the White Horse moving under the Water. The time is coming when the righteous things will be submerged; for the cleansing; for the purifying; for things that are going to go to Heaven. Listen to Me My People; for the Word of God is True, Straight, and to the Point. The calamity of the World is here.

I know—that most of you do not believe. I know—that most of you want to know, but only those that have morals—Christian Morals—those who have the Love of Jehovah, the Love of Jesus Christ, the Love of the Holy Spirit will be Saved. You can't say you are Christian, and walk with the world. You can't walk with the world, and claim that you are saved. These are simple Words that are very hard for some people to accept. For they are used to the things of life, their possessions. These possessions will be taken away in an instant! I know you cannot comprehend what I am saying, but you will—when it happens!

I am going to strip this world naked, and I am going to make you look at your nakedness with the Shame. I want you to see your Shame! I want you to see your Sin! For some of you, it will be nothing. For you are righteous, you are clean, and there is nothing to expose. For the rest of you; you will see with clarity your nakedness, your dirtiness. You believe you can do what you want with the things I have given you, and run and play with the devil. I will allow you to do what you want, but I will have the final Word.

I see, and I hear people who are lesbians welcomed in the White House with opened arms. I see, and I hear the revolting things that these women do. I see, and I hear the revolting things that homosexuals do. Yes they are having fun; they are having pleasure, but there will come a time I will strip them naked before Me; and I will show them their Shame!

This Country—and other Countries that have lost all their Morals, all their values are going to see the Wrath of God. But the leaders who allow; who encourage such acts; I am going to stump them with the Heel of My Shoe, and grind their heads into the ground. Any leader, any person, who encourages such a thing will be hearing from Me.

I created a beautiful man in My Image. I created a woman for his partner, so the both could become one. With the help of the devil, with the help of the wickedness of man; they made dirty; they made evil; what I made beautiful in the beginning. People of the world must be really blind to believe that I do not see these things. But I tell you as My Name is Jehovah, with My Son Jesus Christ of Nazareth, with the Power of the Holy Spirit; your President or any President who allows such things will see the Heel of My Shoe.

We are not playing games. This is not a fun and game thing! But there is a win and lose situation. The union between a man and a woman is sacred. It was made for a man and a wife, with the husband at the head, in union with his wife, both of them working as a unit. Why is that so hard to understand? But I tell you people of the world; that the time of your fun and games is almost over. For My Heel is ready too. With one Breath—things will begin to happen, and I will begin to clean this filthy little planet that you call earth.

But My Eyes see what is clean; what is righteous; what is pure, I know My Followers, My Lambs, My Sheep, and I will protect them. No matter what happens, I am going to save them from what is dirty; from what is evil. This planet is going to be ravished beyond your comprehension to the point that you wished you were not born. The devil is going to be locked up with all of his people. You think I am kidding? Keep doing what you are doing, and We will see who becomes the winner. You have not seen Power. You have not seen Anger. You have not seen Wrath, until you have seen the cleansing of this world.

I tell you this from the Lips of Jehovah, from the Lips of Jesus Christ of Nazareth, from the Lips of the Holy Spirit. We are not playing your dirty game. I am telling My prophet Reymundo to type up this prophecy today because the urgency of this message must be sent out to My Lambs, My Sheep, for We are closer each day to the abyss.

And My Sheep and My Lambs, you better wake up. You better do more than you have been doing. You better pray. You better evangelize, for your leaders are not doing their jobs. Did you hear My Words? I want you to go door to door, anywhere, where you work—tell anybody, and everybody that you know: "That your Lord and Savior is Coming with the Wrath and the Vengeance of God." So be it! So be it! So be it! (over)

1038. Vision given to Raymond Aguilera on 29 April 1997 at 9:00 PM.

The Lord gave me a vision of two figures that looked like Angels. Both figures were wearing White looking sheets or a type of White Robes. They were standing outside near a campfire or open fire. As I watched, I noticed that they pulled out this White Sheet that was as Clean and White as the Robes they were wearing. With their hands, each Angel held one corner of this open White Sheet, and they laid the White Sheet over the flames of the open fire. Then the vision stopped. (over)

1039. Prophecy given to Raymond Aguilera on 6 May 1997 at 11:08 AM. in Spanish.

Hear Me, this minute! Hear Me! Hear Me! Hear Me, this minute! Yes, Hear Me! It has arrived the things that I have told you in the past days. You have to place your ear to the ground, for I am going to tell you things. I know that the world doesn't hear the things of God. The climate is going to change more in the coming years. Yes, the Climate is going to change. I am going to show you with the climate that the whole world is in My Hands.

You believe you can do what you want, but I am going to show you; I have the last Word, and that all is pointed. I, and My Son, and the Holy Spirit are ready. The devil is ready. All is ready! But look—you have to hear Me because it has arrived the day that you are going to have to choose, of all that is good or of all that is evil. For you know, and I know that the things of God are Clean and are Exact. They are from the Holy Spirit. They are from the Father. They are from the Son. But if you do not hear Me, and if you do not pray, and if you do not eat the Communion, and if you do not do the things of God; you are going to suffer.

For now, the devil wants to choke you; he wants to do what he wants with you. But if you choose the devil, **the easy road**, I am going to leave you, but I am going to cry. But I know—that I gave you the chance; My Mind is clean. For the things of God are the things of God. You know, and I know, that this Word is from the Father for your spirit is going to radiate with the things of God if you are Mine. If you are not Mine, you are not going to sense a thing. You are going to be asleep. For that is the way it is with the things of the devil, they are asleep, and they do not do a thing. And that sleep is going to find you the pit.

But you know, and I know, that the things of God are going to happen. For all of My Words happen Exactly and to the Point. I know that Christians are seeking Me, but they seek Me with the eyes and the ears of man. But everything is going to change in the coming years, for the Force of the Holy Spirit is going to burn their hearts. They are going to seek Me with a hunger. But I know, which ones are Mine, and which ones are the devil's. And the ones who belong to the devil are going to make war with the ones who are good, and many are going to die. For they didn't look for the things that are good. They sought the things that are of the devil. And the devil is going to want to eat all that is good.

Did you hear Me to the point? But if you did not hear Me, that is another thing. You are going to have to learn these matters the hard way—you alone. For I only protect what is Mine. Did you hear Me? Did you hear Me? Did you hear Me, this minute? This is all that I want to tell you, with My prophet Reymundo. (over)

1040. Prophecy given to Raymond Aguilera on 7 May 1997 at 1:10 AM. in Spanish.

It is I. It is I, My son. I know that you are tired. That you cannot keep your eyes open; for you are so tired. It has arrived, Reymundo, it has arrived the present that I was going to give you. It has arrived. The present is ready, and I am going to give it to you with the Love of your Father, with the Love of My Son, with the Love of the Holy Spirit. You know that I am saying the truth, but when your present arrives; you are going to know, that all that I have said to you in the years past is going to happen. It is going to happen to the point. I know that you do not want to hear Me for you are so tired, but I tell you the truth. I tell you the things of Heaven.

You are My beloved. You hadn't been born; the day that I appointed you, so you could carry My Word. But I knew, that the day was going to come, when the Two of Us were going to talk, and the Two of Us were going to Cry. We are going to cry for the people who do not want to hear Me. We are going to Cry, for they do not want to hear the Father, the Son, and the Holy Spirit. But I knew many years before, that this date was going to arrive to the point. But make yourself strong Reymundo, and remember that I hear your tears.

But people have such hard heads, and such hard hearts, that no one can change them, I know that it hurts your heart. Make yourself strong, for things are going to become hotter, day by day, hour by hour, minute by minute. It has arrived; the end of all that is bad. It has arrived the end of the devil. I am going to hit him like a fly. There are people in the world, that do not believe Me. They believe that you, Reymundo, are crazy with all of the Words that you say, and in all the manners that you say them. But I am going to show them how crazy you are. For all that I have said to you, and all that you have written is going to happen, to the letter, to the point. That's why you have to make yourself strong, for they are going to get mad with you. But remember I am going to give you the present. Yes! I am going to give it to you.

I know this minute, what you are saying to yourself. "What is My Father talking about this present? I didn't know nothing about a present."

Yes, I know what you are saying, Reymundo! I have told you, but you have not heard Me. Do you remember the promises? So you remember, My Word? It has arrived the day that I told you. Raise your hands right now! And I will tell you the truth for your present has arrived. All! All! All! All is going to go well, you just have to do what I have said to you. I will protect you; you and your friend, and all those who help you, I am going to protect. For they are taking care of the Word of God with the Force of the Holy Spirit, I tell you the truth. It has arrived the match. Remember the match that I told you about years ago. It has arrived.

I know what you are thinking; for I am showing you some onions. But remember from where the onion comes from. The onion comes from the ground. That's way it is going to happen. I am going to take them out like an onion. All that are! Remember, all that are, I am going to lift up. Like an onion. Hurry sleep, and rest for I know that you are tired. (over)

1041. Vision given to Raymond Aguilera on 7 May 1997 at 1:20 AM.

The Lord gave me a vision of outer space. I saw a black whirlwind spinning on top of the planet earth. As I watched, I saw a White Cloud appear, and the White Cloud got bigger and bigger. It covered the whole planet until the planet earth could not be seen. (over)

1042. Prophecy given to Raymond Aguilera on 7 May 1997 at 8:13 AM. in Spanish.

Shasta! Shasta! Shasta! It has arrived; all that I have told you about the mountain Shasta. It has arrived the flame, the earthquake, the star of Shasta, the mountain of Shasta. Hurry run and hide yourself if you can. For here comes the rocks of Shasta. The mountain that is going to lose all that it has with the Force of God, with the Force that is going to clean all that is filthy, with the Force of God. Hurry—if you hear My Word—run, and hide yourself. For it has arrived, the star of Mt. Shasta. The devils that live in the town of Mt. Shasta are going to be the first who are going to see the Force of God. For God is going to hit it like a fly. Yes, I am going to hit them—like a fly! For they believe, and have the nerve to do filthy things. They believe they are god.

But I hear all, and I see all, and I have the LAST Word with all that is Mine. I tell you clearly! I tell you to the point! I tell you the Word of God! It has arrived, the day of Shasta. Remember that I told you to hide yourself from the rocks of Shasta, of all that is filthy. For here comes the Force of God that is going to FRIGHTENED THE WORLD! If you do not believe Me; that is what you have to live with; for it has arrived. What I am going to clean-up with the mountain of Shasta.

What a shame—that all that is beautiful and clean is going to suffer for all that is filthy. But the people of the world, I tell them, and I tell them, and I tell them, and they plug their ears, and they place their hands over their eyes, and they do not want to hear Me. But they cannot say that I did not tell them the truth, the Word of God, the Word of the Father, the Word of the Son, the Word of the Holy Spirit.

Hurry—pick-up the Bible, and read it with the Heart of God, with the Eyes of God, with the Ears of God, with the Spirit of God, and you are going to learn that what I say is the Truth; and is going to happen, ALL OF IT! The devil will not be able to help you; he is only going to help you to take you to the pit. In that way the two of you can have a party in the same pit; for the two you love each other so much. These Words I just have said hurt Me, but if you do not seek Me; I am going to send you with your friend, the devil, to the pit, when I hit Mt. Shasta. Yes, Yes, Yes! (over)

1043. Vision given to Raymond Aguilera on 7 May 1997 at 2:02 PM.

I saw a vision of a fireman's water hose with a trickle of water coming out of the nozzle. (over)

1044. Vision given to Raymond Aguilera on 8 May 1997 at 1:35 AM.

A vision of a woman's white high heel shoe with a brick in front of the shoe. (over)

1045. Vision given to Raymond Aguilera on 9 May 1997 at 8:00 PM.

A vision of a map of the world, then a bloody knife carved up the map. (over)

Vision:

A vision of the planet earth, but the surface of the earth had the same surface appearance as the surface of a human brain.

1046. Prophecy given to Raymond Aguilera on 11 May 1997 at 8:00 AM.

Castro, Castro, Castro. Fidel Castro will die for what he has done. Bill Gates is nothing. Bill Clinton is nothing.

Reymundo, I want you to go to Mt. Shasta and make Three Stone Altars—One to the north, one to the east, and one to the south. On these Stone Altars, I want you to pour on each Altar one pint of the best olive oil you can buy at the local store. (over)

1047. Vision given to Raymond Aguilera on 11 May 1997.

A vision of part of the Pacific Rim geological plates the area between Washington, Oregon and Northern California they looked like they were ripping apart or separating. (over)

Vision:
Then I saw a river of lava and above the river of lava, I saw Three Ringing Golden Bells. Then the Lord instructed me to also Anoint with oil Mt. Lassen, Crater Lake, and Mount Saint Helens.

1048. Prophecy given to Raymond Aguilera on 12 May 1997 at 12:30 AM. in Spanish.

The rat is under the table. Look at him. Look at how he runs from here to there, the rat that is under the table. Look for him, and catch him, for if you catch him you will have something to eat tonight. Hurry! He went over there! Get your knife and cut his throat and in that way we will have something to eat tonight. Yes, Reymundo, that is the way it is going to be in the days that are coming.

They are going to eat rats. They are going to eat what they can find. But I tell and I tell this world, that the hard days are going to come, but do you believe they hear Me. No! No! No! They have other things to do.

They have to have fun. They have to go here and there. They do not have the time to pray. They do not have the time to read the Bible. Lets see if they have the time to catch the rat to eat in the days that are coming. Like I told you—the letter of God is to the point, and is going to arrive, and is going to hit this world. I told you in the Bible many years ago that I was going to send My Word in the last days. And I told you that many were not going to believe Me. You are in those days NOW!

For I am sending My Word with the Force of the Holy Spirit, but the people who believe that they know, they are not going to hear Me; they are going to get mad. For they do not know the God, the One who made the world, the stars, all that you see, all that you touch. They believe they know, but they do not have the Heart of God. What a shame! But it is the Truth of the days that you are living in. All of the pastors, the ministers, know the words, they know how to move their hands, they know how to put on their elegant clothes, but they do not have the Heart. They forgot to put on the Heart of God.

But the end has arrived. It has arrived THE END of the Word that I said many years ago. And do not say that I did not tell you. You had the eyes, you had the ears to see and to hear the Word of God for many, many years. And the time I gave you is almost over. But if you want to suffer, that is your thing. But the ones who want to save themselves; they have to seek Me, for there are many who are sending out My Word with the Force of the Holy Spirit. Lets see who is going to eat, if you are going to catch the rat to eat or if the rat is going to catch you to eat? Wake-up, and hear the Words of God. Read the Bible and repent, for here comes My Son Jesus. (over)

1049. Vision given to Raymond Aguilera on 12 May 1997 at 3:45 PM.

The Lord gave me a vision of a safety pin, and in-between the safety pin wires; there was an image of a volcano. (over)

1050. Occurrence given to Raymond Aguilera on 16 May 1997.

From Prophecy #1046
Reymundo, I want you to go to Mt. Shasta and make Three Stone Altars, one to the north, one to the east, and one to the south. On these Stone Altars, I want you to pour on each Altar one pint of the best olive oil you can buy at the local store.

When I received the above Prophecy, I prayed to the Lord for a confirmation because I did not have the money for such a trip. Then within two days someone who I had never heard of sent enough money to make the Anointing trip.

After receiving the confirmation, I decided to leave on May 16. I discussed the trip with Ron Viessman and asked him if he wanted to go, but he had some class exams the following week. After discussing the trip further, we came up with the idea of having Ron follow me to Mt. Shasta on Friday, and have him return by Sunday, in this way we could use his Jeep on the dirt mountain roads around Mt. Shasta, after the Anointing the Altars. For we both knew my car was not able to get through the mountain roads to the locations that the Lord wanted Anointed. We began to prepare and left at 1:00 PM. on Friday May 16.

As with the other such trips the spiritual warfare began to increase. Even now, for several days I have been trying to type this material for the Prophecy Book, and the spiritual warfare has really increased. I wonder if Christians really know this type of spiritual warfare. For I have never heard of it taught or mentioned in churches. It seems all I ever hear in churches is your going to be blessed, your going to be blessed, but never about the reality of Satan and his forces. Oh well, lets move on.

Mt. Lassen Altar Anointed on 16 May 1997 about 4:30 PM
When we arrived at Mt. Lassen, we found the Park road up to the Mountain closed due to snow, but the area that the Lord wanted an

Anointed Altar built was open. So we collected the first stones for the first Altar and Anointed it and prayed at the site, and left for Mt. Shasta.

Mt. Shasta South Altar Anointed on 17 May 1997 at 1:00 PM

When we arrived in Mt. Shasta City we parked my car and left in Ron's Jeep, and purchased the Anointing Oil at a local store and proceeded toward the dirt mountain road (logging road). Once we arrived at the first Mt. Shasta location (South side), we had Communion and Anointed each other with oil. Then we built the Altar to the Lord out of the local stones, and Anointed it with the olive oil. For some reason I was led to photograph the Anointing Altars. As we had expected the logging road was very bad. In some areas the Jeep almost could not go through for the road was very narrow. At one point we had to build a rock bridge to cross this stream of water to get to the second location on the East side.

Mt. Shasta East Altar Anointed on 17 May 1997 at 4:00 PM

It took us about 2 1/2 hours to build the rock bridge and another half an hour to get to the second location. It did cross my mind several times. "What in the world are we doing out here?" We were pretty tired after building the rock bridge, but we built and Anointed the second Altar to the Lord on the East side of Mt. Shasta. I photographed it 6 days later on my return trip home for I had run out of film after I had photographed the first Altar on the South side of Mt. Shasta.

Mt. Shasta North Altar Anointed on 17 May 1997 at 5:00 PM.

We found the third site a side sandy road off of highway 97. We searched for stones and built the Altar on the North side of Mt. Shasta as we had done the other two sites with an opening on the top to hold the upside down bottle of Olive Oil. But at this Northern Altar the Lord instructed me to make a 6-foot Cross in the dirt in front of the Altar extending North. So I carved a large 6-foot dirt Cross with my shoe on the ground surface extending North. Then the Lord instructed me to walk around the Cross, and the Altar Three Times. So we started to walk around the Altar and Cross in a counter clockwise direction, and the Lord stopped us, and told us to walk around the Altar and Cross in a clockwise direction. After we had walked around the Altar and dirt Cross Three Times, the Lord said, "The Cross represents the Hammer that was going to be used to nail the coffin of Satan."

Then the Lord instructed me to take the bottle of Wine that we had purchased for Communion and to pour it over the image of the Cross. So I pour the whole bottle of Wine over the image of the 6-foot Cross. Then the Lord said, "The Wine represents the Seal of the Lord."

Then Ron took me back to my car and he went home, and I proceeded to Anoint Crater Lake and Mount Saint Helens as per the Lord's instructions. Since now I was in my car with some photographic film, and on the way to Crater Lake, I returned to at the northern side Altar, and photographed the Altar and Cross. For it was close and just off of Highway 97.

Crater Lake Altar Anointed on 18 May 1997 at 3:10 PM. (Sunday)

When I arrived at Crater Lake, I found most of it under snow. This made it harder for me because I could not find any stones, and wherever the ground was showing there were people everywhere. But I finally found a place and built an Altar and Anointed it next to the road. This Altar was much smaller, but I Anointed it in the same manner, in the Name of the Father, and of the Son, and of the Holy Spirit. This spot that I found was on the top rim of Crater Lake. The next stop was my sister's house for a stay over and prayer for direction for the other locations or Mountains.

19 May 1997 (Monday)

On Monday the Lord instructed me to go to Mount Saint Helens. I arrived at Mount Saint Helens late so I camped there for the night.

20 May 1997 (Tuesday)

In the early morning hours before the sun came up, the Lord SURPRISED me, and woke me up. He told me to fill my air mattress with air. (I hadn't been blowing up the air mattress, and only using it to lay my sleeping bag on it, to keep any water out that might come under my tent.) During this communication with Lord, the Lord wrote in the Spirit the name "HOOD" in capital letters, which told me to go and build an Altar at Mt. Hood. Then He wrote the letters "OK" over the words "Mt. Rainier." So now I knew, I had to go to Mt. Hood and Mt. Rainier after I Anointed the Altar at Mt. Saint Helens. This information was good because I was planning on going home after Mt. Saint Helens.

You have no idea, how hard it was for me to get my tired body out of that warm sleeping bag, and blow air into that air mattress that night, but I did it. Then I tried to get some sleep, and wondered why the Lord wanted my air mattress filled with air. I might add here, that the Lord did frighten me little for I was in a dead sleep state when He awoke me. For after replacing the front brake shoes on my car in front of my sister house that morning, and driving straight for about 5 hours, I did not expect to be awakened in the early morning hours. I'll never understand the "why" of some of these things.

Mt. Saint Helens Altar Anointed on May 20 at 12:30 PM.

At Mt. Saint Helens, I was not allowed to get any closer to the mountain than the distance we were from Altars we built around on Mt. Shasta. I hiked about .8 of mile along a trail next to a cliff facing the side of where Mt. Saint Helens blew up. I Anointed the Altar at Mt. Saint Helens at 12:30 PM and photographed the site. All of these photographs will be placed on the web site soon, I hope.

Mt. Rainier Altar Anointed at 4:55 PM.

I Anointed the Altar at Mt. Rainier high on the Volcano's southern side. I had a hard time here too finding some clear ground without snow, but I found a spot near the road.

Mt. Hood Altar Anointed on 21 May 1997 at 1:54 PM.

At Mt. Hood the ground was also covered with snow, and I had a hard time finding clear ground with some stones for the Altar, but I found a large rock over hanging a cliff off the road. So I carefully climbed on to it, and built and Anointed the Altar there. I had to be very careful for this cliff went down hundreds of feet. But over this large hanging rock the Altar was built, and I headed for home.

I was also hoping to back track for 2 hours and stop long enough to photograph the Eastern Altar at Mt. Shasta, the only Altar I had not photographed because I had run out of film. I was frightened of this because it was suppose to rain that afternoon, and I didn't have Ron's Jeep. If I got caught on those dirt logging roads during a rain, I wouldn't be able to get out until the muddy roads dried out. For no one else would be able to use the roads either. But I figured, I could get in and out in 2 hours if I didn't get lost, and getting from that side of Mt. Shasta the roads were a little better. Well two times, I almost decided to return and try to find the Highway 97 for thought I was lost, and the weather looked pretty bad. But I kept praying and praying to the Lord to help me, and He did so. I photographed the Eastern Altar and headed out for home. Praise you Lord!!!

I kept wondering while I traveled across California, Oregon, and Washington, why did the Lord need me to Anoint these places in the first place? And the only answer that even came close was, "He told me too, so I had to do it." Who really knows the Mind of God. (over)

1051. Prophecy given to Raymond Aguilera on 28 May 1997 at 6:56 PM. in Spanish.

Look My son it is not important how you look. And it is not important, that you place your photograph (web site #1050 Occurrence) in what happened. What is important is; what you did! It is not important to Me, what you look like. I know, that you believe that you are a little over weight (little fat), but to Me it is not important. People who see things like this—do not see with the eyes of God. They see with the eyes of the world. That is why, I am telling you not to place your photograph (in #1050 Occurrence); for I like what I see. Did you hear Me, Reymundo?

I know that the devil was hitting you, when you were writing about, when you went to the mountains. But this minute—the devil is crying. For he knows, and I know; what you did with the Oil. I give you My Thanks—for doing what I told you. I know, that you do not understand what happened, but it is not important if you understand it or not. What is important is; that you did it! For you have the Love of God from the top of your head to the bottom of your feet. Oh—the things We could do, if We had more soldiers, who did what I told them. But that is not important, for all will go how I said it, in My Word—to the Point! All is going to happen to the Point. Hurry—rest! I know, that you are tired. Until another day, I will call you with the Lips of God, My beloved. (over)

1052. Prophecy given to Raymond Aguilera on 30 May 1997 at 8:23 PM.

The Lord said, "Ray, the demonic attacks on this prophetic ministry are coming from the continent of Africa." (over)

1053. Prophecy given to Raymond Aguilera on 30 May 1997 at 3:53 PM.

During prayer the Lord said, "The power of the Cosa Nostra will increase in the coming months." (over)

1054. Vision given to Raymond Aguilera on 2 June 1997 at 2:37 PM.

The Lord gave me a vision of a beach, and on the brown sandy shore, there were piles and piles of dead baby pigs. These pigs were pink in color. (over)

1055. Prophecy given to Raymond Aguilera on 2 June 1997 at 11:45 PM. in Spanish.

Africa has the cannon of the devil. Africa—did you hear me, Reymundo? Africa has the cannon of the devil. (over)

1056. Prophecy given to Raymond Aguilera on 8 June 1997 at 3 AM.

The Lord said, "Come, come—come to My Holy Hill, My Holy Mountain—come. Come to My Holy Mountain and build Me an Altar and Anoint it with Oil." Holy Ground. Holy Ground. (over)

Comments:
The Lord meant Mt. Zion.

1057. Prophecy given to Raymond Aguilera on 10 June 1997 at 4:15 AM.

Then the Lord said, "Pennies from Heaven." (over)

1058. Vision given to Raymond Aguilera on 12 June 1997 at 2:16 PM.

I was given a vision of a plumb bob, with the plumb line extending from the top with a Gold Ring going through the plumb line. (over)

1059. Prophecy given to Raymond Aguilera on 13 June 1997.

The Lord gave me Chapter One of the Book of Zephaniah:
From KJV Bible:
Zep 1:1 The word of the LORD which came unto Zephaniah the son of Cushi, the son of Gedaliah, the son of Amariah, the son of Hizkiah, in the days of Josiah the son of Amon, king of Judah.
Zep 1:2 I will utterly consume all things from off the land, saith the LORD.
Zep 1:3 I will consume man and beast; I will consume the fowls of the heaven, and the fishes of the sea, and the stumblingblocks with the wicked; and I will cut off man from off the land, saith the LORD.
Zep 1:4 I will also stretch out mine hand upon Judah, and upon all the inhabitants of Jerusalem; and I will cut off the remnant of Baal from this place, and the name of the Chemarims with the priests;
Zep 1:5 And them that worship the host of heaven upon the housetops; and them that worship and that swear by the LORD, and that swear by Malcham;
Zep 1:6 And them that are turned back from the LORD; and those that have not sought the LORD, nor inquired for him.
Zep 1:7 Hold thy peace at the presence of the Lord GOD: for the day of the LORD is at hand: for the LORD hath prepared a sacrifice, he hath bid his guests.
Zep 1:8 And it shall come to pass in the day of the LORD'S sacrifice, that I will punish the princes, and the king's children, and all such as are clothed with strange apparel.
Zep 1:9 In the same day also will I punish all those that leap on the threshold, which fill their masters' houses with violence and deceit.
Zep 1:10 And it shall come to pass in that day, saith the LORD, that there shall be the noise of a cry from the fish gate, and an howling from the second, and a great crashing from the hills.

Zep 1:11 Howl, ye inhabitants of Maktesh, for all the merchant people are cut down; all they that bear silver are cut off.

Zep 1:12 And it shall come to pass at that time, that I will search Jerusalem with candles, and punish the men that are settled on their lees: that say in their heart, The LORD will not do good, neither will he do evil.

Zep 1:13 Therefore their goods shall become a booty, and their houses a desolation: they shall also build houses, but not inhabit them; and they shall plant vineyards, but not drink the wine thereof.

Zep 1:14 The great day of the LORD is near, it is near, and hasteth greatly, even the voice of the day of the LORD: the mighty man shall cry there bitterly.

Zep 1:15 That day is a day of wrath, a day of trouble and distress, a day of wasteness and desolation, a day of darkness and gloominess, a day of clouds and thick darkness,

Zep 1:16 A day of the trumpet and alarm against the fenced cities, and against the high towers.

Zep 1:17 And I will bring distress upon men, that they shall walk like blind men, because they have sinned against the LORD: and their blood shall be poured out as dust, and their flesh as the dung.

Zep 1:18 Neither their silver nor their gold shall be able to deliver them in the day of the LORD'S wrath; but the whole land shall be devoured by the fire of his jealousy: for he shall make even a speedy riddance of all them that dwell in the land.

(over)

1060. Prophecy given to Raymond Aguilera on 14 June 1997 at 1:45 AM. in Spanish.

You know what? You know what? You have to hear Me, for the time has now arrived, the time of the computer, the time you have to use the Mind of God. For all of the Words I have given you, and you have written on your computer are going to live in the hearts of My Sheep. That is why, I want you to buy a new one (computer). I do not care how much it costs you. For everything belongs to God. I know that you believe, that it is a lot of money, but you have to remember—that everything belongs to Me, and I am going to tell you more of the things of the end.

For I know that you are frightened—where I am going to send you, but do not worry Reymundo! All will go well, and to the Point. I will show you when you arrive—the things of God, in the place that My Son walked. I know that your heart is radiating. Your heart is radiating, for I am sending you there. But We have to shut this Book in this world, of the things of the devil, of the things of God, ALL to the Point.

I know the map, and I will POINT you where to go. And I am going to tell people, your brothers and sisters, to send you more money. For I am going to move more DIRECTLY, and more POINTED. For I am going to move this world up and down, and from one side to another with the Force of the Holy Spirit. It has arrived the Hammer of God! (over)

1061. Vision given to Raymond Aguilera on 14 June 1997.

I see a vision, but I do not know how to explain it, but the Lord is showing me a virus. It starts off with the shape of a flower, and the Lord is telling me that it is going to go all over the world.

1062. Occurrence given to Raymond Aguilera on 14 June 1997.

The spiritual warfare has really increased in the past week. One early morning before the sun came up, I was awaken with a strong pain in my chest. I felt like I was going to have a heart attack. I was really frightened, so I began to pray to the Lord for help. Slowly, but surely the pain left. I hate those kinds of attacks, but the Lord always removes them. Then, the next two days, after awaking from my afternoon nap, I felt like I was hit with a sledge hammer in the middle of my back. And the other day on the way home from the Post Office, I could feel the Angels of God, and the angels of the devil fiercely fighting around the outside of my car. What ever is going on, I seem to be in the middle of it or in the middle of something. (over)

1063. Vision given to Raymond Aguilera on 15 June 1997 at 11:30 PM.

During prayer, the Lord showed me a vision of some sort of stand. It had the shape of a horseshoe with the opening facing up. On top of the two horse shoe ends, I could see two probes facing each other. And in-between these two probes there was an enormous ball of light or energy. Then the Lord impressed it on my spirit that in-between the probes, this ball of light or energy, was the whole universe, EVERYTHING that EXISTS was that energy looking cloud or ball of light!

1064. Vision given to Raymond Aguilera on 16 June 1997 at 8:45 PM.

During worship, the Lord gave me a vision of a Door, and this Door had a large brass looking doorknob and lock. As I watched the lock, this thin handle Key was placed in the Key Hole and the Key was turned. (over)

1065. Vision given to Raymond Aguilera on 23 June 1997.

The Lord gave me a vision of Three Whirlwinds spinning at the same point on the ground.

1066. Prophecy given to Raymond Aguilera on 23 June 1997 at 6:56 AM. in English.

I am, Reymundo! I am what you see; what you touch. Everything that is; that was; that is going to be. The Ark will be established again. Like I told you earlier in another Prophecy, but remember the beast. The anti-Christ will be established as I told you earlier in another Prophecy too.

I can feel your anxiety of going to Israel. I can sense your doubt. I can sense your strengths. I can sense your amazement. But look, just do as I say, and everything will be done at the right time, at the right place. I have chosen you to open the Door to the next event that will happen in the spirit world. The human mind cannot comprehend or understand what you are about to do. But All the Power, All the Forces of the universe are going to be watching what you do, on that day, on that hour, at that minute. You will sense some things that you have never sensed before, but trust Me. All will go right! All will go well! For the Hand of Jehovah is upon you through the Power of the Holy Spirit, through the Power of My Son, Jesus Christ of Nazareth.

I will send All the money, All the strength that you need in the coming months, in the coming years. You will never understand while you are alive; what you will do or what you have been doing. But that is of no consequence, the important thing is that you OBEY! I know things are hard. I know you are bewildered, but I—My Son, and the Holy Spirit are with you every step of the way. I know—I know you are concerned about your health—I know! But do not worry for all will go well. I have not forgotten your promises, and I have not forgotten Mine. You will sense the Power of the battle between Good and evil, but My Heavenly Angels will make a path wide and straight to the appointed place of the anointed altar. Nothing will happen that was not destined to happen. Remember the Ark. Remember the Ark, the Ark of My Covenant. Remember the Ark. So be it. So be it. So be it. (over)

1067. Vision given to Raymond Aguilera on 26 June 1997 at 5:52 PM.

The Lord gave me a vision of a bull's head. All I could see was the top of the bull's head as the bull moved from the west toward the east. The left horn of the bull caught my attention, for it was all black, except for a burgundy-red band with a white strip on each side of the burgundy-red color. (over)

1068. Prophecy given to Raymond Aguilera on 29 June 1997 at 6:52 PM in Spanish.

The Lord said, "Cosa Nostra, Cosa Nostra, the Cosa Nostra is agria (Spanish word: "Agria"—sour, bitter, disagreeable). The Cosa Nostra is agria. (over)

1069. Prophecy given to Raymond Aguilera on 29 June 1997 at 7:23 in English.

The big battle, the battle of Armageddon will be fought will be won by the Lord of Lords, the King of Kings. Push the button, and you will see the Power of God. Remember push the button, and you will see the Power of God, the Maker the Breaker of the universe; the One that was—that is, and will always be.

The Day of Glory has come. The Day of Vengeance has come. The Day of Days is here.

Open your Bibles and read about the Power of your God from the beginning to the end. For as the Lighting strikes from the west, and is seen from the north, from south, from the east, from the west; so shall it be—instantaneous the Power of Jehovah, the Power of Jesus Christ of Nazareth, the Power of the Holy Spirit.

If you want to save yourself open the Bible and read. Point everything you have toward My Son Jesus Christ of Nazareth, and you will find the Father, the POWER OF POWER, the GLORY OF GLORY. Through the Power of the Holy Spirit you will be saved.

Remember have Communion, Repent your sins, look-out for your brothers and sisters, and you will find the Glory of Glories, the Maker, the Breaker of the universe; Who has the Heart; Who is the Love of Love.

Vengeance is Mine, saith the Lord. Vengeance is Mine, saith the Lord. Vengeance is Mine, saith the Lord. So be it! So be it! So be it! (over)

Vision

I had a vision of a nuclear smoke stack. As I watched the large round smoke stack, the smoke stack opening reduced in size, and the image changed into a volcano. (over)

Nuclear smoke shack changed into volcano.

1070. Prophecy given to Raymond Aguilera on 8 July 1997 at 8:15 AM.

The Lord gave me the scriptures from the Book of Ezekiel, Chapter 7.

From the KJV Bible:

Ezek 7:1 Moreover the word of the LORD came unto me, saying,

Ezek 7:2 Also, thou son of man, thus saith the Lord GOD unto the land of Israel; An end, the end is come upon the four corners of the land.

Ezek 7:3 Now is the end come upon thee, and I will send mine anger upon thee, and will judge thee according to thy ways, and will recompense upon thee all thine abominations.

Ezek 7:4 And mine eye shall not spare thee, neither will I have pity: but I will recompense thy ways upon thee, and thine abominations shall be in the midst of thee: and ye shall know that I am the LORD.

Ezek 7:5 Thus saith the Lord GOD; An evil, an only evil, behold, is come.

Ezek 7:6 An end is come, the end is come: it watcheth for thee; behold, it is come.

Ezek 7:7 The morning is come unto thee, O thou that dwellest in the land: the time is come, the day of trouble is near, and not the sounding again of the mountains.

Ezek 7:8 Now will I shortly pour out my fury upon thee, and accomplish mine anger upon thee: and I will judge thee according to thy ways, and will recompense thee for all thine abominations.

Ezek 7:9 And mine eye shall not spare, neither will I have pity: I will recompense thee according to thy ways and thine abominations that are in the midst of thee; and ye shall know that I am the LORD that smiteth.

Ezek 7:10 Behold the day, behold, it is come: the morning is gone forth; the rod hath blossomed, pride hath budded.

Ezek 7:11 Violence is risen up into a rod of wickedness: none of them shall remain, nor of their multitude, nor of any of theirs: neither shall there be wailing for them.

Ezek 7:12 The time is come, the day draweth near: let not the buyer rejoice, nor the seller mourn: for wrath is upon all the multitude thereof.

Ezek 7:13 For the seller shall not return to that which is sold, although they were yet alive: for the vision is touching the whole multitude thereof, which shall not return; neither shall any strengthen himself in the iniquity of his life.

Ezek 7:14 They have blown the trumpet, even to make all ready; but none goeth to the battle: for my wrath is upon all the multitude thereof.

Ezek 7:15 The sword is without, and the pestilence and the famine within: he that is in the field shall die with the sword; and he that is in the city, famine and pestilence shall devour him.

Ezek 7:16 But they that escape of them shall escape, and shall be on the mountains like doves of the valleys, all of them mourning, every one for his iniquity.

Ezek 7:17 All hands shall be feeble, and all knees shall be weak as water.

Ezek 7:18 They shall also gird themselves with sackcloth, and horror shall cover them; and shame shall be upon all faces, and baldness upon all their heads.

Ezek 7:19 They shall cast their silver in the streets, and their gold shall be removed: their silver and their gold shall not be able to deliver them in the day of the wrath of the LORD: they shall not satisfy their souls, neither fill their bowels: because it is the stumblingblock of their iniquity.

Ezek 7:20 As for the beauty of his ornament, he set it in majesty: but they made the images of their abominations and of their detestable things therein: therefore have I set it far from them.

Ezek 7:21 And I will give it into the hands of the strangers for a prey, and to the wicked of the earth for a spoil; and they shall pollute it.

Ezek 7:22 My face will I turn also from them, and they shall pollute my secret place: for the robbers shall enter into it, and defile it.

Ezek 7:23 Make a chain: for the land is full of bloody crimes, and the city is full of violence.

Ezek 7:24 Wherefore I will bring the worst of the heathen, and they shall possess their houses: I will also make the pomp of the strong to cease; and their holy places shall be defiled.

Ezek 7:25 Destruction cometh; and they shall seek peace, and there shall be none.

Ezek 7:26 Mischief shall come upon mischief, and rumour shall be upon rumour; then shall they seek a vision of the prophet; but the law shall perish from the priest, and counsel from the ancients.
Ezek 7:27 The king shall mourn, and the prince shall be clothed with desolation, and the hands of the people of the land shall be troubled: I will do unto them after their way, and according to their deserts will I judge them; and they shall know that I am the LORD.

1071. Prophecy given to Raymond Aguilera on 13 July 1997 at 9:55 AM. in Spanish.

The White House is of the heart of the devil. Hear Me! Hear Me! If you have your eyes clean, and you can see clearly; you are going to know of the things of the White House are of the heart of the devil. The White House changed many years ago. At one point in time they sought, and looked for God, but on this day, on this date, they have the heart of the devil. They do not look for the things of God. They do not want to hear the things of God. The men of the White House, they only think of the things they have; the things that they want. They do not have the Mind of God, and they do not WANT the Mind of God.

Hear Me! Hear Me! The things that I tell you are the truth—they are clear! I know, the DATE, that is going to come with the Force of God, and they will not be able to save themselves. For what I say, is going to happen to the point. The people of the White House are blind, and they believe they can save themselves with the force of man. But the force of man is NOTHING for here comes the Day of God with the Force of God!

Here comes the day, Reymundo—that the Words you have written are going to be on the minds of all the world with the Force of God. There are people who are going to get mad. There are going to be people that are going to have joy; for they are going to see with the Eyes of God at the things of God. I know that these past weeks have been very hard, but I told you, I was going to give you the money for the taxes, and now that you have paid them. You can go to the mountain of God, with the Force of God. I tell you clearly and I tell you to the point. On that Day, on that minute, that you place the OIL on top of the Rocks of God, the things of the Spirit are going to change with the Force of God.

I know that you are still frightened of the things that have happened, but ALL that I have told you in the past years are going to happen. I am going to give you the wife, I am going to give you the money, I am going to give you the Mind of God. I am going to give you the Force of God to the point. All the things of the world are going to change. All the things of Heaven are going to change. Do not worry, all will go well. All will go to the point. Remember, all that you need; I am going to give you. All of the world is going to change. All of Heaven is going to change. All is written in the Bible to the point.

I liked the way you did the (Prophecy) Book. I am going to send people to help you send the Book with the Force of God, but the war around you is going to become higher. But do not worry, for you are in My Hands. Did you hear Me? With the Force of God, the Father, the Son Jesus, and the Holy Spirit, I tell you the things of Heaven.

Remember—nothing good comes from the White House; nothing good comes all the governments of the world. For no one seeks the God, Who made the world, the stars, all that you see, all that you touch. They do not seek Me with the Heart of God. But this is all that I am going to tell you this minute at this date. Hurry, write what I have told you, and send it with the Force of God. (over)

1072. Prophecy given to Raymond Aguilera on 14 July 1997 at 9:30 AM.

This morning, I prayed to the Lord about my Israel Mount Zion Anointing trip. I asked the Lord to show me in the Bible something about this mission trip. So I opened my new Bible, and it opened to the Book of Micah, and the Lord led me to Chapter 4.

From the KJV:
Micah 4:1 But in the last days it shall come to pass, that the mountain of the house of the LORD shall be established in the top of the mountains, and it shall be exalted above the hills; and people shall flow unto it.

Micah 4:2 And many nations shall come, and say, Come, and let us go up to the mountain of the LORD, and to the house of the God of Jacob; and he will teach us of his ways, and we will walk in his paths: for the law shall go forth of Zion, and the word of the LORD from Jerusalem.

Micah 4:3 And he shall judge among many people, and rebuke strong nations afar off; and they shall beat their swords into plowshares, and their spears into pruninghooks: nation shall not lift up a sword against nation, neither shall they learn war any more.

Micah 4:4 But they shall sit every man under his vine and under his fig tree; and none shall make them afraid: for the mouth of the LORD of hosts hath spoken it.

Micah 4:5 For all people will walk every one in the name of his god, and we will walk in the name of the LORD our God for ever and ever.

Micah 4:6 In that day, saith the LORD, will I assemble her that halteth, and I will gather her that is driven out, and her that I have afflicted;

Micah 4:7 And I will make her that halted a remnant, and her that was cast far off a strong nation: and the LORD shall reign over them in mount Zion from henceforth, even for ever.

Micah 4:8 And thou, O tower of the flock, the strong hold of the daughter of Zion, unto thee shall it come, even the first dominion; the kingdom shall come to the daughter of Jerusalem.

1073. Prophecy given to Raymond Aguilera on 17 July 1997 at 1:30 PM. in English.

The Lord said, "The media, the movie makers, are going to want you to look to outer space, for other Beings, they call them Aliens. What I am telling you is—Do not look to outer space—look to inner space, for that is where they are. The spirit demons, the things that are not of God, the things that will destroy you. So look to the Bible; look to Jesus Christ of Nazareth; look to the Father; through the Power, through the Eyes of the Holy Spirit—you will find Heaven. Listen to My Words–Clearly and to the Point: Inner space, inner space, inner space—is where the devil is. So be it. So be it. So be it." (over)

1074. Prophecy given to Raymond Aguilera on 22 July 1997 at 8:04 AM. in English.

Who are those who come against you My son? Who are those who confront you, who blaspheme the Name of the Lord by their wicked ways? Who are those who dare confront the Lord; God Jehovah, Jesus Christ, and the Holy Spirit, with their evil manners, their evil thoughts? Stand firm My son, for you are on the side of righteousness. Be bold, be strong, for the hour is approaching that My Son will appear on the eastern sky with the Power and the Might of Heaven, with the Power and the Might of the Throne of God.

Who are these people who dare confront their God with the words of the devil, the serpent, the dragon of the pit? Mark My Words—nothing in the universe will stop Jehovah. Nothing that man can do or think—or plan, will have anyway of affecting the Word of God. What the Lord has said will happen to the Point, to the Letter.

Be strong, be brave, for the Power of the Holy Spirit is around you! The Power of the Holy Angels will protect you. The Power of My Word, which is ABSOLUTE! Be brave, be strong for here comes the King of Kings, the Lord of Lords, to clean, to correct all that is dirty, all that is filthy, all that is of the pit. Who DARES! Who dares to confront The God Jehovah. Have him step forward, and We will see who will be left standing! Who DARES!!! So be it! So be it! So be it! (over)

1075. Prophecy given to Raymond Aguilera on 22 July 1997 at 8:20 AM.

The Lord gave the scripture from the Book of Matthew 6:12.

From the KJV Bible:
Mat 6:12 And forgive us our debts, as we forgive our debtors. (over)

1076. Prophecy given to Raymond Aguilera on 25 July 1997 at 4 AM. in Spanish.

It fell the "posta" (Spanish word) fell. Yes, here—the "posta" fell. Yes, it has arrived the flame. It has arrived. If you open your eyes, I will show you the things of God with the Force of God. It has arrived—the entire Bible; all of God to the point. The hammer has arrived, and the box has arrived. The tears of the world have arrived.

The whole world believes they know it all, but I, the Father, with the Son, with the Force of the Holy Spirit, I am going to show everyone, with My Word, with My Force—the Hand of God. Yes—the Chicken is ready for the knife. And the knife is at the neck of the Chicken.

The world does not believe in God. The world is going to see the Force of God. The birds are going to eat the flesh, the meat of the ones who do not believe. With the Force of the Holy Spirit, I am telling you the truth. ALL—exactly to the point, I am telling you the truth. I am not playing a game. These things are exactly to the point, with the Force of God, I tell you the truth.

All is going to stop in one minute. All are going to get frightened at that same minute. When they see My Son, with all of the Angels, with the Force of the Holy Spirit, fighting for the things that are His. And I know—for I gave it all to Him. For what is Mine, I can give away. Hurry—sleep and rest, Reymundo, we have started the Word of God.

1077. Prophecy given to Raymond Aguilera on 25 July 1997 at 5:30 AM. in Spanish.

It is I, My son. It is I. Why is it that you cannot sleep (Reymundo)? Go on rest! We have things to do. You have to make yourself pointed (focused). You have to make yourself strong. Come on—rest, for the New Day has arrived, the Day of God. Come on—rest! For the things of God have arrived. Yes, yes, yes. (over)

1078. Vision given to Raymond Aguilera on 25 July 1997 at 6 AM.

The Lord gave me the same vision He gave on:

728. Vision given to Raymond Aguilera on 20 May 1995 at 7:30 PM
I had a vision of a upside down fish, surrounded by a pink cloud or some sort of pink fog. The top of the tail was showing, but the body of the fish was hidden in the cloud.

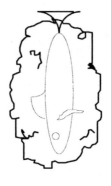

(over)

1079. Vision given to Raymond Aguilera on 25 July 1997 at 6 AM.

The Lord showed me the twenty-four chairs of the twenty-four elders from the Book of Revelation. But the chairs were not yet filled. (over)

From the KJV Bible:
Rev 4:4 And round about the throne were four and twenty seats: and upon the seats I saw four and twenty elders sitting, clothed in white raiment; and they had on their heads crowns of gold.

1080. Prophecy given to Raymond Aguilera on 25 July 1997 at 6 AM.

The Lord gave me a Word for someone who lives in Australia. He or she is on our e-mail list. I do not know who it is, but he or she sent some money to cover some of the expenses for this Israel mission trip.

The Lord said, "I am going to bless you, and I LOVE YOU!" (over)

Comments:
On this man or woman from Australia, the Lord somehow showed me His Love for this person. It was so BEAUTIFUL, PURE, AND CLEAN; it made me want to cry. This event was indescribable. (over)

1081. Prophecy given to Raymond Aguilera on 25 July 1997 at 6 AM.

This Prophecy came in Non-understandable Tongues.

1082. Prophecy given to Raymond Aguilera on 25 July 1997 at 6:30 AM. in English.

The mark of the beast will be implemented with force. (over)

1083. Prophecy given to Raymond Aguilera on 26 July 1997 at 1:45 AM. in English.

Just because the rabbit can go in his hole and hide, does not mean I do not know where he is at! You sinners, you pagans, you idol worshippers, you satan worshippers, your time has come! The day of vengeance is here! So saith Jehovah! You were warned, and you were warned, and you closed your eyes and your ears and you denied My Presence! You denied My Word. So by that Word, you will be Judged without mercy.

The End is upon you! The Hour, the Time will not be reveled until it is to late! It will be upon you like a thief in the night. So you were warned again! By the Power of the Holy Spirit, through My prophet, Reymundo, through the Prophets of the Bible, through the Word of My Son, Jesus Christ of Nazareth. Beware! For the fox can find rabbits and Jehovah, Jesus Christ of Nazareth, and the Holy Spirit can find you. (over)

1084. Vision given to Raymond Aguilera on 26 July 1997 at 3:30 AM.

I see an image of Jesus Christ walking behind a light complexioned man with reddish-brown hair, and kind of balding on the top, with a mustache. This man is somewhere in his forty's. (over)

1085. Occurrence given to Raymond Aguilera on 26 July 1997 at 2:53 PM.

The Anointing of Mount Zion:
I awoke early this morning, and the Lord instructed me to thoroughly wash myself, and to Anoint myself with the same bottle of Olive Oil I purchased the day before. He instructed me to Anoint myself, on the forehead, hands, and both feet in the Name of the Father Jehovah, Jesus Christ, and the Holy Spirit. Then He told me everything would go well.

This morning our tour group was going out early. We planned to cover the old town of Jerusalem. And we would end up going through Mount Zion. I prayed to myself the whole day for instructions on where, and how to Anoint Mount Zion. The Lord kept me uninformed the whole day. Since the Lord was not saying anything. I just figured He wanted Mount Zion Anointed the next day, since I had a free day to do what ever I wanted.

Well, we were coming to the end of the Mount Zion area. And still the Lord was silent. I had my Anointing Oil in my pocket, and my camera ready to photograph the site. Then, when our tour guide said we were heading for the tour bus, I began to get nervous! For one thing, there weren't many rocks around to gather, and there were many people around looking at everything! I had noticed what I thought was a rest room, and since Jerusalem was very hot, and we were all drinking a lot of water, I asked the tour guide if I could go to the rest room before I got on the bus. I was hoping the Lord would show me the Anointing Site with some stones before we left Mount Zion!

Anna the tour guide said, "Yes, if you really need to."

And for some reason, I handed her my camera, and left running for the rest room. I could not find the rest room I had seen earlier, and I hurriedly began to pray to the Lord for the location, and the day of the Anointing.

Then my brain went into gear, "You stupid person! Where is your camera? You dummy." I said to myself!

So I concluded, the next day was the day of the Anointing of Mount Zion. But I kept praying in the Name of the Father, the Son Jesus Christ, and the Holy Spirit—to tell me what to do! I knew everyone was on the bus by now, and waiting for me, so I headed back. Then, I saw a group of stones on the ground, on a clean and well kept area. Then I knew that was the place for the Anointing! I didn't know how I knew, but I KNEW that was the Anointing site.

So quickly into my pocket my hand went. Out came the Anointing Oil, and within thirty seconds, the stones and ground was Anointed. I could not believe how fast the whole thing went! Then as I threw the empty bottle of Oil onto the Oiled stones and ground, I began to feel guilty. For I remembered, I did not have my camera to photograph the Anointed site. All that kept going through my mind was, all the months, money, and film for that moment in time, and it was lost. In my heart I felt so bad, and sad, and I guess my heart tried to apologize to the Lord for failing Him.

When I reached the bus people were still trying to settle in. And Anna looked at me and said, "That was quick!"

But all that was on my mind was that I had to rent a cab tomorrow, and come back with my camera.

Once everyone got settled on the bus, Anna said she had a special treat for us, and asked if we wanted to see the Garden of Gethsemane. That location wasn't on our tour. But she asked us if we wanted to go. Everyone said in a loud "Yes!" And off we went. I was happy to go to Gethsemane, but my mind was still back at Mount Zion.

The Garden of Gethsemane is a beautiful little place with olive trees, and a church on the grounds. Once our lecture on the church, and the grounds was over, we were release to explore. I felt so bad. I could of cried thinking about how stupid I was in giving my camera to Anna. I kept telling myself over and over—tomorrow I'll get a cab, and come back, and photograph the Anointing site. I went inside the church and began to pray, and apologize to the Lord for failing him. Then during the prayer the Lord spoke and said, "No, you do not have to go back, and photograph the Anointing site. Not all things and locations were meant to be shown. Now, I release you—go, and enjoy yourself and have a good time the rest of the trip."

I Anointed Mount Zion on 26 July 1997 at 2:53 PM., and I finally realized it was the Lord who made me give Anna my camera. I will say it again—I will never understand why the Lord does certain things. (over)

1086. Prophecy given to Raymond Aguilera on 26 July 1997 at 8:17 PM.

Mister Juan Lopez, and Peter Sanchez, from Argentina. The Lord says, "Be careful, be righteous and the Lord will be with you. For the cross that you bear will be lifted, but you must stay in prayer, and you must seek righteousness in the mind, and your spirit will reveal your blessing in the coming months, in the coming years." (over)

1087. Occurrence given to Raymond Aguilera on 27 July 1997 at 3:30 AM.

On Sunday evening I prayed, and stayed up late watching television, until I could not keep my eyes open. I had been feeling very old and lonely these past few months with all of this traveling, camping in tents, and sleeping on the cold hard ground, and not really understanding why except that I was order too by the Lord. And now here I am half way around the world, in Israel, wondering, "Why"? Then I started to wonder. When was the Lord going to give me that special woman, and wondering if it was my friend from many years ago, I remembered looking into the mirror a few days ago, and not liking what I saw. All I could see, was one tired fat numb old man, (though I don't really believe I am old), seeking God, with a HUNGER that my flesh could not understand.

After taking a deep breath, I tried to focus and began to pray. I said to the Lord, "Where I am going to find this special partner you have been telling me about all of these years? For if I was a woman, I wouldn't want me. And look at my hair or what is left of it. It is all white. And most people think I am nuts, and should be locked up! So Lord, since there is no one here but you and I—please give more hair and a righteous woman who can help me through this crazy Christian walk! (I guess after writing this, I am not alone anymore.)" So after my other nightly prayers—for the people on the e-mail list, family, friends, and people who are seriously sick, I fell asleep.

Then during the early morning hours, I was suddenly awakened. I was sleeping on my back with my hands at my side, and this incredible force bound my hands and paralyzed my body to the bed. All that ran through my mind was—"Lord—I am in trouble. Something has me frozen to the bed. HELP ME!!!" No matter how hard I tried to move my body, my body would not move. What was so strange, I kept having this image of Daniel. When the Angel of the Lord appeared to him, and he fell down on his face in fear—this kept running through my mind.

I felt a woman's hands holding my two wrists. I also felt this peace. The whole room was filled with this incredible power. I still did not know if this presence was friend or foe. But I could feel the smallness of the two hands that were holding my wrists. And I could not see anyone.

So I asked, "Who is this?"

And a voice said with power and authority, "This is Ruth."

At first I did not know if it was a demonic force, or some Angel named, Ruth. I struggle at first for I was so startled. Then Ruth of the Bible came to my mind or my spirit. I do not know which. Also, slowly I was able to raise both my hands, with these spiritual woman's hands holding on to my wrists.

So I said to myself, "If this is Ruth I can say, I love Jesus, I love Jesus, I love Jesus?"

So I began to praise the Lord Jesus Christ of Nazareth, over and over. So with both my hands raised in the spirit, I began to wave them, and I kept praising, and moving, and waving them into the air, with Ruth's hands holding my wrists. I could also feel this heat, or warmth come upon my body. Just as suddenly as they appeared they disappeared, and my hands fell back to the bed. This really scared me!

But all I can say, "I love you Jesus Christ of Nazareth. I give you all the praise and the honor, and the glory—Now and forever and ever. Amen."

Comments:

I remembered that I had prayed earlier to the Lord about my old feeling body and my white hair. Well, two interesting things happened when I got home. My mother called me early Sunday morning to see if I got back safe and she told me she had a VERY, VERY vivid dream during my Israel mission trip. She told me that one night she had this dream of seeing me in my twenties and that I looked very young. She said what caught her attention was my hair—That I had such a full head of very black hair, with a big wave on one side. That—then she knew I was safe from the bombing they had in Jerusalem. She said it was so real that she awoke my dad and told him her dream, and that she could not go back to sleep that evening.

Then when I was home my brother Ted came over and late that same evening we were talking, and he said, "You know Ray, I had a vivid dream when you were in Israel. I saw you in this dream and you were a little baby, and someone was holding you in his arms, but what was so unusual; you had a full head of dark brown hair with a wave to one side. The dream was so realistic it woke me up." What are the odds of two people having the same kind of dream.

A short note my daughter Cynthia gave me after reading my comments notes.

July27, 1997 at 8:00 AM

My father (Ray) telephoned me, direct from Israel, to inform me that there had been two bombings in Israel a few hours earlier. He told me that I would hear about it from the news media sometime that evening. He also told me that he had been at the place where the bombs went off, and had left that bombed area two days prior.

That morning, I phoned my grandmother to let her know that my father (Ray) was okay, and not to worry, because the news media was informing the world about the bombing. My father was concerned that the news would give my Grandmother grief.

When my Grandmother and I were talking that morning, she told me that she had a clear dream of my father, the night before. My Grandmother told me in her dream that she told my father, that she was very worried about him leaving the country. Ray (my father) told her (in her dream) not to worry Mother, I am okay I'll be fine. I m here for you. Please don't worry. I am coming home. (My Grandmother told me that his looks were like when he was young, when he was newly married to my mother). She was shocked to see him so young. And his hair was very dark. After her dream, she felt much better. And her dream gave her great comfort. (She told me this in her own words).

1088. Vision given to Raymond Aguilera on 27 July 1997 at 3:45 AM.

I saw a vision of a dark black hill or a mountain with a hole on top of it, with a river of flowing bones, skulls, and arms. They were bleach white, and coming out of the top of the hill. (over)

1089. Vision:

I kept having all kind of visions and things I do not understand. I had a vision of this white cross, and it was stuck into the ground upside down at an angle of 45 degrees. And this cave or the ground opened, and this white light came out, and the cross was forced in the ground upside down. (over)

I can also see this large hole in the ground. It is much larger than a well hole. It looks like it is 50 feet in diameter. And in the center of this large hole I could see the Star of David. Now I see a rope extending down towards the hole.

1090. Vision:

A vision of some cast Iron gears. On the side of gear teeth there was a fish. At first I thought the fish was moving the gears, but it wasn't. The fish was just on the side of the gears. (over)

1091. Vision:

Now I see this large round black kettle full of water and on top of the water there is a black cross. This kettle reminds me of those large black kettles they use in cartoons where they place people inside and cooked and ate them. (over)

1092. Vision:

I see a pole in a vertical position and it has a cross on top. It reminds me of a street sign with the street names on top. (over)

1093. Vision:

Now I see a vision of a woman from the eighteen hundreds, and a sword splits her in half from the forehead down to her feet. And now I see a lit White candle in-between the two pieces.

1094. Vision:

Now I see the words "Swords into plowshares" from Isaiah 2:4. (over)

1095. Vision:

A vision of an elephant stepping on a high platform with it's two back legs on the ground, and one front leg on the platform and the forth on top of a golden tea pot. (over)

1096. Vision:

I see a saucer shape with a black candleholder underneath with a lit candle. And the Candle was heating up the saucer shape as it moved from side to side over the flame. (over)

Comment:
The sun is coming up I better get some sleep. (over)

1097. Vision given to Raymond Aguilera on 28 July 1997 at 1:20 AM.

The Lord gave me some kind of letters that looks like this:

The Lord gave me the letters Z and C, but the two letters were touching. (over)

The Lord gave me the Greek letter π. (over)

1098. Prophecy given to Raymond Aguilera on 28 July 1997 at 1:20 AM.

The Lord said, "The turtle's head will be cut off." (over)

1099. Vision given to Raymond Aguilera on 28 July 1997 at 1:20 AM.

A vision of an egg standing on it's point with blue and white rings around it. (over)

1100. Vision given to Raymond Aguilera on 28 July 1997 at 1:20 AM.

A vision of some kind of musical horn, and on the end of it; it has a black plug. When the black plug is removed the musical horn is polished. (over)

1101. Vision given to Raymond Aguilera on 28 July 1997 at 1:20 AM.

I saw a vision of a large area of darkness. It was ALL black except for a pinhole of White.

1102. Occurrence given to Raymond Aguilera on 28 July 1997 at 4:15 AM.

I was praying and praising the Lord, telling Him that I was nothing, and that He was everything, and I repeated it and repeated it. Then this Power; I do not know—this lifting Force came into the Hotel room. It felt like—it was shaking the bed in the real world, and in the spiritual world, at the same time. I felt myself spinning and elevating higher, higher, and higher in the spirit someplace. Then the Lord started showing me, people and places, that I have never seen before. Then He told me, these places are going to be destroyed. Then next thing I knew—I was back on top of my bed. (over)

1103. Prophecy given to Raymond Aguilera on 28 July 1997 at 4:30 AM.

The Lord said, "My Hand goes straight to Israel." (over)

1104. Occurrence given to Raymond Aguilera 29 July 1997 at 10:36 PM.

I was laying in bed and something grabbed my left foot and would not let me go. I bound it, and ordered it to leave in the Name of Jesus Christ. What was so unusual was that I was not in my Hotel room, I was somewhere else in the spirit. I cannot explain it other than that. (over)

1105. Vision given to Raymond Aguilera on 30 July 1997 at 3:25AM.

The Lord gave me a vision of a shuttlecock that is used in badminton except the image of the planet earth was the end of the shuttlecock. (over)

1106. Vision given to Raymond Aguilera on 30 July 1997 at 5:03 AM.

I saw a vision of Three Horses pulling one Chariot.

1107. Prophecy given to Raymond Aguilera on 3 August 1997 at 5:20 PM. in English.

My People of Israel—listen to My Words. This is your God, the Father of Abraham, the Father of Isaac, the Father of Jacob. Why! Why do you do such ungodly things before My Eyes? Many of you claim to know—God. Many of you claim to know—the Word of God. WHY! Doesn't the scriptures say you shouldn't make an Altar of stone worked by man's hands. And yet for years and years, I have watched you pray at the Wailing Wall, and you place your little prayers, your little notes in-between the stones. What foolishness! Don't you know the Word of God? How the Altar of God should be made! Why do you do such blasphemous things?

You have created an Altar using the ways of man. You pray to a stone wall, which can do nothing. You say you are waiting for the Messiah, yet you do not follow the Laws of God! So—I am telling you this minute, this second—STOP YOUR FOOLISHNESS! Now—and build Me My Temple, and do it correctly. For the foolish things of man will amount to nothing! I will tell your elders, your leaders in the coming months, in the coming years, where to build My Altar. Where to build My Temple. So STOP these foolish things of praying to a wall which can do nothing!

How many centuries have you used idols? When will you ever learn? There is only One God—Jehovah, Jesus Christ, and the Holy Spirit. Though you do not believe in the Trinity, it is a FACT! So be it! So be it! Those who listen to My Words will be on the side of God. Those who do the things of man will be on the side of the serpent. Nothing has changed since the time of My Son. You still follow the law according to man. You turn your head, you turn your back on the ways of your God—then you get into trouble. You expect your God to bail you out. You are running out of time! The time of the Temple is here! You have the specifications. You have the know how. Remember the Arc of the Covenant, the time of the Temple is here! (over)

Comments:
The Lord gave me the scripture Exodus: 20:25

From KJV Bible:
Exo 20:22 And the LORD said unto Moses, Thus thou shalt say unto the children of Israel, Ye have seen that I have talked with you from heaven.
Exo 20:23 Ye shall not make with me gods of silver, neither shall ye make unto you gods of gold.
Exo 20:24 An altar of earth thou shalt make unto me, and shalt sacrifice thereon thy burnt offerings, and thy peace offerings, thy sheep, and thine oxen: in all places where I record my name I will come unto thee, and I will bless thee.
Exo 20:25 And if thou wilt make me an altar of stone, thou shalt not build it of hewn stone: for if thou lift up thy tool upon it, thou hast polluted it.

Exo 20:26 Neither shalt thou go up by steps unto mine altar, that thy nakedness be not discovered thereon.

1108. Vision given to Raymond Aguilera on 8 August 1997 at 8:42 AM.

A vision of a bright white human skull with a large diamond placed in each eye socket. The skull was sitting on top of a large wooden oak desk. (over)

1109. Vision given to Raymond Aguilera on 29 August 1997 at 1:14 PM.

During prayer, the Lord showed me a vision of a battle with a dragon. This dragon was fighting many of the Lord's Angels. As the battles progressed, the dragon used the back of it's tail and struck the Continent of South America. (over)

1110. Occurrence given to Raymond Aguilera on 29 August 1997.

The Lord Jehovah took me in the spirit, into outer space to the place where He first introduced Himself to me. From there, He showed me the Toronto trip I went on. He also showed me my trip to Israel and the camping trips—He showed me the process of my training. He showed me the things that had happened and they were very revealing. The Power of God was incredible! (over)

1111. Vision given to Raymond Aguilera on 9 September 1997 at 1:10 PM.

I see the face of a black woman with very short hair about ¼ " high. She has a full round face. That's all that I know! (over)

1112. Occurrence given to Raymond Aguilera on 9 September 1997 at 8:30 PM.

During the Monday night Bible study, the Lord revealed to me that reading the Bible is like going to a movie—where you see the movie from the beginning to the end.

The Lord said, "You don't go to a movie and see the end and bits and pieces of the middle, and bits and pieces of the beginning; and then really leaving the movie knowing the WHOLE CONTENT." He said, "Reading the Bible is the same thing. You can only understand the Bible, when you begin at the Beginning and you stop at that End. This jumping around the Bible will just get you confused."

"I Praise you, Jesus Christ." Amen.

1113. Vision given to Raymond Aguilera on 16 September 1997 at 9:10 AM.

The Lord gave me a vision of Mt. Shasta. In this vision the mountain had an enormous black ball on top of the mountain. I watched this enormous black ball roll off the top of the snow covered mountain, then the mountain exploded! (over)

1114. Vision given to Raymond Aguilera on 27 September 1997 at 7:31 AM.

I was given a vision of some sort of a pit. In the spirit, the Lord revealed—that where people were going to be thrown into. I can see this soldier on top of this thing, shooting people in this hole or pit. But what was so interesting—in the background I could see this enormous White Light. It was the Spirit of God! (over)

8:07 AM.
I see a dark desert with a dark sky. It looks like thunderclouds.

1115. Prophecy given to Raymond Aguilera on 7 October 1997 at 3:36 PM.

The Lord said, "The wolf and the bear will clash in the month of November." (over)

1116. 3:43 PM.

The Lord showed me a pencil with a sharp point. Then the Lord said, "What does the writing point of a pencil have to do with the eraser?" (over)

1117. Prophecy given to Raymond Aguilera on 14 October 1997 at 7:12 PM. in Spanish.

The Lord said, "Shoes, Shoes, the Shoes of God are going to move." The Lord told me this in Spanish, as I was driving home. (over)

1118. Occurrence given to Raymond Aguilera on 20 October 1997 at 12:30 PM.

I would like to share a few things that happened this week. After doing some running around, I came home and I approached my front door. I noticed a very strong odor that smelled like women's perfume. The first thing that came to my mind was, "We have a woman visitor." But as I walked inside the house, I found the house was empty. There was no one to be found. But near the front door in a circular area of about 10 feet inside of the house, it smelled like a perfume factory. But as I walked away from the front door, the perfume scent seemed to get less and less. So I walked back toward the front door and the perfume scent was so strong—one could almost taste it. Your whole body seemed to be able smell it or taste it. I don't know how else to describe it. It smelled like flowers. I even walked back to the front door to smell it to see if someone had poured some perfume on the door, but the front door smell did not have any perfume scent! So then I checked all of the furniture without success. Only near the front door in a circular area of 10 feet was where this Wonderful Scent seemed to be! It seemed to go up into the ceiling. I wish—I could describe it better, but I do not know how else to explain it!

A few minutes later, I told Ron about it, but my mind tried to make some kind of sense of it and figured my daughter or granddaughter had just spilled something. Ten minutes later my daughter came home and I asked her what she spilled in the living room. She said, she didn't know anything about it, for she had been gone all morning. Then I suddenly realized the Scent was TOTALLY GONE!

Then two days later, at almost the same time, the perfume Scent came back and left just as fast, but this time, I had enough time to run downstairs to get Ron. By the time we came back it was almost all gone except for a small amount of it. Very, very strange!

1119. Occurrence given to Raymond Aguilera on 3 November 1997 at 9:00 AM.

I received this e-mail:
>Hi Ray, Sorry to bother you again. I have two items to ask:

>1) Has any one compiled a list on the animals mentioned in the prophecies and who or what they relate to? i.e. I would believe the bear is Russia, and the Fox could be the anti-christ.
Do you think this could be done? I would like to know what is the turtle, owl and the wolf!

>2) Could you ask the Lord what is going to happen in Australia?

>With Thanks,

>Bill.

So on item #2, I went to prayer, and asked the Lord about Australia, and the Lord showed me an arrow and said, "When the arrow strikes, and hits the bucket." (over)

1120. Prophecy given to Raymond Aguilera on 3 November 1997 at 9:15 AM.

As my prayer proceeded from Occurrence #1119, the Lord said, "When Bill Gates falls, will begin the beginning of the end." (over)

1121. Occurrence given to Raymond Aguilera on 3 November 1997 at 9:15 AM. to 9:00 PM.

After sending out Prophecy #1120 (the prophecy about Bill Gates), even though it only took a few minutes to receive it. Somehow those minutes of receiving it—left me totally exhausted. I only had enough strength to update my web site, and to send it out to the people on our e-mail list.

I do not understand why at times, there is such a physical drain on my body, when some of these prophecies come to me. I have no idea if other prophets experience the same. I was totally exhausted after this Occurrence. My physical strength went to an all time low. After I sent it out, and placed it on the web site, I went back to bed. It was only about 10 or 11 o'clock in the morning, but I felt like I had worked 20 hours. I stayed pretty much in bed most of the day until about 4 PM. Then I started feeling very depressed. So I decided to get dressed and go to a movie. I remembered the difficulty of getting out of my car, and walking from the parking lot to the Movie Theater.

As I sat there thinking of what had happened that morning, and wondered how all of this was changing my Christian walk. I remembered how easy life was before the Lord started speaking to me, and what I had learned and experienced the past eight years.

The movie started, and it was getting interesting, and I began to forget everything that had happened that morning. When all of a sudden the movie camera broke, and the film started flicking. The lights came on, and a employee from the theater told us that the movie could not be completed. Then the manager gave us all a free movie pass for the next showing at 7 PM.

I was very disappointed, and I worked my tired body back home. I laid down once more, but this depression would not leave me. All I seemed to do was toss and turn on my bed until about 6:45 PM. At this point, I made my mind up to get out of bed and go back to the Movie Theater. So once more, I got my tired body out of the car and made my way back to the theater. By the time I got there, the movie had already been running for about ten minutes. Well, I once again, I forgot about my morning occurrence, and got into the movie plot again. Then the theater lights came on, while the film was still running! Then the lights went off; and the curtains closed, then they opened, then the film stopped! Then the lights went back on, then off, everything went crazy! Finally the film, curtains, and lights settled down, and I saw the rest of the movie, and I went home.

As I drove home, I began to wonder if this was all because of the earlier (#1120 and #1121) Prophecies, and began to pray to the Lord for help. (over)

1122. Occurrence given to Raymond Aguilera on 14 November 1997 at 8:30 PM.

For the past two weeks, I have had many people call and write for prayers. I also noticed, that I would cry during most of these prayers. Most of the time I did not even realize that I was crying until well into the prayer. It seemed like they were empathy type of prayers, where your body would physically get into the prayer and cry.

Well—Friday night Carl, a friend of mine, asked me if I wanted to go to hear a well-known prophet speak in San Jose. I told him yes, and then

I proceeded to his house. I noticed the heavy traffic, and mentioned it to Carl. We decided to stay home and pray, and have Communion.

Occurrence/Vision:

During our prayers is when this occurrence/vision happened. Most of the time, I feel like the biggest sinner in the world. I do not know why the Lord does this to me, when I least expect it!

This experience was so real in the spirit I cannot fully explain it in words. But during prayer before Communion, the Lord gave me the "HONOR AND PRIVILEGE", to see Him in the Spirit, during the taking the Holy Wine with His Disciples at the Last Supper in the upper room.

As I looked at the Lord, I could see Him from about the wrist up, but He looked like He was sitting on the floor, but I am not sure. I knew beyond a shadow of a doubt, that it was Him. But, His Body had no shape; you could identify. I know, I sound strange, and not making any sense, but I knew exactly—who He was, and what He was going doing. I also knew that it was the Last Supper of the Lord, and the world's first Communion service given directly by the Lord. This all sounds very strange doesn't it!

What was shown to me was the moment after the taking of the Bread (His Body), and just before the Wine (His Blood) was given out. How—can I explain this without sounding like a crazy man! I was seeing Jesus Christ from the wrist up, but He had no identifiable features in the flesh, in His Face or Body, but I could see His Face CLEARLY in the Spirit. But as I looked at His Spiritual Face, it looked so quite, calm, peaceful, and tranquil, but yet I could sense tears in His Face. As I watched Him, He slowly and patiently took a long deep look at each of the Disciples before He passed the Wine. It seemed to me that He was looking down deeply into everyone soul. It also seemed to me—that this look showed what each Disciple was going to do and suffer for His Namesake. Maybe that was why He had that tone of Tears in His eyes. The whole place became

TOTALLY QUIET; and no one made any sound as if the HOLY SPIRIT was filling the whole room as they watched.

All that kept running through my mind was; "I HAVE NO BUSINESS HERE; seeing such a HOLY MOMENT!" I began to feel so dirty and undeserving seeing this happen. I wish—I could explain all of this in words, but I cannot. These kinds of experiences make me wonder, "WHY me!!!!" For reading it in the Bible was enough, and I believed. That was enough for me! But yet your spirit gets so hungry for a personal closeness to the Lord, that it never gets enough.

It was like—when not a word is spoken, and you see someone with love or pain in his body, and no one has to tell you, but the both of you know what is going on inside the person. I could sense the Lord's Eyes search deeply into the enter depths of each Disciple with the Love of His Heart. Wow, this was great! This whole occurrence lasted about 10 seconds, but it seemed like 10 to 15 minutes.

The hair on my arms started to rise, and I wanted to cry!! Why—am I such a crybaby, when it comes to these kinds of things? All I wanted to do was run and run as fast as I could. Does that sound like a holy man seeking the Lord? Well—I could not type this up until today. I could not even shave my face or take a shower for about three days. I found myself out of focus every time I tried to type it up. But where can a person run or hide from the Lord? And why would they want too! I am WAY OVER my head and body in my Christian Spiritual walk again. I am beginning to believe our bodies are NOT MADE to experience some things in the SPIRIT! For it really breaks us!

I kept asking myself, "WHY", is the Lord doing this to me? I was in such "Awa", at being able to see this occurrence, and at the same time my mind was saying, "I am NOT worthy to see this! Why, is the Lord doing this to me!!! (over)

Vision:

Then I saw the Lord weeping, and I wondered if that was why I had been crying the past several weeks.

Vision:

Then the Lord showed me a nuclear explosion of some sort. Then this pillar of fire came down from Heaven, which extended miles and miles from the sky. It was cylindrical in shape, and the flames circled in this cylindrical shape. And as I watched this nuclear explosion; this pillar of fire went around the perimeter of the nuclear blast. Then the Lord informed me that was why He was crying. (over)

1123. Prophecy given to Raymond Aguilera on 14 November 1997 at 8:30 PM.

During this Communion prayer from the above Occurrences, we also prayed for Carl's church, The Vineyard church of San Francisco. Because it's membership was way down from +700 down to about +300. Then the Lord said, "I am going to prune it back because I have given them many Words and Prophecies, and they did not do what I asked." (over)

1124. Occurrence given to Raymond Aguilera on 14 November 1997 at 11:00 PM.

Well, after returning late from Carl's house, I logged on the Internet and checked my e-mail. I found a e-mail from someone, who wanted me to give him an interpretation of a dream he had had. He gave me the link to his web site, so I proceeded to check it out. I normally do not have the time to surf the Net or check out web sites, but somehow I was still overwhelmed from what I had seen at Carl's house. So, I found myself reading his dream, but it did not have as much effect on me as his links page of other web sites. I found myself being led by the Lord through links on his links page, and there I found a link and clicked on it and found it to be an End Times Ministry Church web site. There wasn't anything there that caught my eyes except their awards page. This web site had many, many Internet awards on it. Then the Lord led me to e-mail him this e-mail.

****

Subj: I love you Brother XXX XXXX!
Date: 97-11-15 02:38:00 EST
From: ReyAgu
To: XXXXXX

Hello brother XXX XXXX,

I was led to your web site by the Lord, and I was wondering of what value are all your web site awards in Heaven. I hope you do not lose your focus.

yours in Christ,
Raymond Aguilera

Seek God (Jehovah, Jesus Christ, and the Holy Spirit) by PRAYING and having FAITH.

Learn about God by READING the Holy Bible from the beginning to the end.

If you believe it or not; The Lord's Truth will not CHANGE!

God bless you all.

Web sites:
< http://prophecy.org >
e-mail: Ray@prophecy.org

Raymond Aguilera, PO Box 20517, El Sobrante, CA. 94820-0517, USA.

Fax 510-222-4969,
****

From the Words about the Vineyard Church and the above web site, all that came to my mind was the Lord is going to clean up His House. (over)

1125. Vision given to Raymond Aguilera on 21 November 1997 at 1:30 AM.

Hello brothers and sisters,

I am starting to get e-mail like the one below. But all that has been coming to my mind are the scriptures about testing. Here are only a few:

From KJV Bible:
Exo 17:2 Wherefore the people did chide with Moses, and said, Give us water that we may drink. And Moses said unto them, Why chide ye with me? wherefore do ye tempt the LORD?

Deu 6:16 Ye shall not tempt the LORD your God, as ye tempted him in Massah.

Judg 6:39 And Gideon said unto God, Let not thine anger be hot against me, and I will speak but this once: let me prove, I pray thee, but this once with the fleece; let it now be dry only upon the fleece, and upon all the ground let there be dew.

Psa 139:23 Search me, O God, and know my heart: try me, and know my thoughts:
Psa 139:24 And see if there be any wicked way in me, and lead me in the way everlasting.

Psa 139:23 Search me, O God, and know my heart: try me, and know my thoughts:

Psa 139:24 And see if there be any wicked way in me, and lead me in the way everlasting.
****
>To: ReyAgu@aol.com

>Mr. Aguilera,

>I am afraid of trusting those who are called prophets. But maybe you are one.
>I don't believe G_D would speak to me directly because I am not worthy.
>So I ask you to speak to HIM for me. I have one question which I would like to
>ask, and a second one so that I will know that the answer comes from HIM.

>1. Will the Menorah witness the passage of Ezra's mountain?

>2. Do you wish me to stay or to go?

>Thank you Mr. Aguilera. G_D Bless you.
****

The Lord answered the above request with a vision:

   In the vision the Lord showed me a wide brandy glass (empty of wine), but INSIDE the brandy glass, there was a fish swimming in the air! Then the Lord used His Shoe and crashed the brandy glass to pieces. Then the fish fell to the floor. Then I saw a woman's shoe come, and step and crash the small fish. (over)

****

>To: ReyAgu

>Hello Ray

>How have you been ? Well i hope. How's The Ministry going ? Thank You for adding me to the Prayer List,You and your Mission are also on mine. I have a favor to ask but not quite shure how to phrase it so here goes, Would you please ask The LORD if i understand correctly about the spring time, i feel i missed somthing but i am not quite shure what. And also the friend.
Thank You
Good Luck and GOD Bless

The Lord's answer:
Subj: Re: The Spring/Reply
Date: 97-11-19 22:58:12 EST
From: ReyAgu
To: XXXXXX

Hi there XXXXX

The Lord said, "Yes to the first thing, and No to the second thing. I am the First, and the Last and the One, who is going to be."
(over)

1126. Vision given to Raymond Aguilera on 23 November 1997 at 10:45 AM.

During prayer, the Lord gave me a vision of a fox. Then I saw a Knife come down from Heaven and cut off half of the fox's left ear. (over)

1127. Vision given to Raymond Aguilera on 28 November 1997 at 8:35 AM.

The Lord gave me a vision of a tree. As I watched the large tree, the ground was removed from under the tree, where I could see all of it's roots.

Vision:

Then the Lord gave me a vision of ship, but on this ship there was another ship. It was a vision of a ship within a ship. (over)

1128. Prophecy given to Raymond Aguilera on 29 November 1997 at 11:15 PM. in Spanish.

Hear—hear My son! Hear all of the Words that I say to you. For this is the Word of your God, the One, who made all, the world, Heaven, all that is, all that you touch, all that is going to be! I am Everything—with My Son and the Holy Spirit. All that I have told you, I am going to give you to the Point!—All the money, your wife, all the miracles, all the things of the Spirit. You are My Word, and I tell you these Words with the Love of the Father, with the Love of the Son, with the Love of the Holy Spirit.

Here comes the point in time, that all that I have told you is going to happen, and all of the world—all that have ears are going to hear. All that have eyes are going to see if they know the Father, if they know the Son, if they know the Holy Spirit. They are going to see and hear, with the Force of the Father, the Force of the Son, the Force of the Holy Spirit. For now all is ready! All is ready—did you hear Me with your ears, Reymundo? I know—that you are praying for the things that you do not have! I know—that your heart has tears. I know—that you do not have the money that you need. I know—that you do not have the strength you need. But I am going to give you the strength! I am going to give you the money! I am going to give you the Heart of God!

For the two, with all of the brothers and sisters, We are going to Point everything We have toward Heaven! I am telling you the Truth and to the Point with the Force of the Holy Spirit! Do not cry anymore, I heard you with My Ears! I heard you with all you have done! I know your heart My son! I know! All is straight! All is clean! But you have to wait and have more patience, and you have to make yourself strong with the Word of God, with the Faith of God, with the Heart of God.

I tell you these things, for I am going to send you to all parts of the world, with the Force of God and I know that you are going to need money! I know, you are going to need strength! I know the things of man! I know the things of the Spirit! But do not worry My son! For all of the brothers and sisters with the Help of the Holy Spirit, We are going to correct with the Force, with the Word, with all that is Clean, with all that is Pointed toward Heaven.

Hear Me! Hear Me! Hear Me, this minute to the Word of God. It has arrived the things that I have promised you. They have arrived! Hurry rest! I know—that the devil is mad, but let him get mad; for it is of no importance to Me! For he is nothing. What is important; is the Word of God with the Force of the Holy Spirit. All is going to happen like I have said—to the LETTER, to the POINT!—With the Love of God, I tell you these things on this night. Hurry, rest My son! I have heard your prayer. I have heard your prayer. Rest My son! (over)

1129. Prophecy given to Raymond Aguilera on 1 December 1997 at 12:10 AM. in Spanish.

How is it going My son? How is it going? You know what? Your heart is pointed. Your spirit is pointed, and I want you to point all toward your Father, the Son, and the Holy Spirit. For the things of the Spirit are going to begin again. And I know, where you are going to go, and I know what you are going to do in the days that are coming.

I know that people are going to get mad, but do not worry, for I am with you with My Angels, to the point. I—with My Word are going to frighten—all of the world with the things that are going to happen in the year that is coming. I tell them and I tell them and I tell them, but they do not want to hear Me! And it has arrived again, the things of the Spirit. I know and you know—that it is going to become hotter with the things of the Spirit. They are going to seek you out with stones, Reymundo! They are going to seek you out! But that is the way it has to be. For they do not want to hear. They do not want to see the things of God. But they cannot stop—what is the Truth and Straight and to the Point. They can jump! They can scream! But they cannot stop the Word of God. Did you hear Me? It has arrived the day of the Spirit. (over)

1130. Prophecy given to Raymond Aguilera on 2 December 1997 at 5:45 PM.

During prayer as I was driving home from a small job, when the Lord said to me, "Raymond, tell Mark, that he has moved from the exposed iceberg to below the waterline."

Then the Lord showed me the iceberg of Vision #808. (over)

808. Vision given to Raymond Aguilera on 3 October 1995 at 12 noon

The Lord showed me an iceberg.

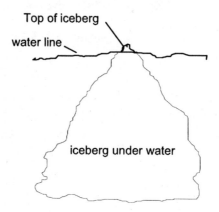

The Lord said, "You see this iceberg?"
I said, "Yes."
"Do you see the TOP OF IT?", He said.

I said, "Yes."

He said, "That is the Body of My Son that people know. Look under the water. That's the real church—the part that's underwater. I am going to awaken it. I am going to direct it, and I am going to use it with the Power of the Holy Spirit, with the Power of Jehovah, with the Power of My Son. This is the Great I am I am, I am I am, I am I am." (over)

1131. Prophecy given to Raymond Aguilera on 3 December 1997 at 11:30 PM.

Saddam Hussein will fall with a vengeance because—he did not keep his agreement with the terrorist. This is the whole Truth, so saith Jehovah. It will happen like a person, who makes butter from milk. Remember the vision of a ship within a ship. (over)

1132. Prophecy given to Raymond Aguilera on 7 December 1997 at 8:30 AM.

The Lord said, "In My Father's House, there are many mansions, and I am preparing one for you."

Vision:

Then I was given a vision of names being placed on something that looked like a rug. This rug was all rolled up except where the names were being placed. It reminded me of rolled paper scrolls that were used in the old Jewish, Roman, and Greek days to write on. But this accounting material looked like some kind of rug like material. I could see the names being placed on it, but I was not allowed to see who was placing the names on this rug or how they were being placed on this material. It almost looked like if they were stamped on with golden letters, but I am not really sure. Though in my spirit, I knew someone was placing them on; I was not allowed to see who it was. Somehow—I also knew in my spirit, that the people of these names had just died. I was shocked to see so many names being placed on this material so fast. This material was extremely large and wide, and as these names were placed on it; it slowly rolled up. (over)

1133. Vision given to Raymond Aguilera on 7 December 1997 at 9 AM.

The Lord gave me a vision of a large Knife being sharpened on a large Stone.
Then the Lord said, "Which is more important—the Knife or the Stone?"
I didn't know what to say. So I said, "I do not know!"
Then the Lord said, "The Stone!" (over)

1134. Prophecy given to Raymond Aguilera on 7 December 1997 at 12:15 PM.

The Lord said, "Those who hear My Voice, recognize Me!" (over)

1135. Prophecy given to Raymond Aguilera on 17 December 1997 at 8:30 AM.

The Lord said, "Merry Christmas, Merry Christmas, Merry Christmas, Merry Christmas, Merry Christmas, Merry Christmas, Merry Christmas, Merry Christmas, Merry Christmas." (Nine times)

Vision:
Then I was given an image of a waterline with water below and air above. (over)

1136. Prophecy given to Raymond Aguilera on 18 December 1997 at 1:30 PM.

During prayer the Lord gave me many visions:
Vision:
I saw a vision of an upside down tripod holding a White Sheet.

Vision:

I saw a vision of a single leather sandal with someone wearing a black sock. Then I saw a large shoe, which had a long spike on the bottom of its heel. The spike was about 6 inches long.

Vision:

The next image was of a black looking object or box. This black box had a white flag on two sides waving in the air asking for mercy, and trying to surrender. Later, the Lord told me the black box was a church. Then this missile came from the sky, and destroyed the black box with the two waving flags. Then I saw another black box with waving white flags, and the same thing happened to it. They were totally destroyed by these missiles from the sky. It looked like there was no such thing "As mercy," coming from these missiles.

After the above visions, more black boxes appeared, but they didn't have waving flags, but some kind of protective dome surrounded them as they came under attack. These domes protected them from these bombing missiles.

Vision:

Then the next vision was of a metal cooking pot being placed on top of a hot cooking stove.

Vision:

Then I saw what looked like a metal medallion or broach with a figure of a cat on it. What was so unusual; it reminded me of the Ford Mercury Cat Logo that you see on their cars. This medallion was around someone's neck with a gold chain. What I sensed in the spirit was—that whoever was wearing this medallion had something to do with this war or it was this company, but I am not really sure. But there was some kind of association with this cat and this war, I was seeing.

Vision:

Then I saw a single White Candle.
Then I heard the Lord say, "Look closely at the UN. (United Nations)"

Vision:

Somehow I could see the upper atmosphere of the earth. I could see that these destroying missiles were coming from what looked like circling satellites. As I looked at these attacking missiles come down, the ground forces tried to shoot them down, and by shooting up larger and fatter looking missiles into the atmosphere. All of this looked like there was some kind of war going on.

Vision:

The next image I saw was of a jet flying high and toward what looked like our sun or a very bright white light.

Then during this occurrence, I heard a Voice identify itself as Ruth. This reminded me of the Ruth Voice that spoke to me in the spirit in Israel. Ruth said, "Do not worry, I will be with you!"

Then the Lord said, "The songs of the dead. The songs of the dead. The songs of the dead." (over)

1137. Prophecy given to Raymond Aguilera on 21 December 97 at 11:15 PM. in Spanish.

Hear the Word of God with the Ears of God! I am—now, I am—now, I am—now! My son, the Body is going to be cleaned. The Body is going to be cleaned, the Body of My Son. He is going to arrive and He is going to clean all that is filthy. He is going to clean the Body to the Point, with Force, with the Holy Spirit! This is your Father. The One who made all, with His Word, with the Force of the Holy Spirit. It has arrived.

Hear! Hear! Hear! Yes, it has arrived the calendar of the New Year. It has arrived to the point. The race, that all run is going to stop to the point! Yes, yes, the day is going to arrive that the Wine is going to run—like the Blood is going to run in the Road. Yes! "The Wine!" I know to the point the things of God and the date of the race.

Hear! Hear! Hear! I know, I know, I know, that the Angels are ready, and that the devils are ready. But nothing is going to happen until I give the Word. Then the fighting will begin until "The End." Did you hear Me with the Ears of God, when I say the Word? Yes! Yes! I know, I know. (over)

1138. Prophecy given to Raymond Aguilera on 22 December 1997 at 1:27 AM.

The Lord said, "Amy Grant's song, Somewhere down the road, is Prophetic." (over)

1139. Prophecy given to Raymond Aguilera on 23 December 1997 at 7:14 AM. in Spanish.

Pastor Alexander is like a doorknob that turns and turns, and opens nothing.

Vision:
Then the Lord gave me a vision of a tongue being cut off.

Vision:
Then the Lord gave me a vision of a dollar sign.

1140. Vision and Prophecy given to Raymond Aguilera on 28 December 1997 at 7:28 AM.

The Lord showed me a Christmas tree and said, "Even though this Christmas tree is nailed onto a wooden cross. It is like the body of Christ, "The church of man". It has no roots". (over)

Prophecy:
The church of man asks you to give ten percent because it said in the Bible, that Abram gave to Melchizedek ten percent, but I tell you giving is good. They are going to love hearing that, but I am also going to tell you. Giving is also like the little widow who gave the two coins. And giving is like Sapphira. It is going to be everything in the middle. (In-between) (over)

From KJV Bible:

Gen 14:17 And the king of Sodom went out to meet him after his return from the slaughter of Chedorlaomer, and of the kings that were with him, at the valley of Shaveh, which is the king's dale.

Gen 14:18 And Melchizedek king of Salem brought forth bread and wine: and he was the priest of the most high God.

Gen 14:19 And he blessed him, and said, Blessed be Abram of the most high God, possessor of heaven and earth:

Gen 14:20 And blessed be the most high God, which hath delivered thine enemies into thy hand. And he gave him tithes of all.

Mark 12:42 And there came a certain poor widow, and she threw in two mites, which make a farthing.

Acts 5:1 But a certain man named Ananias, with Sapphira his wife, sold a possession,

Acts 5:2 And kept back part of the price, his wife also being privy to it, and brought a certain part, and laid it, at the apostles' feet.

Acts 5:3 But Peter said, Ananias, why hath Satan filled thine heart to lie to the Holy Ghost, and to keep back part of the price of the land?

Acts 5:4 Whiles it remained, was it not thine own? and after it was sold, was it not in thine own power? why hast thou conceived this thing in thine heart? thou hast not lied unto men, but unto God.

Acts 5:5 And Ananias hearing these words fell down, and gave up the ghost: and great fear came on all them that heard these things.

Acts 5:6 And the young men arose, wound him up, and carried him out, and buried him.

Acts 5:7 And it was about the space of three hours after, when his wife, not knowing what was done, came in.

Acts 5:8 And Peter answered unto her, Tell me whether ye sold the land for so much? And she said, Yea, for so much.

Acts 5:9 Then Peter said unto her, How is it that ye have agreed together to tempt the Spirit of the Lord? behold, the feet of them which have buried thy husband are at the door, and shall carry thee out.
Acts 5:10 Then fell she down straightway at his feet, and yielded up the ghost: and the young men came in, and found her dead, and, carrying her forth, buried her by her husband.

1141. Prophecy given to Raymond Aguilera on 29 December 1997 at 6:45 PM

The tower of Babel—history is repeating itself. The churches of today are building their towers of Babel, trying to reach Heaven with their doctrine, with their words. And history will repeat itself. I will STOP!—their towers of Babel, so saith Jehovah, so saith Jesus, so saith the Lord. So be it! So be it! So be it! (over)

1142. Prophecy given to Raymond Aguilera on 31 Dec 1997 at 9:15 AM.

If I walked into their churches today, they would not recognize me. They would try to force Me to submit to their covering, to their doctrine. What a shame, what a shame!—That they do not know Jesus Christ of Nazareth. For the hour of the Word, the hour of Power, the hour of the Father, is upon this little planet. What a shame! What a shame! What a shame!—That the leaderships are so blind, so dumb. So be it! So be it! (over)

Remember Carmanlita. Remember Carmanlita, Carmanlita. (over)

1143. Vision given to Raymond Aguilera on 11 January 1998 at 8:01 AM.

I had a vision of a hand. Somehow the skin of the hand was replaced. I could see some white particles of some sort going through the veins. It reminded me of the skin of a snake. (over)

1144. Vision given to Raymond Aguilera on 11 January 1998 at 8:13 AM.

I saw a vision of a woman with red hair giving a man a massage. He was on top of a table. (over)

Vision:
I saw a vision of many boxes or crates. They were full of human bones. And I saw a live man who looked like a skeleton placing these crates on a conveyor belt. These crates were open. (over)

1145. Prophecy given to Raymond Aguilera on 13 January 1998 at 6:45 PM.

During prayer, I asked the Lord, "Can a baby in a woman's womb hear". The Lord gave me the scriptures of Genesis (Gen 1:27), where He made man in His image. Then He gave me the scriptures of Luke (Luke 1:39-41). Then the Lord said, "Life begins at conception, not at the birth of the child. A baby can hear and he has feelings in the womb". (over)

From KJV Bible:
Gen 1:27 So God created man in his own image, in the image of God created he him; male and female created he them.

Luke 1:39 And Mary arose in those days, and went into the hill country with haste, into a city of Juda;
Luke 1:40 And entered into the house of Zacharias, and saluted Elisabeth.

Luke 1:41 And it came to pass, that, when Elisabeth heard the salutation of Mary, the babe leaped in her womb; and Elisabeth was filled with the Holy Ghost:

1146. Vision given to Raymond Aguilera on 20 January 1998 at 11:20 PM.

A vision of a White lit candle. Over the candle there was an up-side down clear drinking glass. (over)

1147. Prophecy given to Raymond Aguilera on 2 February 1998 at 1:10 AM. in Spanish.

My son, My son, My son, the hunger of the tiger is big. Yes! The hunger of the snake is big too! The both of them are pointed. The two of them are waiting! The two of them are waiting for the devil. But they believe they can awaken the things of the world, but all is beneath My Finger. I tell you to the point. I tell you the things of God.

It has arrived, the pencil. Yes, the pencil that is going to write, that is going to begin the war to the point. I tell you correctly! I tell you to the point! All of the world all of the religions believe—they know it all—to save the body. But they do not know that the Father, with the Son, with the Holy Spirit is there in front of their noses. They cannot see with their eyes the things of God, but all is beneath the Finger of God.

It has arrived the Word of God. I tell you these things straight and in the manner of God. But if you hear Me or not, this is not going to change a single letter, a single point of what I tell you. It is the truth. They believe they know it all, but they know nothing. They know nothing, for the things of God, are the things of God, and the mind of man is the mind of man. The two things are not the same!

Like I have told you, there are some who, hug the Word of God. There are others that cry. There are others that get mad, when they hear the Word of God. But I know, that all will go—like the way I put it—to the

Point! And it has arrived, the Force of God in the Manner of God. I know this minute—what you are thinking, when read and hear these Words. For I read your heart, and I know if you are going to cry. If you are going to get mad or if it is going to give you joy! All that happens in your life, I know it. But what I say—and in the manner that I tell you—are going to be the things of God—with the Force of God.

But if you do not seek My Son Jesus, you are going to be blind, and you are not going to be able to see in front of your nose. Read the Bible and Pray—for My Son is ready. Did you hear Me? Did you hear Me? This is your Father, with the Son, and the Holy Spirit telling you the things of Heaven. (over)

1148. Prophecy given to Raymond Aguilera on 6 February 1998 at 9:30AM. in Spanish.

Forgive the nun. Forgive the nun. Forgive the nun. For her eyes are going to radiate (burn), are going to radiate (burn) with the Flame of God. Yes, yes, forgive the nun. It has arrived the days of the eyes. (over)

1149. Occurrence given to Raymond Aguilera on 23 February 1998 at 2 PM.

Subj: O.K.?
Date: 98-02-24 12:36:35 EST
From: XXXXX
To: ReyAgu

Hello Ray
Been kinda worried about ya the last week or so, do'nt really know why, so i Prayed extra for you and your Ministry and thought i'de write and see how your doin. Write if you get a chance,
GOD Bless
lance

Hello brothers and sisters in Christ,

I received this e-mail today and it shows me how tuned in some of you brothers and sisters are. I have been very busy these past few months trying to set something up so I could bring in some money to keep this ministry going. I figured, since the Lord has me on hold, now would be the right time to work on the finances. Well, not much has happened in this area except more bills and work. But for some reason I feel, I should place this on the web site some time today, at least I hope too.

Yesterday at 2 PM one of the things I was counting on the Lord to deliver, and something I had been praying about for nine years—And one of the reasons for trusting and having hope in the Lord, and something that strengthened me in this ministry, was taken away. I do not want to get into the details, but I felt like I was standing on top of the rock of Jesus, when out of nowhere the devil came beat me down to nothing in the matter of minutes.

As many of you believers in Christ know, there always comes a time in our walk, when our flesh and our spiritual walk comes under such a powerful attack, that we feel like the rug has been pulled out from under us—you just want to give it all up. Well, that is what happened to me yesterday. I was even considering removing or closing down the Prophecy web site and all related things. Right now, I am so tired of all of this. But I am going to keep moving forward with the work that Jehovah, Jesus Christ, and the Holy Spirit, has given me. I keep remembering what the Lord told me many, many years ago. NO MATTER WHAT HAPPENS, "Trust in Jehovah, Jesus Christ, and the Holy Spirit". Being a Christian is not easy, I do not care what people say!! These lonely feelings and waiting for the next battle gets very old. May the Lord forgive me for my thoughts, but I am at another major turning point in my Christian walk. Please pray that the Lord's perfect will be done and completed. God bless you all!

Yours in Christ,
ray

1150. Prophecy given to Raymond Aguilera on 24 February 1998 at 10:45 PM. in Spanish.

I am, I am My son. I am the Boat—I am the Boat of Heaven. I know that the water is very hard and very high for you right now. And it is hitting the Boat very fast, but—do not worry for all will go well. For I knew, that the devil was planning this—all that happened yesterday. For many weeks, he was gathering these things to hit you with. But I knew that you were on top of the Rock of God, of My Son. I know that you fell.

I know that your heart is hurting. The devil wants to kill you. He wants to kill you this year. For he knows, that the Word that you have placed on your computer is going to all parts of the world. And that people have a hunger to hear the Word of God. He wants to stop you, Reymundo! He and all of his soldiers are pointed to kill you. He has a hunger for your blood. For he KNOWS that if he stops you, he will stop many, who are seeking God, and many who want to hear the Word of God. That is why, he is hitting you.

And that is why, he hit your friend. Your friend is not doing the things of God. He wants to use her to hit you. I know that you are broken. You are broken, but he is not going to stop you. For I know all that is going to happen to the point. Did you hear Me, My son?

There is going to be a river—and this river is going to branch out to the left and to the right. I want you to go to the right side of the branch. But you have to wait—and I will tell you what you are going to do—and when you are going to do it. The devil is very mad with you. The war of the spirit is very large right now around you! They want to stop you, like

I have told you! They want to kill you! For they know—that if they stop you or kill you. They can stop the Word of God! I am not going to let them stop the Word.

I told you, when We started—that you were not going to stop. You are going to finish the walk, that I told you, and that I have given you. Yes, My Reymundo! I Love you with all of My Heart! But the road is some times very difficult. I know that you cry, and that you burn, but look—the world is going to end. And We have to do some work. Just point your nose toward the Father, the Son, Jesus, and the Holy Spirit. And all will go well.

There are many people who are looking at you. They want to know what you are going to do—if you are going to fall. If you are going to lift yourself up. You do not know—what I know! People radiate in their hearts for God, who made all, with His Word, with His Hand, with the Force of the Holy Spirit. All will go well, My son.

Make yourself strong for here comes the devil again! But he is not going to stop you. For I know—what is going to happen. Yes, My son, I tell you with the Lips of Heaven. I tell you with the Arms of Heaven. When you get to Heaven, I am going to Hug you! I am going to Kiss you! For no one believed—that you could do—what you are doing! Not even you—believed it! You are doing it!

I know that you feel alone, but I am going to give you the wife that I told you about. So she can help you in the manner of God. I know—for I know what is going to happen. Wipe (clean) your tears, and make yourself strong! For here comes the devil with fighting on his mind. Did you hear Me? But do not worry, for I have My Angels around you. And this minute **They** are fighting with the demons of the devil, but nothing is going to happen. But I know—what is going to happen with the devil, to the day, to the minute, to the point. He cannot stop the Word of God! Make yourself strong, My son, My beautiful one, My beloved. (over)

1151. Prophecy and Vision given to Raymond Aguilera on 26 February 1998 at 11:45 PM.

I had a vision of an enormous battle in the spirit. I have no idea where in the spirit or if it is around me or somewhere else but it involves riders on horses. They are coming at each other with great power. I can actually feel or sense this enormous power of good and evil fighting to their maximum; without either of them falling back a micro centimeter. I wonder if this is how it is going to be at the end of this little planet. For there is no way of describing such power hitting each other. If only the people of God could see this, they would most certainly stop "playing church". For sure—the perspective of the leadership would change. (over)

Prophecy translated from Spanish:

How is it going? How is it going My son? I know the fighting that is happening in the spirit. It is Hard and it is Pointed. Yes! Do you know why? For the fighting that is happening around you—the devil has the mind, that he wants to kill you. And he wants to push the force of the demons on top of you. But My Angels are there, all there—around you fighting with the Force of God. For I told you many years ago, that I was going to protect you. That nothing was going to happen to you. This is the Truth! For I do not lie! All is Correct—All is to the Point!

I know that some times you do not believe Me, but this is the Truth! All is going to Happen Exactly to the Point like I told you many years ago. And all of the promises that I told you—are going to come to the Point! I know that you do not believe this—this minute—what I am telling you! But it is the TRUTH! I Love you much, My Reymundo, and I know that you do not believe Me right now. But this is the Truth! That is the way of man, but the things of God, the Father, the Son, and the Holy Spirit—are CORRECT AND TO THE POINT!

Sometimes people die. And sometimes many people die. But the thing is—some things happen—and I let them happen. But the Truth is the Truth; and is—I am there! If it is in the world that people are living or the world where they are dead or in the world of the spirit—I am everywhere protecting what is Mine. It is not important in which world they are in—I protect what is Mine! And I bury—what is NOT! All will go right.

I know that you do not have worries now. For now, you know that you have more Force, than you believed you had. I showed you WELL. I know that you suffered much to learn these things that I have just told you—that I have showed you—and that have happened! We have many things yet to do My Reymundo. The world is going to become hotter for the things that are bad. Some things have just started, but there are many things that are going to happen—that still have not begun. And the entire climate is going to change, and earthquakes. Yes! There is going to much suffering in this world.

But if you (people) are strong in the Father, in the Son, Jesus, and with the Holy Spirit, you (people) can pass through these things with the Force of God. But if you (people) live in the world and you (people) believe in the world. I am going to BURY you (people) in the PIT with the devil. And it does not hurt Me—to say these Words. For what is Mine, I protect! And what is not! I am going to BURY in the PIT!! And I do not care if you are the President or if you are a man who cleans toilets. I look at the heart. I look at the heart. Did you hear Me? I look at the heart! If you (people) seek out My Son Jesus, if you read the Bible, if you (people) have the Communion, if you (people) help the brothers and sisters that need help—I tell you CLEARLY AND I TELL YOU TO THE POINT! The devil cannot do a thing!

Yes! I know that your heart is hurting (Reymundo), but that is nothing; you are going to live, and all will go right! But the devil is not going to live, and he is going to go to the PIT! Do you know what I have told you? Do you know these things differently? You are going to live! And he is going to the PIT! This is CORRECT AND TO THE POINT!

Here comes the day of "Fright" for the world. Yes! I know—the DATE, to the POINT!! But it gives Me Joy, My son—that you are stronger, but I know that your heart is hurting. But it is going to go well, My son. All will go well. Just stand on top of the Rock of My Son Jesus and you can see what your Father, with My Son, and the Holy Spirit—is going to do. He is going to clean all that is filthy. Open the Word with the Force of the Holy Spirit. I tell you the Truth, My beloved. Arm yourself, and I will tell you more on another day to the point the Manner of God. (over)

1152. Prophecy and Vision given to Raymond Aguilera on 27 Feb 1998 at 7 AM.

The Lord awoke me up and told me to have communion. I was half-asleep, and I got up and had communion. Then I went back to bed. Then the Lord gave me a vision of an open umbrella. Then I saw lighting strike the umbrella, but nothing happened to the umbrella. Then the Lord said, "The vision represented Satan striking the umbrella. The umbrella represented prayer cover."

Then He said, "See Reymundo, something simple as umbrella and something as thin as the fabric of the umbrella beat the devil's lighting strike! See what prayer cover can do." (over)

Vision 7:10 AM:

The Lord gave me a vision—of me playing baseball with God. The ball was pitched (by Jesus), and I swung the bat. I hit the ball real hard, and it surprised me, for it went way high, into the sky towards outer space. Then in the spirit, I saw the Lord, Father, catch the ball. Then, I could see myself running to the bases. Then I saw the Father throw the ball back down toward the Earth. As the ball was coming down, I touched first base, then second base, and then third base. Then I saw myself racing toward home base as the ball and I were reaching home plate at the same time. I slid into home plate and the Lord Jesus Christ caught the ball as I slid into home plate. And the Holy Spirit said "SAFE. Reymundo Aguilera won the game!" (over)

1153. Occurrence given to Raymond Aguilera on 27 February 1998 at 5:10 PM.

Hello brothers and sisters,

I think—I could use many prayers on this matter. I have been waiting (on hold) on this, for about nine years, since the Lord first gave me this prophetic gift.

Yours in Christ,
ray

The Lord said, "Reymundo, I release you to seek your new wife. Seek and you will find. And do not WORRY, for I will send her to you". (over)

PS: Why, did He have to say not to worry? For now I know—I will!

1154. Prophecy and Vision given to Raymond Aguilera on 2 March 1998 at 8:00 AM.

The Lord gave Me a vision of a self-inking rubber stamp, during prayer time with a brother in Christ. Then the next morning the Lord explained the meaning of the rubber stamp. That Carl was Marked as His (the Lord's). He explained that the rubber stamp meant—that He was beginning to mark or separate His Lambs or Flock. The Lord also said, Christians around the world would begin to see and have dreams about rubber stamps or being Marked by God or set aside by the Lord. (over)

Comments:
I could use some more prayers—the warfare has really increased and I am having a hard time sleeping and I find myself in constant prayer.

1155. Vision and Prophecy given to Raymond Aguilera on 5 March 1998 at 8:20 AM.

The Lord gave me a vision of a long linked chain. Then the Lord said, "Saddam Hussein is at the head of the chain, and he will break its links. (over)

1156. Prophecy given to Raymond Aguilera on 7 March 1998 at 7:13 AM.

Comments:

After receiving this short Prophecy, I was left totally exhausted and dizzy for about three hours. The Power of the Holy Spirit must really be shaking the spiritual world. The spiritual warfare is still intensifying each day. I must praise the Lord here, for I have no idea how I am holding on. At times, I feel like a mad dog pulling on a rag, and other times I feel like a mad dog running with his tail between his legs. All of this spiritual warfare gives me a spiritual rush, but I know it's nothing that I am doing in the spirit or in the flesh. I am realizing though that this warfare is to the death of all that we know.

Prophecy:

I am the God of Abraham. I am the God of Jacob, the God of Isaac, the God of Moses, the God of Samuel, the God of Ezekiel, the God of Isaiah, the God of Jeremiah, the God of everything that was, the God of everything that is, the God of everything that will be! The only Peace that will befall this planet is the day, is the hour, is the second, that My Son Jesus Christ of Nazareth comes and settles the problems of this world, with the Power and Might of Jehovah, with the Power and Might of Jesus Christ of Nazareth, with the Power and Might of the Holy Spirit. All peace and tranquilly that befalls this planet before that day is not real! It is temporary. For the Love of Jehovah is Peace. For the Love of Jesus Christ is Peace. For the Love of the Holy Spirit is Peace.

MARK MY WORDS! Read the Bible! Study the Book of Revelation. Study the Words of the Prophets. Be meek, be humble, take Communion, and Pray, and Pray, and Pray. For the events that are facing this planet, will be extremely terrible for all concerned, who are not under the Blood of the Jesus Christ of Nazareth, under that Umbrella, under that Word. For the cleansing by fire is upon you. If you believe, your husband, your wife, your church, your government—can protect you. You will be lost! For only Jesus Christ of Nazareth through the Power of the Holy Spirit, through the Power of Jehovah will protect you, through His Words, through His Angels, through His Love. (over)

1157. Prophecy given to Raymond Aguilera on 13 March 1998 at 8:32 AM.

Good morning, Reymundo! How are things going? You have noticed the shock and the repercussions of the blows that the devil tried to implement on you have passed. And the Work of God keeps on going.

The art of man, is to destroy all that is good, all that is righteous, all that is not of God. The art of man—is sin! As you know, and as I know—I have always dealt with the problem of sin. Since Adam and Eve, I have separated and created certain people to follow (Me), to be obedient, to love the things of God. These people will be gathered. These people will be saved. The rest will be placed with the devil in a place—that no one should be!

But as you know, and as I know—the nature of man is sin, and sin produces sin because it is in union with the devil! I have been patient. I have waited for many years for this point in time! As you will see in the coming years the things in the Prophecy Book coming to be with the Power of Jehovah, with the Might of Jesus Christ, with the Love of the Holy Spirit. For We are God!

We do things in an orderly manner, in a Loving manner, but with Power! Some people do not believe this! That is something they have to deal with at the proper time, at the proper place. But whether they believe in evolution, or whether they believe in Jehovah and Christ Jesus and the Holy Spirit, the Truth will manifest itself, and manifest itself to this planet, to your brother, to your neighbor, to your mother, to your father, to everyone who has ever existed. It does not matter whether you believe in God or you do not believe in God. What God does and what God performs and what He will do—will happen—through His Word, through Love, through His Power, through all that is Righteous, through all that is Clean, through all that is of God.

Nothing in this planet happens, or comes to be without My Knowledge. Whether it is good, whether it is bad! If you want to save yourselves, you are going to have to choose—good or evil. For there is no such thing as maybe! "Do you hear My Words?" Either you are for Me, or you are against Me! That is simple. That is direct. That is to the Point! What is so hard to understand about that! I understand, and I have a Loving Heart. I know you—all you can do is try, and try, and try to be good. That is all I ask! Because sin is sin—and man has sin. You try and I will do the Rest! Because that tells Me—You want to be righteous! You are seeking Jesus Christ of Nazareth. You Love the Holy Spirit. And through those things, that tells Me—you love Me, Jehovah. That is not hard to understand. If you fall—you repent! I will forgive! And We will keep on going!

For the end is before you. Some of you are beginning to sense it. Some of you are beginning to dream about it. Some of you are beginning to see it. Seeing, and hearing, and believing are Powerful, but many of you are blind. Many of you are chasing doctrine. Many of you are chasing your pastors. Many of you are doing things that are not Godly. But the simple fact is—the end will come! And your decision will be good or bad. Either you go to this place, or you go to that place! I hope—I have made My Point Clear and to the Point! For you are going to cross many hard days, many hard weeks, many hard months, many hard years. Where the things, that you have always depended upon, will be taken from you. Sometimes it is your mother. Sometimes it is your father. Sometimes it will be your son and daughter. Sometimes it will be the money you love so much. Sometimes it will be your life.

Things will be as they should be. The accounting of all that was created is coming to a point. Well—that is all for today! Tomorrow will bring some good and some evil, but you have to make a choice on—who is your God, and on what you will do. This is your Loving Father giving you a Loving message from Heaven. (over)

1158. Prophecy and Vision given to Raymond Aguilera on 17 March 1998 at 3:34 PM.

Note:

I feel like SCREAMING at the top of my lungs, and I do not know why. Since I posted the last Prophecy the next day I hurt my back. I have spent a lot of hours in a hot tub of water or trying to rest in bed. I was working around the house, when suddenly my back started hurting. Now the Lord has given me this Prophecy—Vision and I can hear the neighbor dogs fighting, and what seems to their death. My dog seems to be barking at something inside my house. Then last night, I had a nightmare about my brother dying. And also, last week I was given 15 days to pay my electric bill and yesterday I received a 48-hour notice that my electricity will be turned off for non-payment. These things are important, but not life threatening, and for some unknown reason I woke-up with this almost uncontrollable anger. The devil believes, he is so slick, but I remember Ephesians 6:11-18.

From the KJV Bible:

Eph 6:11 Put on the whole armour of God, that ye may be able to stand against the wiles of the devil.

Eph 6:12 For we wrestle not against flesh and blood, but against principalities, against powers, against the rulers of the darkness of this world, against spiritual wickedness in high places.

Eph 6:13 Wherefore take unto you the whole armour of God, that ye may be able to withstand in the evil day, and having done all, to stand.
Eph 6:14 Stand therefore, having your loins girt about with truth, and having on the breastplate of righteousness;
Eph 6:15 And your feet shod with the preparation of the gospel of peace;
Eph 6:16 Above all, taking the shield of faith, wherewith ye shall be able to quench all the fiery darts of the wicked.
Eph 6:17 And take the helmet of salvation, and the sword of the Spirit, which is the word of God:
Eph 6:18 Praying always with all prayer and supplication in the Spirit, and watching thereunto with all perseverance and supplication for all saints;

Vision:

I had a vision of woman. I am seeing it from an unusual angle. I am viewing this vision from a few feet off the ground level. I can see this woman from her knees up into reddish-orange sky in the background. This sky is very strange in Color almost like those colored dyed T-shirts of the 1960's.

Prophecy:

Then the Lord said, "The tiger and the woman will clash and fight until the end and the determination of the fight will be determined by the sitting sun. (over)

1159. Vision given to Raymond Aguilera on 18 March 1998 at 4:00 PM.

During prayer, the Lord gave me a vision of a Large White Ball that was about 5 foot in diameter. I could see it on top of this platform, and this platform had some kind of track attached to it. As I watched this Ball, it began to roll onto this track which had all kinds of twists and turns. I could also see the track had a loop in the middle of it. This Ball went through all the movements on the track and the vision stopped. (over)

Then the Lord showed me a beautiful shapely woman with red hair. She was wearing a very lightweight dress that went down to her knees. What was so unusual, she had no face. The place where her face should have been was blank, and only her beautiful curly red hair could be seen. (over)

1160. Occurrence given to Raymond Aguilera on 19 March 1998 at 7:30 PM.

This is for the few Christians, who do not believe in spiritual warfare or spiritual warfare in the flesh. This is a short list of three things that happened to me after receiving, Prophecy: 1157, 1158, 1159.

After receiving and sending out Prophecy 1157:
Somehow my back got hurt, and I was in bed for about 4 days.

After receiving Prophecy 1158:
I went to visit my friend, Jerry. We had a gathering with two other brothers in the Lord. When the first brother arrived, he closed the front door. A wall clock fell off the wall and hit me right on the top of my head. The battery fell out of the clock with the impact, but I was not hurt. We anointed the two brothers and prayed, and talked about the Lord most of the night.

After receiving and sending out Vision 1159.
I went back to Jerry's house for some more rest and relaxation, and on the way, while I was approaching a stoplight. I noticed that the stoplight was red, and there was only one car stopped in my lane (a van). When I reached about five car lengths or 50 feet from the stoplight. This van placed it in reverse, and proceeded at a high speed backwards toward my car. I sounded off my horn, and the van stopped about one foot from the front of my car. We were the only two vehicles on the road. The van was placed in forward drive and left as if nothing had happened. (very strange!)

1161. Prophecy given to Raymond Aguilera on 21 March 1998 at 8:00 AM.

The Lord said, "The only chicken soup that President Clinton will get—will be a pot!"

Then the Lord gave me a vision of someone carrying a 2.5-foot high ceramic pot on top of their head. (over)

1162. Vision given to Raymond Aguilera on 22 March 1998 at 9:49 PM.

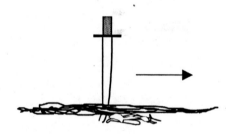

I had a vision of a sword moving over the top of an ocean. The blade was cutting the water as it moved.

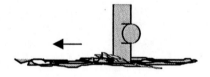

Then the vision changed into a submarine periscope moving over the water.

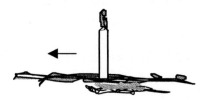

Then that vision changed into a White Lit Candle moving over the top of the water. (over)

Vision:

A vision of a truck laying on its side, on the side of the road. Then this enormous hook (that looked like a fishhook), but this hook was twice as large as the truck—came out of the ground, and hooked the truck in the middle. The hook then forced the truck into the ground, and ripped the ground open in the process.

1163. Vision given to Raymond Aguilera on 25 March 1998 at 12:56 AM.

The Lord gave a vision of a submerged volcano under the ocean. (over) Then the Lord gave me a vision of a Large Capital J.

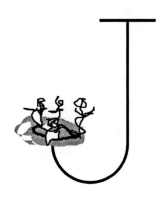

And on the loop of the J, I saw some sort of life raft with some people sitting on it. (over)

1164. Vision given to Raymond Aguilera on 3 April 1998 at 10:00AM.

During prayer the Lord gave me a vision of the planet earth. In this vision, I saw Seven Swords moving side by side digging or craving the surface of the planet.

Vision:

Then I was shown a Wine Glass and a tongue licking the Wine Glass. Then the Lord said, "There will come a day, when you will thirst for My Blood".

Vision:

Then I saw a pair of large Cymbals hitting each other.

Vision:

Then a Large Flood Light was turned on.

Vision:

I saw a vision of a transparent earth. (over)

Comments:

I almost over looked this Vision—Prophecy. I had received these visions and prophecy during prayer at Carl's house, for they were not on my tape recorder, but Carl had written them down after our prayer time. I found them later, after placing the other visions on the web site.

1165. Vision given to Raymond Aguilera on 6 April 1998 at 8:30 AM.

A vision of a plumb bob being held by a White Rope or String of some sort. (over)

1166. Vision given to Raymond Aguilera on 14 April 1998 at 9:45 PM.

The Lord gave a vision of a Madonna (mother and child). As I watched this vision, I saw hundreds or maybe thousands of black birds flying in the air. They looked like one black moving cloud, as they moved from the right to left.

Then the next vision was of another Madonna (Mother and Child), but this one was a little smaller.

Then the next image was, of a grave with a gray headstone. In front of the gravestone (where the dirt covers the body on the ground), looked black or charcoal in color.

Then the next image was of another Madonna. The face looked like it was not there. There was no face, only a black shadow where the face should be.

Then the next image was of another grave next to the previous grave (grave with gray headstone). Except this other grave had a pure White headstone, and it had many, many beautiful fresh colorful flowers (every color you could think of), were in front of it. It was so beautiful and clean. Then the image stopped! (over)

1167. Vision given to Raymond Aguilera on 30 April 1998 at 9:30 PM.

During prayer the Lord showed me a vision of the bottom half of the Eiffel Tower in Paris. On top of this half base there was some kind of round clear transparent ball of some kind.

Vision:
Then later the Lord showed me His Hand holding this big black ball. In the spirit, I asked the Lord, "What was the black ball?"
Then the Lord said, "The ball was black because of all of the sin in the world. The ball is the planet earth."

1168. Vision given to Raymond Aguilera on 4 May 1998 at 5:20 PM.

A vision of an aquarium filled one third with dirt. In the center of the aquarium the dirt began to be disturbed like what a gofer would do in the ground. The dirt was being pushed up. But no animal could be seem and the aquarium was shallow about 3 inches. (over)

1169. Vision given to Raymond on 9 May 9:32 AM.

The Lord gave me vision of some sort of a circular (but round in shape) crystal which had facets on it that looked like what you see on a diamond. This round crystal emerged from under some water or lake. (over)

1170. Occurrence given to Raymond Aguilera on 13 May 1998 at 8:17 AM.

I had a very unusual evening. I got attacked in the middle of the night. This evil presence came into my room and started hitting my head. Then I felt like some kind of sore was developing on my tongue and it burned, and it burned. I still feel it right now! Every time I tried to fall asleep, this whatever it was would try to attack me. I had taken Communion earlier, and I prayed for my family members, who live with me, but this evil presence was so strong, I had to get up again and anoint my forehead, hands, and feet. Then I went back to bed and began to pray against it aloud! It seemed that the Lord could have taken care of the situation, but I did have a very realistic strange dream.

I really do not understand what is going on, but I believe this attack has to do with the Bible Study Notes on the end times, I am uploading onto the web site. I have been having so much warfare over it—it is so unbelievable. So the other night I asked the Lord to give me a sign or a confirmation. That what I was doing was correct! I prayed and I prayed and I prayed and I asked the Lord—that I wanted to see lighting and hear thunder as a confirmation. So I waited and I waited, for it was raining; and nothing happened! So I prayed myself to sleep.

Then the next morning I read in the newspaper, and saw on television that lighting struck and burned this multistory building's deck or awning in San Francisco. It cracked part of the building, and totally destroyed the deck or awing and it fell off the upper part of the building and hit the street below. Then I remembered my prayer, but I did not know if that was my confirmation from the Lord.

Then the next day we had four or five twisters (can you believe it—in the San Francisco Bay Area!). We never have tournedos in the San Francisco Bay Area. It blew some roofs off a few houses and uprooted some trees. All of this happened within a fifty-mile radius of my house. Then the Lord placed it in my spirit that this had to do with what I was doing. And you better believe it scares me! For I saw them on the television and these things were real! This one news program even instructed people on what to do in case a tornado hits your area. This reminded me of the spiritual attack last night, it was real too! So I am getting a different perspective on these Bible Study Notes on the end times that I am preparing concerning what I studied two years ago! (over)

1171. Prophecy given to Raymond Aguilera on 28 May 98 at 8:00 PM.

The Lord said, "Ishmael will come from the north."
Vision:
Then I had a vision of an army of tanks in the desert.

1172. Vision given to Raymond Aguilera on 1 June 1998 at 9:45 PM.

A vision of a half-full Wine Glass. As I watched the Wine Glass in the spirit, I saw a Hand come out from under the Wine in the Glass. (over)

1173. Vision given to Raymond Aguilera on 3 June 1998 at 12:15 AM.

The Lord gave me a vision of a lit candle. As I watched the white lit candle the wick was separated from the white wax, and stood upright next to the wax and it was lit. (over)

1174. Prophecy given to Raymond Aguilera on 3 June 1998 at 9:15 PM. in English.

Ring the Bell! Ring the Bell!
The time is here for bringing the saints together.
Ring the Bell!
For the calamity before you will be unbelievable; will be direct; will be to the point!
Ring the Bell! Ring the Bell!
For the hour and the day have been appointed.
Ring the Bell! Ring the Bell!
The darkness will befall the planet, when the moon and the sun are lined up one before the other at that point in time.
Ring the Bell! Ring the Bell!

The hour and the day is here.
Ring the Bell! Ring the Bell!
If you love your life, you will lose it.
Ring the Bell! Ring the Bell!
If you hate your life you will find it.
Ring the Bell! Ring the Bell!
Each day that goes by will be a blessing.
Ring the Bell!

For there will come a day when the blessing will end. Did you hear what I have said to the point? Come! Open your Bibles and read from the beginning to the end. Read every Word! Remember as much as you can! For the easy life, the easy days are going to leave you. You will be left empty. You will be left helpless if you do not read the Bible from the beginning to the end.

Remember the antichrist.
Remember the false prophet.
Remember your arch enemy, Satan, the devil. Who has his fangs focused at your throat with pleasure to lick your blood.
Remember the Bible.
Remember My Son, Jesus Christ of Nazareth. For the days that will befall this little planet will be the worst than man has ever seen.
Remember! The end is before you.
Remember the ten virgins.
Remember the watch tower.
Remember the seeds that fell on good soil.
Remember all that is before you! The weather will change more. More people will die by earthquake, by changes in the weather.
Remember the birth pains of change.
Remember My children, I will never desert you, but the fulfillment of prophecy is coming to bear. The focus of the devil is going to become

more clear in the coming years, but remember no matter what happens I am with you.

Remember plant the seeds! Plant the seeds!

Remember that mustard seed. Remember the mustard seed.

Help those who need help. Take care of the sick. Take care of the wounded. Focus your eyes, your ears, your heart, and your spirit only toward My Son, Jesus Christ of Nazareth. In that way you will find salvation. You will find Me, Jehovah. For man will disappoint you. For man will take you through the wide gate. Many will seek Me. Many will not find Me. Go through the narrow gate. It might be bumpy. It might be hard. But salvation is close at hand. Bring the Body together and help each other with the Love of Christ, with Love of Jesus, with the Love of the Holy Spirit, which means the Love of Jehovah.

Make yourself strong! Make yourself bold! Be radical for Jesus! Be firm! Be righteous! Be clean! All will go well.

Remember I love you! Remember I love you! Remember I love you!

My Son, Jesus Christ of Nazareth, will be at the proper time; at the proper place, with the Power of the Holy Spirit. Try and try and try to be clean, to be righteous. Repent of your sins. And I will do the rest! (over)

1175. Prophecy given to Raymond Aguilera on 5 June 1998 at 4:42 PM. in Spanish.

The House of God is very hard! Yes! The House of God is very hard! And all that is not Mine, I am going to kill and I am going to put it in the jail, the Jail of God. But you have to read the Bible to know what I am telling you. For if you do not read the Bible from one point until the end—you are not going to know! Read about the Jail of God where I place them—those that I kill. Clearly it is there in the Bible, the Jail of God.

I know the problems you have Reymundo! I know that the devil is mad! But all will go well to the point. No one can stop the Word of God!

When I say it—it begins the righteous things, the things pointed with the Force of the Holy Spirit. Yes! The things I tell you and things you have; have the Force of God. That is why the devil hits you. For he believes he can stop you! But you know and I know—that he has already lost the war. But the day is coming—that I am going to place him in the Jail with the chains. Yes! I am going to tie him from the neck to his feet. Yes! I am going to tie him like a dog! But there comes the day that I am going to let him loose. Did you hear Me, Reymundo? I am going to let him loose for a short time. Then I am going to hit him on top of his head with a hammer! Then I am going to kill him for all the time that there is time.

He believes, he has the nerve to stop the Word of God. But I, with My Son, with the Holy Spirit—We have the Force of Force, and he is nothing! He believes he "is", but you and I know he is nothing. I am going to stop him like a fly. Did you hear Me, Reymundo? Point everything in the manner of God, and all will go well. But I want you to open your eyes and your ears, for I am going to send you your wife. Did you hear Me? Here she comes with the love of God. And here comes THE END of all that you know, of all that you touch, of all that you see. Here comes THE END of the world, to the point, to the time of God, to the minute of God.

The world is all closed. For the devil closed the eyes, closed the ears, closed the heart of all who are in the world, with all that is bad, with all that is of the devil. And he believes he has won, but he knows nothing! For Reymundo with My Word, with your help—We are going to tell the whole world the Word of God. And I do not care, if they cry, if they scream, if they throw stones at you. For I am going to clean all! All that is bad and I am going to correct it! And I am going to hit all that is filthy with My Hand. For here comes "The End".

My Angels are ready! My Son is ready! The Holy Spirit is ready! We just have to awaken the Body of God with the Force of God. But all will go well My son—like I told you years ago. I know that you have suffered. I know your tears. I know your heart. But all that I give you is from God, the love, the affection—the kisses come from the Lips of God. Hurry rest a little bit, but I want you to start once again. I will send you the money that you need. I will send you the strength that you need. I will send you the wife that you need. I will send the Angels that you will need. With the Blood of My Son, with the Word of God, with the Force of the Holy Spirit, We are going to finish all that We have started. Did you hear Me, Reymundo? These are the Words of God with the Lips of Love of all that is good, of all that is correct. (over)

Daily Communion

Communion Bible Scripture
(KING JAMES VERSION)

1 Cor 11:24 And when he had given thanks, he brake it, and said, Take, eat: this is my body, which is broken for you: this do in remembrance of me.
1 Cor 11:25 After the same manner also he took the cup, when he had supped, saying, This cup is the new testament in my blood: this do ye, as oft as ye drink it, in remembrance of me.
1 Cor 11:26 For as often as ye eat this bread, and drink this cup, ye do show the Lord's death till he come.
1 Cor 11:27 Wherefore whosoever shall eat this bread, and drink this cup of the Lord, unworthily, shall be guilty of the body and blood of the Lord.
1 Cor 11:28 But let a man examine himself, and so let him eat of that bread, and drink of that cup.
1 Cor 11:29 For he that eateth and drinketh unworthily, eateth and drinketh damnation to himself, not discerning the Lord's body.
1 Cor 11:30 For this cause many are weak and sickly among you, and many sleep.
1 Cor 11:31 For if we would judge ourselves, we should not be judged.
1 Cor 11:32 But when we are judged, we are chastened of the Lord, that we should not be condemned with the world.
1 Cor 11:33 Wherefore, my brethren, when ye come together to eat, tarry one for another.

1 Cor 11:34 And if any man hunger, let him eat at home; that ye come not together unto condemnation. And the rest will I set in order when I come.

Luke 22:15 And he said unto them, With desire I have desired to eat this passover with you before I suffer:
Luke 22:16 For I say unto you, I will not any more eat thereof, until it be fulfilled in the kingdom of God.
Luke 22:17 And he took the cup, and gave thanks, and said, Take this, and divide it among yourselves:
Luke 22:18 For I say unto you, I will not drink of the fruit of the vine, until the kingdom of God shall come.
Luke 22:19 And he took bread, and gave thanks, and brake it, and gave unto them, saying, This is my body which is given for you: this do in remembrance of me.
Luke 22:20 Likewise also the cup after supper, saying, This cup is the new testament in my blood, which is shed for you.

Mat 26:26 And as they were eating, Jesus took bread, and blessed it, and brake it, and gave it to the disciples, and said, Take, eat; this is my body.
Mat 26:27 And he took the cup, and gave thanks, and gave it to them, saying, Drink ye all of it;
Mat 26:28 For this is my blood of the new testament, which is shed for many for the remission of sins.
Mat 26:29 But I say unto you, I will not drink henceforth of this fruit of the vine, until that day when I drink it new with you in my Father's kingdom.
Mat 26:30 And when they had sung an hymn, they went out into the mount of Olives.

Mark 14:22 And as they did eat, Jesus took bread, and blessed, and brake it, and gave to them, and said, Take, eat: this is my body.
Mark 14:23 And he took the cup, and when he had given thanks, he gave it to them: and they all drank of it.

Mark 14:24 And he said unto them, This is my blood of the new testament, which is shed for many.
Mark 14:25 Verily I say unto you, I will drink no more of the fruit of the vine, until that day that I drink it new in the kingdom of God.
Mark 14:26 And when they had sung an hymn, they went out into the mount of Olives.

Daily Communion

1. Read scripture or Pray.
2. Repent sins.
3. Break Bread (The Body of Christ Jesus)
    in the Name of the Father Jehovah,
    in the Name of the Son Jesus Christ of Nazareth,
    in the Name of the Holy Spirit the Counselor.
4. Read scripture or Pray.
5. Drink Wine or Grape juice (The Blood of Jesus Christ)
    in the Name of the Father Jehovah,
    in the Name of the Son Jesus Christ of Nazareth,
    in the Name of the Holy Spirit the Counselor.
6. Read scripture, Pray or Sing.

About the Author

Raymond Aguilera was a Businessman and Sculptor, until his life was changed by a miraculous calling from God. Since 1990, he has documented over 2,000 prophecies/visions while traveling throughout the world on missions for God, and has experienced many supernatural occurrences as written in four Prophecy Books.

Printed in the United States
4127